# Praise for *Celebrating the Duke*

"Like the musicians he wrote about, Ralph Gleason had a unique voice. He gives you the history, geography, sociology, and psychology of jazz—and the poetry." —Ira Gitler

"[*Celebrating the Duke*] is a marvelous anthology. . . . There is not a word in the entire book that does not ring with the enthusiasm, conviction, and feeling that Ralph brought to everything he wrote. . . . The articles abound in the revealing anecdotes that form the life's blood of the history of the music." —*San Francisco Chronicle*

"Nobody was better than Ralph J. Gleason at getting to the man—or woman—behind the music. His piece on Billie Holiday—a difficult, complex and perplexing woman—has made me, if not understand her, at least perceive her better than anything else I have read about her." —Bruce Cook, *The New Republic*

"[Gleason's] writing projects in his readers' minds a sense of familiarity and intimacy with his subjects, the great jazz performers of the last thirty years. . . . The real value of the book is a collection of the cream from the work of one of our foremost jazz critics and writers." —*Library Journal*

"The articles included are well-written and give an excellent insight into the jazz scene. . . . It is a must for the jazz buff." —*Choice*

BY RALPH J. GLEASON

JAM SESSION
THE JEFFERSON AIRPLANE & THE SAN FRANCISCO SOUND
CELEBRATING THE DUKE, AND LOUIS, BESSIE, BILLIE, BIRD, CARMEN,
MILES, DIZZY AND OTHER HEROES

# CELEBRATING THE DUKE

# Celebrating
# The Duke

## And Louis, Bessie, Billie, Bird, Carmen, Miles, Dizzy and Other Heroes

## RALPH J. GLEASON

FOREWORD BY STUDS TERKEL
NEW INTRODUCTION BY IRA GITLER

DA CAPO PRESS • NEW YORK

Library of Congress Cataloging in Publication Data

Gleason, Ralph J.
  Celebrating the Duke, and Louis, Bessie, Billie, Bird, Carmen, Miles, Dizzy, and
other heroes / Ralph J. Gleason; foreword by Studs Terkel; new introduction by Ira
Gitler. —1st Da Capo Press ed.
    p.    cm.
  Originally published: Boston: Little, Brown, c1975.
  Discography: p.
  Includes index.
  ISBN 0-306-80645-2
  1. Jazz—History and criticism. 2. Jazz musicians. I. Title.
ML3506.G58   1995
781.65'09—dc20                                                                    95-21599
                                                                                      CIP

First Da Capo Press edition 1995

Published by Da Capo Press, Inc.
A Subsidiary of Plenum Publishing Corporation
233 Spring Street, New York, N.Y. 10013

Manufactured in the United States of America

# Contents

# Introduction
## to the Da Capo Edition

RALPH J. GLEASON was both avuncular and avant-garde. He was the younger brother of one of your parents who talked to you about things that they didn't, took you places they wouldn't, and brought you presents other than socks or underwear. I didn't have an uncle like that. My older brother, who introduced me to jazz, was the equivalent. By the time I met Ralph I was 29 and he was 41, approximately the same age as my brother. Of course Ralph, unlike my brother, hadn't known me from my childhood. Rather we were adults, professionals in the same field with a mutual love of the music.

In the spring of 1958 I went down to North Texas State to emcee the annual concert by the students of Gene Hall's very fine jazz program. I parlayed this into a west coast trip. Ralph had mentioned my name favorably in *Down Beat* while reviewing some LPs for which I had written the liner notes. We exchanged letters in the aftermath and I let him know I was planning to visit San Francisco for the first time. He gave me his phone number. I dialed him from my hotel room shortly after my arrival, but I certainly wasn't prepared for the two-hour conversation which ensued. In it we reinforced the convergence of our musical tastes and found that we also laughed at the same things. We were contemporaries in thought and feeling, but chronologically, and therefore in experience, I was junior. That's where the avant-garde uncle entered.

In the evening, armed against his diabetes with a container of milk and a banana, he came by to introduce me to the San Francisco scene as part of his club rounds for the *Chronicle*. We went to the Jazz Workshop, The Blackhawk, Enrico's coffee house, and Ann's 440. Lenny Bruce was appearing at the last named and he was completely new to me. We walked in mid-set and I felt Ralph's glee in his role as illuminator when Lenny had me on the floor in nothing flat. Ralph was one of the very first to recognize his genius and to say so in the press. When I wrote for his excellent *Jazz Quarterly*, he rewarded me with something more valuable than the money the magazine could ill afford—a private tape of Bruce's club performances. I used it to spread the Gospel according to Lenny among the Manhattan uninitiated.

Ralph and I continued to correspond and suffice it to say his letters—literate, funny, insightful—remain in my archives. In 1966, on my second visit to San Francisco, I was a houseguest at the Gleasons in Berkeley for several days. This time Ralph took me to the Fillmore to hear the Jefferson Airplane while everything from amorphous blobs of color to old Shirley Temple movies appeared on screens that bordered the dance floor. I never got into rock the way he did, but I understood his embracing the Airplane because of his deep affection for the blues and his involvement with the contemporaneity of the scene. That his children were teenagers had something to do with it, but it went way beyond that.

Our next meeting never took place. In the spring of 1975 I was in Los Angeles beginning work on *The Encyclopedia of Jazz in the Seventies* with Leonard Feather. Those preliminary weeks concluded, I went up to San Francisco in June for a bit before returning to New York. On the first night I spoke with Ralph and made a lunch date for the next day. Before morning he was dead. To say he died too soon is an exclamatory understatement. I walked around town that day and happened upon a street band playing the blues in a raggedy, but heartfelt manner. I didn't know if they were blowing for Ralph, but I felt they were. "This is your city," I mused to Ralph in my mind in the midst of my tears, wishing he could have shared my serendipity but figuring, intuitively, that he probably had known them.

*Celebrating the Duke & Louis, Bessie, Billie, Bird, Carmen, Miles, Dizzy & Other Heroes* was published later that year. It also celebrated Ralph who knew and understood the music in its many aspects and, in doing so, always emphasized the humanity of the people who were in the music as it was in them. No ivory tower for R.J.G.

He began as a founder and editor of the periodical *Jazz Information* from 1939 to 1941. From 1942 to 1944 he was with the Office of War Information. He wrote for *Down Beat* from 1948 to 1961 and for the *San Francisco Chronicle* from 1950. In 1958 he helped found the Monterey Jazz Festival; nine years later he did the same for *Rolling Stone*. He hosted jazz radio shows in the '60s and his *Jazz Casual* series for NET was a model of jazz presentation on television and continues to appreciate in value.

Read his chapter on Lunceford and find out about some of Ralph's jazz roots; the one on Pres for the sense of immediacy he could impart as with the image of a ballroom crowd reacting to the announcement of Pres' passing; and the chapter on Carmen for his recognition that she belonged in the pantheon long before others fully realized her stature. Understand the special relationships he had with Miles and Diz; and, perhaps, above all, the bond with Duke and all things Ellingtonian. Read these chapters; read *all* the chapters and feel the music and the people as much as one can without listening. And then listen well—as Ralph did. With this reissue let us again celebrate Ralph Gleason and his heroes. They are all very much with us.

—IRA GITLER
President
Lenny Bruce Fan Club No. 2
New York City, March 1995

# Acknowledgments

As is always the case, many more people helped me with this project than can possibly be listed. However, there are some to whom special thanks must be expressed and they include: Billy Abrahams, whose aid extended far beyond that of an ordinary editor; Bridget Gleason, June Hiatt, Gretchen Horton, Rose Libby, Beverly Grant and Phil Bray. Patricia Willard, the Ellington historian, was especially helpful, and while it is trite to say that without the help of my wife, Jean, this book could not have been written (nor the original articles, I might add), it is a simple statement of fact. In addition, I am grateful to Debbie Ishlon for commissioning the Billie Holiday and Miles Davis at the Blackhawk essays; to Milt Gabler for the opportunity to write the Lunceford essay; to Jann Wenner of *Rolling Stone* for asking me to write the Louis Armstrong and Duke Ellington articles; to Samuel Grafton, Al Parker and Robert Hallock for the opportunity to write the Black Art/Black Music essay, and to Scott Newhall and Gordon Pates for allowing me the opportunity in the pages of the *San Francisco Chronicle* to make a hobby into a career.

R.J.G.
Berkeley, California
1975

# Foreword

Johnny Hodges was one month dead. In *Rolling Stone*, Ralph Gleason was informing young readers of the artist's life. Few of them had heard *about*, let alone *heard*, Ellington's gifted alto sax player. This Gleason understood. There was no air of the *padrone* to his writing. He felt too deeply to play the role of gray eminence. It was a tender, knowledgeable tribute. Ralph was doing what he has done for more than a generation: chronicling, oh so simply, the popular art of jazz. No critic of our day has approached his craft in quite this manner.

We are told that "sense of history" is what distinguishes a statesman from a political hack. It may be added that "sense of continuity" is what distinguishes a major jazz critic from a lesser one. (It is no accident that Gleason was among the first to understand the phenomenon of rock culture: he was reporting to the outside world the Haight-Ashbury explosion with the insight of James Cameron covering the Bikini blast; while others reported the smoke and the mushroom clouds, he contemplated out loud the effect on our psyches.)

The lack of continuity may, indeed, be one of the causes of the malaise that so possesses us today. Call it rootlessness, call it anomie — it comes down to not knowing where you came from and thus not knowing where you are. Nowhere, aside from politics, is this more evident than in the popular arts. That there is an increasing curiosity on the part of the young about old black blues singers and generation-ago country banjo pickers is in no small part due to observers like Ralph Gleason and, say, Nat Hentoff.

To better understand the meaning of Janis Joplin's short and tumultuous life it is mandatory to read Gleason's liner notes on Billie Holiday in those two memorable Columbia albums.* They were more than bouquets to a Lady; they were letters to a not quite comprehending world. They were about an artist and vulnerability; about art's durability and man's mortality.

As you read *Celebrating the Duke*, you are really listening to a theme and variations on the theme: black life in these parts as interpreted by imaginative artists. You will see — not with the shock of recognition so much as with the recognition of shock — that Louis Armstrong often played the role of Tom, while experiencing hurt and fury. Behind the advertised pearly-tooth grin, you'll notice Armstrong remembering a long-ago southern radio man: "I can't introduce that nigger." You'll hear, as though his trumpet and voice (they were one) were offering "Black and Blue," his weary after-hours voice telling of the white stars who so "loved" him: "Even though I played with a lot of 'em, I don't even know where they live." Most important, you'll understand that it doesn't really matter: when the *padrones* are long gone, it is the artist who will be remembered.

Though the legend "Bird Lives" appears on the occasional wall (that has probably been demolished in the name of urban renewal and the realtor's fast buck), Gleason's tribute to Charlie Parker will still be around. And his pieces on Miles Davis, who

* Included here as "Billie Holiday — Lady Day," page 75.

has foregone Louis' smile though not his art. Again, the matter of continuity.

Within these pages is a gathering of Gleason's writings about jazz and the creative spirits. Like jazz itself, its form is somewhat ad hoc, yet it is arranged. There are essays, liner notes, interviews and appreciations. Together they comprise not so much an analysis of jazz as its felt life. It is a work that one of its heroes, Duke Ellington, would "love madly." Gleason, you see, followed Duke's dictum: Don't analyze, listen.

Ralph Gleason is one month dead as I write this. He was fifty-eight years old. A week before I heard the news, I received a case of whiskey and several boxes of cigars from him, and this letter:

> Now don't freak out because I sent you *both* booze and cigars. It gives me pleasure. It's just what I'd like somebody to do for me sometime.

So today I'm taking a shot of whiskey and smoking a cigar. And remembering Ralph.

— Studs Terkel

# Introduction

WHAT GOT ME STARTED on a life of crime, which is what my mother thought my youthful interest in jazz implied, was a case of the measles when I was fifteen.

Until then I had been an ordinary high school wise guy. Good in the 100-yard sprints, fair at basketball, a terrible football player, but a fast one with what we used to call "the comeback."

However in those days — the early 30s — when you had the measles they put you in a darkened room and you were not allowed to read. And so my mother let me have the Atwater Kent and I lay there, wide awake in the night, picking up those strange sounds in the night — Duke Ellington, Louis Armstrong, Cab Calloway, Earl Hines, Fletcher Henderson.

There were a lot of other sounds in the night, of course, but those were the ones that impressed me. It was just before Benny Goodman, Glenn Miller, Tommy Dorsey and Artie Shaw exploded the big band jazz into the Swing Era, and I had never heard of any of them. There were no fan magazines for music in those days, not even *down beat*, and all I knew was what I heard, and what I heard gave a thrust to my life which has never left it.

Years later in San Francisco, a cleric named Malcolm Boyd made his debut as a nightclub act at the hungry i. I went to hear him and his avowed act of bringing God to the nightclubs, and I was totally turned off. Right then I realized that by some kind of accident — probably some late night show with Earl Hines or Duke Ellington from the Grand Terrace Ballroom — I had irrevocably aligned myself with those who had abandoned the formal aspects of religion and found their idols and their inspiration and their saints in the nightclubs where, refugees from a society built on the standards of advertising agencies, they were bravely struggling with the mixed blessings of truth.

Thus it never seemed to me that there was anything odd in considering Duke's Commandment "It don't mean a thing if it ain't got that swing" on a level with some of the historic Ten. And it does not seem odd to me now, for these men have been my teachers and my saints and my idols almost all of my life. I have learned more from them than I ever did in any classroom and their art has given me a faith in creativity and in life itself that no pulpit has ever offered.

Yet strangely enough — and I have never failed to find it strange — these artists who loom so grand on my own horizon, seem somehow to escape notice in other circles whose inhabitants I also dig. This anomaly has always bothered me. When Lyndon Johnson gave his celebrated culture cocktail party, Dwight Macdonald, one of the brightest critics I have ever read and a man whose writing, especially in his years of editing *Politics*, had a deep intellectual influence on me, wrote a long piece in the *New York Review of Books* lamenting that among all the artists gathered in Washington that fateful day there were no American composers. Then, as I read on, Macdonald described how the best moment of the entire affair was when Duke Ellington's magnificent orchestra played for the guests. It was a profound shock to realize that Duke Ellington, whom I believed (and still believe) to be the most important and the greatest composer ever to have lived on this continent, was not even *considered* a composer by Dwight Macdonald. James Baldwin was right — "Nobody knows my name."

Now that I think about it, I was very lucky that my introduction to this music came from the roots: Louis, Duke, Earl and Fletcher. I was ready for Count Basie when I encountered him and for Jimmie Lunceford as well. Though I enjoyed — and dug — many of the big white bands, it was the sound of Ellington and Lunceford and Basie and Louis and later Billie Holiday that made up the sound track to my young life. I wouldn't change it for anything in the world. They are the great ones in my hagiography and I am proud to have known them even a little bit.

So what began as relief from the monotony of the measles ended as a lifetime activity. I could no more stop listening to music than I could stop breathing, and they will both happen at the same time when they do. I started to write about jazz just as soon as I could get someone to print it and that was when I got to Columbia in 1934. Robert Paul Smith (*Where Did You Go? Out. What Did You Do? Nothing*) was writing the jazz column in *Columbia Spectator* when I got there and I had to wait until the next spring before I could take his place. That was in 1935 and I've been writing about jazz and about popular music (among other things) ever since; and from an initial fan magazine attitude and a fan's adulation, it has gradually worked itself around to a view of life which I hope is reflected in some of the pieces in this book.

After *Spectator*, I had no forum for a while until Gene Williams, Ralph de Toledano and I started a magazine called *Jazz Information*, which was the first U.S. jazz magazine. From there I went on to write for *down beat* and other publications and eventually for the *San Francisco Chronicle*, where I was able to concentrate totally on writing about the music I loved and no longer had to do it as an avocation while earning a living elsewhere. For that I will always be grateful to Scott Newhall and Gordon Pates, the editors who gave me that chance and who suffered my proselytizing and my propagandizing down through the years.

Later in *Jazz, A Quarterly of American Music* (a short-lived attempt to give jazz the kind of "respectable" treatment I mistakenly thought it ought to have) I began to see the music as much more than pure music, as a sociological phenomena in its own right. And then in *Rolling Stone* there has been the opportunity to acquaint new, young audiences with the joys of a music most of them automatically rejected because it represented a past from which they wished to break.

But music spans all gaps, generational or otherwise, and once the music of Duke and Louis and Bird and Miles and the rest has a chance to be heard on its own terms, it can reach anyone open to music at all. I have to say, parenthetically, that there are people — for whom I feel very sorry — to whom no kind of music that is a straight-ahead emotional hit is attractive. I think they are frightened by it. Some of my very best friends, in those days when John Coltrane was carving out his new sounds (and James Baldwin was explaining the sociological and poetic background), insisted that the New Jazz was a music of hate, and no amount of pointing out that Coltrane's own words unalterably categorized his music as a music of love could change their opinion. Basically, they were reacting to a new world in which their values and security were threatened by something strange and foreign to them. It was to be repeated a few years later when adult rock music emerged.

I am indebted to organist Ray Manzarek of the Doors (that strange rock group in which Jim Morrison sang "Light My Fire") for the concept that jazz is America's classical music. I had never thought of it quite that way, and of course he is right. What has passed as American so-called classical music is really only an imitation and extension of European music. Jazz is the true classical art music of this society, and as such it has always given us, when we were perceptive enough to see it, a pointed guide to what was happening or about to happen in our culture.

In the 30s and early 40s, jazz was an attempt, knowingly or unknowingly, by black musicians to assimilate into the white society. The style of presentation, the format and the ritual were borrowed from whites. Then, with the emergence of the bebop or modern jazz era of Parker, Gillespie and the rest, it was the beginning of a new system of values for black people, the elevation of their musical creativity to art and the last drive towards integration.

When that integrated jazz world fell apart, it foreshadowed the end of the civil rights movement as it had been structured, and both races fell away into a deeper exploration of their own inherent urges and drives.

From this emerged two things: a white music that was individual and original and unashamed — adult rock. And a black music that created an entirely new set of standards, sounds and ideals which, beginning with Coltrane and Miles, went on to establish a black artistic standard of supreme importance.

Today, in what quite possibly is an indication of what will come, there is an entirely new ambience to jazz. The "free form" players have gotten beyond race, in a sense, to a music of basic human values in which white and black alike can function freely, and the reason that this is possible is that they approach the problem of playing together as equals. The blacks are not trying to be anything but themselves and the whites are not trying to be black. For the first time in music, white players, playing their own true inspiration, can be absorbed into black groups or perform under black leaders without apology or inhibition of any kind, since both are aimed in the same direction and at the same goal of pure art.

It is a new music and one which is strange and, again, frightening to those who are insecure. But it is a true music and despite the fact that, as of the moment, it has little if any box office appeal (i.e., it is all but impossible to make a living playing it, as Archie Shepp, Cecil Taylor and the other pioneers in its style prove), it is a music which gives every indication of lasting.

My hope is that the pieces in this book will serve several functions. They should set the scene for readers young and old who may be aided thereby in listening to *all* kinds of jazz. The generation of rock fans who have raised the long-forgotten music of the Delta bluesmen, such as Robert Johnson, to a new status may find that Robert Johnson is much closer than they might suspect to Louis Armstrong and Duke Ellington. On the other hand, the older generation (raised as I was on Duke and Louis) may find that the new jazz is just as aesthetically rewarding as the sounds that attracted them in the first place.

In addition, by bringing together these glimpses of the great creative artists from the earliest right down to the most modern jazz, I would like to assist in placing all of them on the broad cultural stage in their proper perspective.

This book is dedicated to those musicians present in its pages (and those who unfortunately are not) for all the great moments, the magnificent highs of listening, for all I have learned from them, my true teachers, and above all for their clear instruction in how to live.

R.J.G.

# I
# Jazz:
# Black Art/
# American Art

EVEN THE ETYMOLOGY of the word itself is dim. We don't know who named it or why. Was it a sexual association tracing back to *jasm?* Was it derived from the Creole *chasse-beau?*

We don't know where it was born (although the first authenticated appearance of the word "jazz" in print was in the *San Francisco Call,* March 6, 1913) and we certainly don't know the first players, those forgotten men who started it all. Legend has it that the first jazz musician was Buddy Bolden, a New Orleans trumpet player before the days of phonograph recording, who went mad and died in a Louisiana insane asylum in the 30s.

And we don't really know, despite the legend, that New Orleans was even its true birthplace.

What we *do* know is that this music has spread throughout the world in the twentieth century; that American jazz musicians are treated as major artists everywhere but at home; and we know that in an era in American history when our government representatives

3

abroad are stoned and picketed, when even presidential visits to friendly countries are canceled, the jazz musician is welcomed everywhere.

Everyone has seen — or seen pictures of — the legend YANKEE GO HOME scrawled on some wall. It crops up all over the world. Yet no one has ever reported seeing a similar legend reading YANKEE JAZZMAN GO HOME, though jazz has always been synonymous with America.

Jazz had to wait for a Frenchman, Hugues Panassié, and a Belgian, Robert Goffin, for the first books about it. Louis Armstrong — who was the sensation of London in 1932 in his first appearance at the Palladium there, who played before royalty in England and Italy, who was the guest of honor at a special reception at the Palace of Fine Arts in Brussels, who played for the League of Nations delegates in Geneva — went back home to New Orleans after his European triumph. Following a huge street parade and reunions with childhood friends, Armstrong and his band were to play in the Suburban Gardens and to broadcast from there, one of the first black bands to do so. As the white announcer began to introduce Armstrong he suddenly turned away and said, "I haven't got the heart to introduce that nigger!" Louis knew he was home.

Jazz was born in New Orleans, Ferdinand La Menthe "Jelly Roll" Morton, the late composer and pianist, told us in his Library of Congress recordings of his reminiscences of the early jazz days. Morton's version squared with the legend, even enhanced it, lending the touch of first-person authenticity to rumor. But we really don't know. It is demonstrable, of course, that many of the first jazz players were from the New Orleans area. Of all the jazz musicians listed in the first edition of the *Encyclopedia of Jazz* who were old enough to have been playing when Louis Armstrong first began to hear them, an overwhelming majority were from the New Orleans or southern Louisiana region.

And of course the functional use of jazz music in New Orleans was certainly a larger part of that city's ghetto life than any other's, though such jazzmen as Willie "The Lion" Smith place hearing what they remember as jazz close to the turn of the century in New York and elsewhere.

4

A revisionist school of jazz historians in recent years has dedicated itself to destroying the theory of jazz's origin in New Orleans. But acceptance of that position almost makes it mandatory to accept a giant conspiracy on the part of all the musicians and fans and the early writers who have really been unanimous in crediting New Orleans as the source.

The legend goes further, however, than naming the city. It says that jazz was born in Storyville, the red-light district of New Orleans, child of the fancy brothel and musical accompaniment to the sporting house entertainment of the turn of the century's walk on the wild side. Again, we know that there certainly was jazz in the New Orleans Storyville district before World War I. Survivors of the era have eloquently testified to that as well as to its use in street parades and funeral processions. Increasingly, though, musicians tend to believe it was born in the church, where the African heritage flourished. Whether or not this is the fruit of a desire to rid jazz of its pejorative associations is open to question. But there seems to be reason to accept Duke Ellington's observation, made to the California Arts Commission several years ago, that while there was jazz in Storyville's brothels, the musicians "didn't learn it there."

We never will know precisely and it really doesn't matter anymore where jazz came from. It is obvious today, no matter what its origin, that jazz is an art, that it is the creation of black musicians and a music completely original to the United States of America. Its first creators were black and its most important innovative players, the delineators of all its styles and the greatest of its solo performers, right down to last night's session on the concert hall or the nightclub stage, have all been black men. White musicians have played jazz on an artistic level with blacks — Bix Beiderbecke, Benny Goodman, Jack Teagarden, to name three — but as Archie Shepp, the controversial black playwright and tenor saxophonist has remarked, "They are very few." It is even possible to speculate that all the white jazz musicians could be eliminated from the history of the music without altering its development in any significant way.

So take New Orleans at the end of the nineteenth and the beginning of the twentieth century, with its heritage of French and

Spanish culture, with its spicing of Caribbean mixtures of Africa, France and Spain thrown in, and you have a multiracial cultural melting pot that spawned the music. Curiously, Mobile, Alabama, founded by a brother of the Sieur de Bienville who founded New Orleans and seeded with the same cultural traditions and racial mixtures, did not produce the early jazzmen. History shows us that New Orleans did.

The city was a harbor, a river city, and the river was the roadway to the North, and the black men went North and took that music with them, to Memphis (where W. C. Handy wrote down the first blues) and on to Chicago where King Oliver and Louis Armstrong made their first records and their reputations.

The first white Americans who picked up on jazz music were the ones who took it out to the world at large. They were the Original Dixieland Jazz Band, a group of New Orleans youths who heard the music in the black ghetto and began to play it. They had been preceded in New York — then as now the show business capital of the country — by the black originals, Freddie Keppard and "That Creole Band"; but it was the white players who made the front page with jazz, who made the first hit jazz recordings and who brought it worldwide attention, albeit as a novelty craze.

Curiously, World War I had taken some jazz to France with James Reece Europe's Hellfighters, the band of the 369th Infantry, which had played concerts in the final days of the war throughout France. In the first years following "the war to end all wars," Sam Wooding's orchestra, among others, toured Europe with the Chocolate Kiddies revue and even performed in Russia. The trumpeter Tommy Ladnier was with this band and so was Sidney Bechet, the virtuoso clarinetist and soprano saxophonist. Somehow, however, these early bands, while they were successful, missed. It was the Original Dixieland Jazz Band that made the big impression and began the syndrome of white musicians becoming huge successes playing music originated by black men who remained in relative obscurity.

History lends itself eagerly to "what if." And the question haunts us about jazz. "What if" Keppard and his Creole Band, by all contemporary accounts a marvelously inventive group, had

6

recorded when they had the chance — before Victor recorded the Original Dixieland Jazz Band — would *they* have been the ones? "What if" Jim Europe had not been stabbed to death in Boston in a backstage brawl after his return from France? In the event, Europe died at forty and Keppard did not record, fearful, the legend says, that his music would be stolen if it were to be permanently available on record. And what Keppard feared has been the story, literally and symbolically over the years, of jazz in America.

Freddie Keppard, who battled King Joe Oliver for the crown of jazz in New Orleans after the reign of Buddy Bolden, knew his city's music was something special. So did the young composer and critic Ernest Ansermet (later to become world-famous as a symphonic conductor with the Orchestre de la Suisse Romande) when he heard New Orleans jazz. Ansermet encountered it in the person of Sidney Bechet who, despite his skill on the clarinet and soprano saxophone, did not read music but played it all by ear. Bechet, who died in the mid-50s in France after becoming something of a national celebrity there as an American expatriate, played a concert in Europe with the Southern Syncopated Orchestra in 1919 and Ansermet wrote of Bechet's solos:

"They gave the idea of a style and their form was gripping, abrupt, harsh with a brusque and pitiless ending like that of Bach's second Brandenburg Concerto . . . what a moving thing it is to meet this very black, fat boy. . . . who can say nothing of his art save that he follows his 'own way' and when one thinks that this 'own way' is perhaps the highway the whole world will swing along tomorrow."

So the music crept out of New Orleans. The street parades and the funeral marches, with their pageantry and ritual ("We'd play the slow marches on the way to the graveyard, dead marches like 'Flee as the Bird,' and on the way back we'd play 'Didn't He Ramble . . . he was a good man 'til the butcher cut him down. . . .'" Kid Ory, the trombonist, recalled years later) became part of the New Orleans mystique. The sporting house piano players and the bordello bands from Storyville moved, without a break in rhythm, to the Prohibition underworld of Chicago and other northern cities. En route they played briefly on the Strekfus Mississippi

River steamship lines. Musicians still talk of the night Emmett Hardy, a white cornetist of the Midwest, sat in with Louis Armstrong on a Strekfus riverboat and Bix Beiderbecke, the hero of Dorothy Baker's *Young Man with a Horn*, sat at the feet of Armstrong when the boats came to Bix's hometown of Davenport, Iowa. But the first great spurt of jazz into the consciousness of America and the world was through the Original Dixieland Jazz Band. They became international figures, as a vaudeville novelty to be sure, but also as phonograph recording artists for Victor.

While they were headlining in New York and London, the black entertainment circuit spawned hundreds, perhaps thousands, of singers, musicians and composers, lost now in the mists of history. Many played out their entire careers before black audiences. Others broke through into the white world to make their names known there.

They made their living from a string of nightclubs, dance halls and tent-show stands throughout the South and in the northern city ghettos. Sometimes they recorded, but always for what were called "race" records, a term used to designate records produced for the black audience — "the race" — and sold exclusively in the black neighborhoods.

Gertrude "Ma" Rainey, who toured that circuit for years with her show, The Rabbit Foot Minstrels, had such musicians as the tenor saxophone stylist Coleman Hawkins working for her. Ma Rainey was the teacher of Bessie Smith but she was absolutely unknown in the white entertainment world. A singer of amazing power and capable of evoking deep, almost mystical emotion, she survives on a few records, in a few photographs and in the memories of jazz musicians.

Bessie Smith, Ma Rainey's protégée, became the most successful of all the blues singers. She was known as The Empress of the Blues and, unlike Trixie Smith, Maggie Jones, Victoria Spivey, Mamie Smith and Ma Rainey who were her peers, Bessie broke through, or rather almost broke through, into the aboveground world of music. Her active career lasted on into the late 30s. She recorded a marvelous series of discs for Columbia, one of that company's most profitable items during the Depression, and many of her discs are still available on Columbia albums of jazz classics.

By the time she was the top-selling blues artist on records and one of the leading black vaudeville performers, Bessie Smith began to be noticed by white society. Carl Van Vechten photographed her. Members of the New York literary set, as part of their interest in the Black Renaissance, talked about her, and she even sang one Sunday night at a Fifty-second Street nightclub, The Famous Door, during the late 30s and was mentioned in *The New Yorker's* Talk of the Town!

She made her last recordings on that New York trip and then went back on the road again and had a fatal automobile accident in her native Tennessee. Bessie died after that accident, bleeding to death when a white hospital would not admit her.* Ironically, a similar fate ended the life of the inventor of the blood plasma process less than a decade later. He was also black.

Ethel Waters, long before she starred on Broadway and in films, made records as a blues singer and toured the black vaudeville circuit, Theater Owners Booking Association, known in the vernacular of the black entertainment world as TOBA, "Tough on Black Asses."

Though New Orleans has become glamorous in memory, the diaspora of prostitutes and musicians from Storyville during World War I, caused by an armed forces drive to clean up the city, was not the sentimental event Hollywood made of it in the film *New Orleans*. It did add additional force to the drive to break out that motivated the most talented New Orleans musicians. They went north seeking what James Baldwin was later to call "the gimmick" in order to escape.

Papa Mutt Carey, originator of the growl trumpet style, and Jelly Roll Morton went to the West Coast; Kid Ory, who wrote "Muskrat Ramble" and "Savoy Blues," went to Chicago along with Johnny and Baby Dodds, the clarinet and drum–playing brothers; Johnny St. Cyr, the banjoist; Bud Scott, who stopped playing piano after he heard Jelly Roll and took up guitar; Sugar Johnny, Punch Miller, and Henry "Red" Allen, the trumpeters; Jimmy Noone, the clarinet player who inspired Goodman; Barney Bigard, who joined Duke Ellington for a decade as featured clari-

---

* Recent research indicates this was not true; she was dead on arrival. R.J.G.

9

netist after working with Oliver and Morton; Minor and Tubby Hall, the two brothers who played drums; George "Pops" Foster, who made the string bass into a solo instrument; Zue Robinson and Honore Dutrey, the trombonists; Tommy Ladnier and Sidney Bechet . . . the list is long and sparkling with talent.

Bechet, Armstrong, Oliver and Jelly Roll Morton were the first quartet of New Orleans musicians to establish themselves in the North, and of them only Armstrong survived. Louis not only had the talent to survive but he emerged at the right time. Oliver brought him up from New Orleans and Louis arrived with his cornet in a paper bag, frightened of the big city and terrified that he could not survive there. But he met Joe Glaser, manager of the Sunset Café who became Armstrong's manager, guiding his career all the way to the top of the entertainment world.

Oliver continued after Louis left him, but his recording career died out and he lapsed into obscurity, eventually dying in the late 30s after spending his last years eking out a meager living as a porter in a dance hall.

Bechet, demonstrably as much a virtuoso soloist as Armstrong — after all, he was recognized by the European critics years before Louis — gave up entirely at one point in the 30s and became a tailor after a brief period in the pit band at Billy Rose's Diamond Horseshoe in New York. Bechet returned to jazz later, then went to France and in the 50s became a celebrity there, even making the cover of *Life* shortly before he died.

Morton, like Oliver an organizer and a composer, saw his recording career, like Oliver's, shrivel up and disappear. He died in obscurity in California in the early 40s after contributing to some of jazz's greatest legends. For instance, there was Morton in the 30s, telling everyone who would listen that he, not Paul Whiteman, was the King of Jazz, and that he, Jelly Roll, had actually invented it, in fact. His claims seemed extravagant. They still do. But there was substance in them as he showed when he turned on the radio and picked up the Benny Goodman orchestra playing one of its first hits, Morton's own composition "King Porter Stomp!" Morton turned from the radio to announce disgustedly, "Chicago style! New Orleans style! Hell! It's *ALL* Jelly Roll style!"

Another Morton anecdote contains the answer to why the early recordings of other bands — the records by James Reece Europe and W. C. Handy, for instance — did not have the effect the New Orleans records (even those by the Original Dixieland Jazz Band) had. "Play some of Mr. Handy's records and then play some of my own," Morton declared saltily when asked if he thought the others were jazz.

Looking back now on what went on in the early years of jazz, with the expanded vision of hindsight, it all begins to take shape.

In an America coming of age at the turn of the century, seeking its identity as a world power, European music was *the* standard for culture; it was "classical" and "good." Anything American, therefore, must be somehow less valuable, especially anything which came from the black citizens who, so recently as to be within the memory of a majority of the adult population, had been slaves and officially only three-fifths human at that.

So the music of the black artists — jazz music — was not to be respected. To be enjoyed, certainly, and to be used in the settings of nightlife and underworld, of prostitution, gambling, and vice. UNSPEAKABLE JAZZ MUST GO, the headline in the *Ladies' Home Journal* said in December 1921. Jazz was "jungle music." Even the line in the hit song "Birth of the Blues" implied it, ". . . the wail of a downhearted frail. . . ."

But the white man was invariably drawn to the music of the American black man, just as he was drawn to the sexuality of black women, to the vitality of black slang and even today to the taste of black cooking. White Americans found the world implied and represented by the music to be exciting and fascinating and valuable. They found it to be more honest, more poignant and more dimensional than their own world. Even in slave times, it seemed, the slaves appeared to have more fun, when they had fun, than did their masters.

So, increasingly, the strange process of crossing the color line in reverse began, with whites imitating black speech, dress, style and music. When Louis Armstrong left King Oliver to go out on his own in Chicago, one of his first white friends was the Jewish clarinet player Milton Mezzrow, who declared officially that he was more at home with black friends and musicians than he was with his Jewish family and neighbors. Once, when he was arrested, Mezzrow even put "Negro" in the space marked "Race" on his prison registration card.

The strength of the artistic drive of these musicians is quite remarkable, looking back at it now. American popular song, as it developed, was a wildly Freudian wish-dream fantasy world so thoroughly euphemistic that it seemed determined to have no connection with reality. Yet the black musicians took that music and, despite all difficulties, made it real. It wasn't only Louis Armstrong singing and playing "I'm Confessin'" or "Song of the Islands" or "Stardust," it was the classically trained pianist Fats Waller doing "I'm Gonna Sit Right Down and Write Myself a Letter" and Duke Ellington performing "In the Shade of the Old Apple Tree."

But what does the ordinary American, even today, think of when you say "jazz" to him? He thinks of Louis Armstrong on the Ed Sullivan TV show rolling his eyes and making jokes about Man-Tan or he sees, on the late night show, the cannibal costumes in some faded film reflecting the Hollywood stereotype of the black man as subhuman savage.

He doesn't think of Louis Armstrong singing "Coal Cart Blues," which is a pure folk song written out of Louis' own experience as a juvenile in New Orleans at Andrews Coal Company, hauling hard coal at 15 cents a load, making about 75 cents a day. "Coal Cart Blues" is not only a poignant personal story but a remarkable vehicle for Armstrong's trumpet improvisations.

On the late movie he certainly doesn't see *The Louis Armstrong Story*. He sees the films made of the lives of Benny Goodman, the Dorsey brothers and Glenn Miller but, good musicians as they were and good as their bands were, they had less relationship to the truth of jazz during their time than the fiction in *Family Circle* magazine has to the American novel. It's just that it was possible, given the social attitudes in this society, to make the Goodman, the Dorsey and the Miller stories in Hollywood, but to have made *The Fats Waller Story* or *The Louis Armstrong Story* would have necessitated facing up to what America is all about.

The pattern was repeated again and again through jazz history.

In Chicago, white jazzmen literally copied King Oliver's numbers and issued them as their own. Benny Goodman's career was based on original compositions (however well he played them) that were written by Edgar Sampson and Chick Webb, black musicians who played in Webb's band at Harlem's Savoy Ballroom and who produced "Stompin' at the Savoy"; by Jelly Roll Morton who wrote "King Porter Stomp"; and by Fletcher Henderson (who had led one of the first swing bands, but could not be accepted for the radio show which launched Goodman), whose arrangements were the core of the Goodman band's repertoire. Later, when Goodman's band began to decline in popularity, it took on new life and vitality with the compositions of the black Kansas City musicians, Count Basie and Jimmy Rushing.

Goodman was not alone in this in the Swing Era. Tommy Dorsey made one of his first commercial hits with a song called "Marie" in which the singer, Jack Leonard, sang the lyric while the band, acting as a chorus, sang offbeat riffs in answer to him. It had to be played five, six, ten times a night at the original Dorsey engagement at the Commodore Hotel's Palm Room in New York. It was so successful that it led to a whole series of ballads treated in a similar fashion which were also Dorsey hits. The thousands of white collegians who flocked to hear Tommy Dorsey do "Marie" never knew it was an original arrangement, note for note, by Doc Wheeler's Sunset Royal Serenaders Orchestra. Dorsey played opposite the Sunset Royal group at a Philadelphia theater, heard the arrangement, liked it and made a trade — eight Dorsey arrangements for a hit. Doc Wheeler and the Sunset Royal Serenaders were black.

The Swing Era of Goodman, Dorsey, Miller and the others came more than fifteen years after the first novelty explosion of jazz, but it made the big band adaptation of jazz into the most popular music in America. The success of the leading bands — the white bands — was so great (Goodman and Dorsey, for instance, actually became millionaires) that even the black bands became what was for them financial successes. Yet Count Basie, whose concept for big band jazz is the prototype swing band, was victimized when he made his first records. Basie was actually paid less than the standard musician's union scale for the recording sessions and the American Federation of Musicians later had to force a readjustment.

Even Glenn Miller's huge success was in part founded on the contributions of black musicians. His big hit "In the Mood" was written and arranged by Joe Garland, the tenor saxophone player in Louis Armstrong's big band of the time, and "Tuxedo Junction" was a number Miller picked up from Erskine Hawkins, a black bandleader who never really made the big time but played in New York dance halls. Dorsey, too, altered his band's style in the late 40s by hiring Sy Oliver away from Jimmie Lunceford's band and Harry James' debt to Count Basie was demonstrated over and over again through the years. Even Woody Herman was part of the syndrome. His first big hit was "Caldonia," which he first heard done by the man who wrote it, Louis Jordan, who led small bands on the black vaudeville circuit.

By the beginning of the 50s, jazz was pretty well established as a part of American culture. Books, articles, lectures, and a multitude of recordings contributed to it, but the image jazz had with the average American again was less than pretty. When the ordinary person thought of jazz, the immediate connotations were narcotics and dissipation. The tortured career of Billie Holiday, the gifted blues and ballad singer whose disc of "Strange Fruit" was one of the first pure, uncompromising jazz performances to become even a minor hit in the phonograph record field, made continual headlines. Arrested for narcotics, institutionalized in Lexington's rehabilitation center, "Lady Day," as all the jazz musicians called her, confirmed all the stereotypes not only by her actions but also in her autobiography, *Lady Sings the Blues*. Charlie Parker, the alto saxophonist from Kansas City and one of the originators of the modern jazz style called bebop, was another admitted narcotics addict. Other artists from De Quincey to Baudelaire to Maugham have used drugs and have been considered its victims. They have not had their art judged by their habits. But jazz is a short word, adaptable to newspaper headlines, and every time anybody owning a musical instrument was arrested he was called a "jazz" musician.

Billie Holiday was the bridge between the blues singers of the

14

Bessie Smith generation (Bessie and Louis were her inspirations) and today's popular music and she influenced so many singers herself that one could truly call her the main influence of an entire generation. Even the recent pop favorite Donovan has been influenced by her, as was Frank Sinatra.

Billie Holiday was one of the sacred trinity of jazz artists of the post–World War II years along with Lester Young, the wispy tenor saxophonist, model of the central character in John Clellan Holmes' *The Horn,* who died alone in a New York hotel room after setting the style that made others famous; and Charlie Parker, found dead under mysterious circumstances, an admitted teenage junkie who devised a style of playing jazz that is heard today in almost every television sound track, just as Lester Young's tenor style is heard in the big bands on all the late night TV talk shows. Early in 1969, a jazz/rock band named Blood, Sweat & Tears released an album which became the best-selling album in the country. On it was a long alto saxophone solo so derivative of Parker as to sound like his ghost.

Parker and Dizzy Gillespie, and the moody and opaque pianist Thelonious Monk, developed the modern jazz style by extending to the furthest limits all the things that could be done with the standard ballad form and the standard European, popular music harmonies. Parker was called "Bird," and the famous jazz nightclub Birdland was named after him. When he died, Lennie Tristano, one of the truly original white jazz pianists, said sadly that all the players who soloed in that club every night ought to have paid Parker royalties, they borrowed so much from him.

After Parker and Monk, the younger players such as Charles Mingus and Miles Davis began to create their own literature, no longer content to improvise, however brilliantly, on the scores of others as had the bebop era jazzmen even when they made an intellectual game out of creating new compositions from the chords of old. Davis and Mingus created a body of emotion-packed recordings based on the blues form as well as original structures and became international stars, Davis even evolving, after the white jazz pianist Dave Brubeck opened the door, into a college concert favorite and one of the few black players to become wealthy.

In the 60s, jazz assumed a militant tone, reflecting the new attitudes of the black people. No longer is there any attempt to structure the music in the framework of European music. The new jazz creators, startlingly brilliant musicians such as pianist and composer Cecil Taylor, Archie Shepp, Ornette Coleman, John Coltrane and Sun Ra have, by and large, abandoned even the traditional restrictions of chord structure and tonality. Instead they now play what they call "free form," completely extemporaneous improvised music.

Unusual it certainly is, but it is no less effective at its best than the classical Louis Armstrong solo on "Song of the Islands" or Coleman Hawkins' "Body and Soul" or Dizzy Gillespie and Charlie Parker on "Groovin' High" (their improvisation on the chords and melody of the old ballad "Whispering"). Yet even today the music suffers from an inability of the white community to accept it unless it is watered down.

John Coltrane is a hero to young black Americans and is almost as widely known as some of the great figures of the black revolution such as Malcolm X. One of the first of the jazz musicians to abandon the traditional methods of improvising and to work towards the new "free form" style, he has been accused of "playing hate." I once had a long discussion about this with a highly intelligent man, an executive in a large corporation dealing with the news, who was convinced that Coltrane's music was "a music of hate." What he really meant was that Coltrane's music was far different from that of Armstrong and Basie. The melodies were not familiar and the sounds were sometimes harsh by his standards. Even more, the titles of the compositions and the totality of the music's sound had a non-European, non-American cast to it. In a word, it made him uncomfortable not only because of how it sounded, but because other kinds of nonverbal communication went with it — Eastern beaded headpieces, the new black "natural" hair style.

The truth is that Coltrane's music was openly and obviously a music of love. His most famous original composition, "A Love Supreme," was a tone poem to his God and he defined that God, both in the music itself and in the accompanying poem, as a God of love.

Art precedes social change as well as mirroring the society from which it comes and the turbulence and strident tone that accompanies some of the black struggle for true freedom is found in modern jazz. But that is a part of life and thus as valid as any of the other aspects of the music.

If jazz is America's classical music, then the blues is the folk music of jazz, full brothers though they may be. Like jazz, blues emerged anonymously in the antebellum South and was not, despite another legend, invented by W. C. Handy. Handy wrote down what he heard, but somebody else before him started it.

The blues is a feeling and a form. It is singular and plural at will and it is the story of a man and his troubles in life, his personal story. The great blues singers of the 20s and the early 30s bred the jazzmen, but they also bred a line of itinerent musicians who sang and played only the blues.

Huddie Ledbetter, "Leadbelly," one of the first to become known to the white world, was a pardoned murderer who sang the blues and work songs of the chain gangs in the nightclubs of New York and wrote two songs which were hits long after he died in the early 40s. They were "Rock Island Line," which the British singer Lonnie Donnegan made into a hit in the 50s, and "Goodnight Irene," which was earlier put firmly on the nation's jukeboxes by the Weavers, the prototypical folk singing group. It is interesting to note, again, how Leadbelly's songs were unpalatable in the original but not in the toned-down white versions. Similarly, Duke Ellington's own recorded versions of his songs were never played on one of the biggest independent radio stations in the country in the 50s because they were "too noisy." Black, even then, automatically was equated with "loud" and "raucous." The "jungle music" syndrome again.

Big Bill Broonzy, another powerful and creative blues singer and guitarist, made a series of records in the 30s which became part of the inspiration for today's young musicians of the pop world. Although he toured in Europe after World War II, Big Bill shared the common fate of so many black artists: He died in poverty. One of the leading folk musicologists of America once praised a western university for its interest in folk music shown as long ago as the

30s when it had Carl Sandburg on the campus. Big Bill got on a university campus, too, shortly before he died. But he got there the hard way — sweeping the floors as a janitor.

Sam "Lightnin' " Hopkins, who was a link between the folk/ blues of the 30s and the rhythm and blues of today's black community, was resurrected in the autumn of his life by young blues fans. He has been touring folk music clubs and appearing in concerts in recent years. Howlin' Wolf (Chester Burnett), another blues singer of seminal importance, made a startling appearance before white America when The Rolling Stones insisted on bringing him onstage for a TV show during one of their U.S. tours — his first American television appearance! Howlin' Wolf, like many other black musicians, was better known to British youth than he was in white America.

Ray Charles, the blind pianist and singer, was one of the heroes of black America before the white community's radio stations would play his music, but Charles' career, unlike those of Leadbelly and Big Bill, came at a time when the black radio stations had emerged and could bring his music to the masses. Eventually he became, like James Brown and Otis Redding, one of the top show business figures. Nevertheless, his early career, and the period many consider his most original and productive, was spent playing on what Lou Rawls, another black singer, has immortalized as "the chitlin' circuit," the small bars and dance halls that dot the ghettos.

Muddy Waters is relatively famous today, though almost never seen on television, due to the upsurge of interest in blues in the past two years resulting from its advocacy by the British pop musicians and their American followers. As McKinley Morganfield, he made Library of Congress folk music discs from a prison farm over twenty years ago and many of his blues songs have been revised and recorded under other names as the compositions of other people. B. B. King, known as "King of the Blues" and the originator of the electric guitar style heard today in thousands of white rock bands, made his first American television appearance on National Educational Television as recently as 1968.

Today Europe, which has been so kind to black musicians through the years since Jim Europe and the other exegetes first played there, treats the blues singers and instrumentalists like Muddy Waters, Howlin' Wolf, Chuck Berry, John Lee Hooker and Willie Mae "Big Mama" Thornton as artists of the first rank and they regularly appear in concert halls there.

Two other jazz groups deserve special mention, for they are not only great artists but unique even within this unique art form. They are Duke Ellington and his orchestra and the Modern Jazz Quartet.

Ellington celebrated his sixty-ninth birthday in 1969 at a special White House dinner at which President Nixon presented him with a Presidential Medal of Honor. Great as this honor must have been, it can scarcely obliterate the slur a few years earlier, when the Pulitzer Prize committee voted to give no award in music at all rather than a special one to Ellington.

One of the most prolific writers of popular melodies as well as a composer of major stature, Ellington has utilized his songwriting and his nightclub career to subsidize his "traveling workshop," his orchestra, for over thirty years. Despite his recognition in Europe, Ellington has had to remain on the road, working steadily all of his life with no leisure to compose. His masterpieces have been written on buses and trains and in hotel rooms or in backstage waits at nightclubs. He has contributed a series of compositions unparalleled in American music for their eloquence, their depth of emotion and their lasting qualities. In 1965 he brought back his early-40s composition "New World A-Comin' " for his Sacred Concert and audiences found it refreshingly appropriate to the mood of the day. In 1969 he began to perform again his "Tone Parallel to Harlem," another early-40s composition, which had renewed relevance to today's urban problems.

America has long neglected Duke Ellington. London had an apartment house named for him in the 30s and he has played command performances for the queen. Oddly, his autumnal recognition does not come as a serious composer, though Ellington himself said, "There has never been a serious musician who is as serious about his music as a serious jazz musician," a comment that said it for all jazzmen for all time. He was invited to write but once for a symphonic group, the NBC Symphony of the Air, and he composed "Night Creature." But Ellington would have enhanced the musical reputation of any American orchestra had their prime interest been in other than traditional European music.

Ellington is beyond styles and fads. His music has been a part of a general artistic viewpoint since the beginning and is all related. His success as an entertainer has enabled him to give us some of America's most profound musical expression, whether in his songs or in his longer works.

The Modern Jazz Quartet was formed in the early 50s by four graduates of the Dizzy Gillespie big band: pianist and musical director John Lewis, bassist Percy Heath, drummer Kenny Clarke and vibraharpist Milt Jackson. They set out to train themselves to do two things: to improvise as a free swinging jazz group with full virtuosity but to make it appear effortless through practice, and to perfect a musical unit for the compositions of Lewis.

Both projects were fulfilled. The Modern Jazz Quartet ranks as the supremely polished small jazz unit today. Its performance of film scores by Lewis, longer works by him and an extensive library of jazz numbers has put the Modern Jazz Quartet, like the Ellington organization, in a class by itself. Completely abandoning any attempts to entertain, the Modern Jazz Quartet insisted on its music being heard and judged on its own standards alone and time has proven that assessment of its merit to be correct.

At a recent two-day festival at the University of California in Berkeley, produced by the Afro-American Students Union, an exciting series of black musicians appeared. Archie Shepp, the saxophonist, played with his group and read excerpts from a long poem concerning the black man in America; Sonny Rollins, one of the most brilliant of all tenor improvisors, played a tour de force of twenty minutes' length all by himself, alone on stage. Albert King, the blues singer and guitarist, shouted his songs; Nina Simone sang melodies to words of Paul Laurence Dunbar and Bob Dylan as well as to her own originals; Julian "Cannonball" Adderley played a "soul" song written by his Viennese pianist Joe Zawinul; Max Roach and Abbey Lincoln performed variations on gospel songs; and the festival ended with the Edwin Hawkins Singers, a church choir, raising the audience to ecstasy by its thrilling gospel songs. It had been a triumph for black musicians who had played, as the opening benediction by the Reverend Belcher had urged them to, "for Jesus, Malcolm, and Martin," combining Martin Luther King, Malcolm X and Jesus in the invocation.

Later, some jazz critics criticized the festival for mixing "blues" and "gospel" and "soul" as well as for having a program on which there were less than half a dozen white jazz players, and these in subsidiary roles.

Jazz still seeks its own from white America. The black audience at the festival was at ease with the different kinds of black music, seeing it all as parts of a whole. Similarly, they were at ease with the invocation linking the names of Christ, Malcolm X and Martin Luther King, seeing them all as martyrs for mankind. And they evinced no objection to the cries of "Free Huey" which rang through the amphitheater from time to time. Jazz is black music and as such is part of black culture, which encompasses what is being called these days "the black experience." It represents a world other than that reflected in the organs of the white society.

The *Times* of London, in its survey of America in the early 60s, "The American Imagination," noted that "the white man's idea of the Negro, often operating below the level of consciousness, stands for freedom. This is what drew the flappers of the 20's to the world of Harlem Negroes and jazz. This is what draws the young and the not so young, all over the industrialized world, not only to the excitement of Negro music but to the rebellious jargon of city streets that goes with it. . . . the new Bohemians are vehement in rejecting Ford and Edison, the inventors, the explorers, Teddy Roosevelt and his Rough Riders, all those Americans who by aggressive self-reliance and guts have made modern America what it is. To take the side of the Negro is, for them, to take the role of protest and freedom."

The sociologist Horace Cayton added weight to this observation when he pointed out that "the jazz fans and the rock 'n' roll youth really have joined the Negro underground."

Europe's strictures drove the first settlers to this continent to find freedom. Curiously, the freest art form developed in America, and obviously the most original, had to go to Europe to be recognized.

21

The first serious treatment of jazz as art came in the discussion of the Frenchman Hugues Panassié and the Belgian Robert Goffin. Duke Ellington played for royalty in Europe before he ever got on the stage of Carnegie Hall (and when he did, his manager told him to stop playing his more ambitious works and get back to "nigger music").

Even Nazi Germany was unable to suppress jazz. Lectures and recorded concerts of jazz were given all through the Hitler era by German jazz critic Dietrich Schulz-Koehn. During the Occupation of France, Django Reinhardt and the Hot Club of France continued to play and Radio Paris broadcast Louis Armstrong records saying "ici, un jazz." They did not say "un jazz Americain."

Today jazz is taught by jazz musicians in the school system in Poland where, despite the rigors of the Iron Curtain, there are almost twenty thousand members of the Polish Jazz Federation who met in cellars to play contraband albums during the years immediately after World War II.

Three American jazz groups have appeared in Russia. Benny Goodman toured there (his men suspected of being CIA agents by some Russians, which was greeted as a value judgment by caustic American jazz critics) and Earl Hines, the Chicago pianist, toured there with great success. In 1965, Charles Lloyd, the modern jazz tenor saxophonist, took his quartet to the Talinin Jazz Festival (even Russians have jazz festivals!) and made international headlines with his success.

Jazz groups from Czechoslovakia and Poland have recorded and there have been jazz festivals in those countries as well as in Russia. The Voice of America jazz programs have the most attentive audiences of any U.S. broadcasts. When Dave Brubeck's quartet played in Poland in the late 50s, crowds of young people ran after the train when he left from the Warsaw station. Today only China remains impervious to jazz. Everywhere else — in Japan, Australia, South America, India, Pakistan, Turkey (the Bolshoi Ballet, playing · in Istanbul, came backstage to hear the Dizzy Gillespie orchestra), Finland and the Scandinavian countries — all hail America's music in the most enthusiastic terms.

Yet in America, the Federation of Musicians classifies a jazz concert as a variety show and insists on additional musicians in many concert halls rather than allowing it the "concert" classification it gives to a string quartet or a symphony.

Until very recently in America, jazz was all but ignored in the curricula of American colleges and universities. A professor of music at the University of California answered the question of why there were no courses in jazz by saying "We don't have courses in plumbing, either."

Today, as the black American's drive for wider recognition gains momentum, black jazz musicians are beginning to be in demand for positions in black studies programs. Archie Shepp has served on the faculty of New York State University at Buffalo, and John Handy, the alto saxophonist who played with Mingus, has taught at San Francisco State College. But these are the exceptions. Professional jazz musicians have not yet entered the faculty class in any number, though there are indications that this may be changing. Julian Adderley, whose quintet is one of the most successful in modern jazz, now offers a weekend seminar as part of a concert proposal to colleges and includes lecture demonstrations on various instruments as well as a discussion of the sociological and cultural aspects of the music. John Lewis of the Modern Jazz Quartet is now on the Board of Trustees of Manhattan School of Music, and Tulane University and Rutgers both have jazz archives.

There is no point in claiming that jazz is the only valuable music in America. But it is the only music completely original to this society, child though it is of the black portion of that society. But when we think of American music, we ought to think of those great artists whose names we have not known in the past though the rest of the world knew them very well. When we hear America singing, we might think of it as does Julian Bond, the black Georgia state legislator, who wrote the following verse with its multiple references to artists and compositions in the paper of the southern Student Non-Violent Co-ordinating Committee — SNCC:

> *I, too, hear America singing*
> *But from where I stand*
> *I can only hear Little Richard*
> *And Fats Domino.*

> *But sometimes I hear Ray Charles*
> *Drowning in his own tears*
> *Or Bird*
> *Relaxing at Camarillo*
> *Or Horace Silver doodling.*
> *Then I don't mind standing*
> *a little longer.*

Jazz could do worse than that for an epitaph.

And for a prophecy, I will settle for Baby Dodds' remark to me and Bill Russell after a concert in 1944.

"This ain't the LAST night! This stuff will be heard all over the world, I mean all over the country, I mean EVERY night will be the last night and that ain't never gonna *become*! And the thing about it, ain't gonna be no finish on this stuff, 'cause it's gonna be done and be heard for years and, Oh, I mean a LONG time. . . ."

Amen.

1969

# II
# Heroes

# 1.
# Bessie Smith

SHE SANG OF PAIN and of torment as truly as anyone ever did. There was little humor in her songs as there was little humor in her life. But there was plenty of hurt in both.

She was flamboyant. She had the power and she was as self-destructive as any artist who ever faced the anonymity of the mechanized medium. "If blues was whisky, babe, I would be drunk all the time," one of her poetic children sang. And she was. Most of it.

You can say all of those things about Bessie Smith but it doesn't give you even a glimpse of the incredible concentration of emotion which wells up through all of her songs. Her music swells from below, from something deeper and perhaps even apart from the possibilities of the song itself. It doesn't make very much difference, once you have tuned your ears in to her frequency, whether or not she is singing a good song or a banal one or whether or not the track on the album ends up being one of her more effective performances. Bessie Smith, like any artist, was never limited to one level at a time. Nor was she ever obvious.

Connee Boswell, who was a member of the Boswell Sisters, a vocal group which in the 30s had great success, said it very plainly about Bessie Smith: "I listened for the sound, not the lyrics." And Billie Holiday, whose own vocal style was essential to American popular music of the 40s and 50s, said that she, too, got her inspiration from Bessie's sound.

She was erratic. Art is never consistent and sometimes she would sing a song or make a record that she couldn't dig into with the same fervor as she could others. But beneath the mere performance of even lesser songs, going down from that level to another one which is almost mystical, Bessie Smith always, in everything she ever recorded, communicated that timeless feeling of frustration and of torment that has marked the role of women in this world.

"If he can stand to leave me/ I can stand to see him go."

What a line! But Bessie's music was full of lines like that, with their echoes of almost medieval language cadence expressive of the endless seasons of the earth. By and large, the Bessie Smith records are folk songs, but that is not what makes them important. Their value lies in the fact that they can effect change and make impression upon artistic talents and thus carry an impact for the future in more ways than merely by their own direction. James Baldwin, John O'Hara, Carl van Vechten. Those are merely a few of the names of artists who were not musicians who were affected by what she did. The list in music is all but endless and it rings right down through the years from Louis Armstrong to Randy Newman, whose songs and sound today could not be what they are were it not for Billie Holiday, and Billie's sound could not have existed without Bessie.

When she was at her prime, Bessie's audience was almost totally black. Her records found their way into shacks and boardinghouses in urban ghettos throughout the United States. She made the circuit of shows and clubs and theaters long before Lou Rawls tabbed it "the chitlin' circuit." She came from there and she sang of the people in those audiences, giving back to them — at her best — stories of their own lives.

It was no accident that Janis Joplin paid her homage in the final months before she died, herself a victim of the ancient women's role in art. Janis knew where she came from even if her audience did not.

Bessie Smith's voice was deep and heavy. She sang with a rhythmic pulse that predated the gospel triplets and 6/8 time and she didn't snap and twitch with accents as do the singers who came after her. But her era was a slower one and she is closer to Robert Johnson and Blind Willie than to Muddy or their urban descendants. Closer in pulse, that is, they are all the same family; she is but the older sister with slightly different ways.

Recording in the professional studios of the time, Bessie Smith took with her some of the trappings of vaudeville, of the TOBA circuit. She sang with a piano and horns rather than with a guitar. And the voices of the horns, especially the trumpet, ritualistically played an obbligato to what she sang. When the horn player was Louis Armstrong, the result was not only different but qualitatively better than when it was Joe Smith or any of the others who accompanied her. But the essential elements never changed. Not even when she went out of her way to try, when her career was collapsing, to adjust to what she was persuaded was a changing time.

When Bessie Smith was recording, records weren't available to the general public in anything like the quantities they are today. Records were sold only in special music stores. There was only a handful of labels. The retail dealers were franchised, which meant you never found two outlets selling the same labels in the same neighborhood. And if the artist was black and the music classified as "race" records (which was the jim crow bag Bessie was placed in), then the records were not available at all in the white sections, at the big department store record counters or anywhere at all outside the ghetto. Despite that, she was a hit artist. Despite that, her music — like Louis Armstrong's music — made a deep and lasting impression upon the world. That alone to some degree measures its strength.

Today, in a project that has the same kind of artistic value as does the reprinting of the complete novels of Faulkner, Columbia is making available the full list of 160 performances by Bessie Smith which are in their archives. Her work began in the early days of the phonograph record, before electric recording devices, and Columbia has arranged them in an order which begins at each end of her career and comes back to the middle.

Time is the best critic of all and the Bessie Smith records have stood that test superbly. It does not make much difference at which point one enters the music she created. Many of her white devotees from the 30s began their acquaintance with her by way of "Empty Bed Blues," a remarkable performance on two levels, at least. It was cut at the end of the 20s and it sold for years. It was especially popular with the underground audience of the Eastern colleges at that time because, in a world in which sex was never referred to openly ("It," they called it — Clara Bow had "It"), Bessie Smith's record let it all hang out.

The success of this disc (and of some of her others with the same audience) has led some critics to think of her as a black woman singing suggestive songs (whatever they are) for a white audience. But it is open to question whether or not that audience, of which we now know through the works of O'Hara and others, ever made itself known to the artist at all. She did know she had wide acceptance among jazz musicians of all colors. They showed up wherever she sang, and Bix Beiderbecke's legendary gesture of throwing a week's salary on the floor of a Chicago speakeasy to hear her sing one number is true, even if it never happened.

The way to listen to Bessie Smith is to get any of the Columbia packages (all of them eventually, of course) and just let the music play. It will take a bit of adjustment for some because of the ancient recording technique (although they have done wonders with the remastering). But ears which can accept the rural blues singers of that same period can accept Bessie Smith with a little patience. Once you are accustomed to both her sound and the recording, her records — all of them — bear repeated listening, as more and more comes from them with familiarity.

One of the levels on which her records surprise on initial listening is the encounter with dozens of phrases from the blues rhetoric which are now current. It will take scholars generations, one supposes, to establish who sang them first — if that is important.

30

What I think is important is that once you hear Bessie Smith sing them, they are hers.

Entering into her world through these records is a way to ease the pain. Knowledge of them is not essential to existence, nor to creativity. But knowledge of them can enhance both and we are all in Columbia's debt for making them available once again. And specifically we are indebted to John Hammond, who made Bessie's last records as well as Bob Dylan's first, for pushing this project through.

1971

Louis Armstrong

# 2.
# Louis Armstrong

WHEN JAMES BALDWIN wrote *The Fire Next Time,* an editor of a leading daily paper noted for its liberal, sometimes even mildly radical, but always civil libertarian viewpoint, remarked "If they felt this way why didn't they ever tell us?"

Daniel Louis Armstrong, a trumpet player and international figure for decades, "told" *them* once in plain English how he felt — though the music he has played for over fifty years has told and retold his feeling and his story to the world.

You have seen him periodically on Ed Sullivan or during the past year on the TV talk shows, clowning with Dick Cavett late at night and playing a few notes or singing while he wipes the sweat away with a gleaming white handkerchief.

He sits there, when he's not singing or playing, and tells stories of the old days in New Orleans, of street marches and funerals, of tailgate trombones and Buddy Bolden, of Mississippi River steamships with bands playing all night long and of the time in Chicago when he showed up carrying his trumpet in a paper bag, a twenty-one-year-old green youth from New Orleans making his debut in the big city.

And Louis' appearances on these shows, just as his thousands of concerts and nightclub performances and his hundreds of records over the years, reassures the insecurities of ·WASP America because Louis is safe. Louis is, like a kind of musical Rock of Gibraltar, always there, always smiling, singing, playing and *never* rocking the boat.

So the first time Louis ever rocked the boat he really raised hell.

Governor Faubus (whom Mingus immortalized in "Fables of Faubus") had just fought integration to a standstill in Arkansas. President Eisenhower, rather than take the step the world longed for and lead a little child by the hand up the steps to one of Little Rock's schools to inspire humanity, instead had decided to do nothing at all, and in such a situation, doing nothing was tantamount to encouraging the racists.

Louis, on one of his interminable road tours of the United States (he worked without respite, playing night after night on the road all over the world, right up until his final illness which came upon him last year), blew his stack.

It was September 18, 1957, and Louis was in that cultural center of the Great Plains, Grand Forks, North Dakota, for a concert. "The way they are treating my people in the South," he told a reporter for the *Grand Forks Herald*, "the government can go to hell!" President Eisenhower, Louis said (unknowingly echoing the sentiments of many others), "has no guts."

And then Louis promptly canceled a tour of the Soviet Union which had been set up by the U.S. State Department, refusing to go on the road for a government led by such a President. Louis, a veteran performer on the European concert circuit, plaintively said, "The people over there ask me what's wrong with my country. What am I supposed to say? I have had a beautiful life in music, but I feel the situation the same as any other Negro. My parents and family suffered through all of that old South and things are new now."

The White House, naturally, refused to comment. Louis' road manager, an ancient white named Pierre Talliere, told all the

34

media Louis had been "led" into saying those things and didn't mean them, but Louis told everybody, yes he did so mean them, Talliere was prejudiced, and then he added, "What I've said is me!"

It caused quite a ruckus. Jim Bishop, a Hearst columnist, attacked him viciously for being "an ingrate" and the University of Alabama canceled a concert despite a petition by students to let the show go on.

Louis, however, like the Mississippi, just kept rollin' along, making those incredible one-nighter jumps from Tokyo to Toledo, from London to Los Angeles. And now and then he opened his great mouth and growled some nitty-gritty truths about the country in which he was born. To the AP in Copenhagen during the Selma, Alabama, march in 1965, Louis burst out again. He was sick to his stomach, he said, after watching the TV news coverage of the event. "They would beat Jesus if he was black and marched," he told an interviewer.

But that was about the end of it. Louis hasn't opened his mouth publicly to discuss anything but music, food, the old days in New Orleans, and his panaceas for health since then.

Well, almost.

Some years ago I came across a short interview Louis did with Max Jones in England. Louis' band, which for years has been an integrated unit, had run into trouble in Louisiana. The state had a law against "mixed race" public performances and Louis was sore. Louis is a Louisianian, born in New Orleans in 1900, and he said, "I don't care if I ever see the city again. Honestly, they treat me better all over the world than they do in my hometown. Ain't it stupid? Jazz was born there and I remember when it wasn't no crime for cats of *any* color to get together and blow. I ain't going back to New Orleans and let them white folks be whipping me on my head!"

Something about the juxtaposition of Louis and London and New Orleans clicked in my mind and I started rooting around in all my files and books until I found what I was looking for.

Robert Goffin wrote the first book about Louis Armstrong, based on interviews and his own personal experiences living with Armstrong on tour in Europe and for a while in the United States.

In it, he told about Louis' return to his home city of New Orleans in 1931. Hundreds of people met him at the train. Members of his family, musicians he had grown up with, all paid him tribute in a parade down Canal Street with a banner stretched across the street — WELCOME TO LOUIS ARMSTRONG — THE KING OF PERDIDO. It was an orgy of nostalgia because, of all the musicians bred in that musical city, Louis was the one who had really made it in the outside world and they were welcoming him home. His band was to play a week's engagement at the Suburban Gardens and a crowd of almost ten thousand blacks had gathered outside the club, across the parking lot behind a fence, hoping to hear a note of his music when he played.

"It was a white man's place," Louis has said. "No Negro band had ever played there before. Opening night came and the place was packed. The folks knew I had been up North, been a big hit there and had even been out to Hollywood.

"All of New Orleans high society was there. The Suburban Gardens had its own radio program. They had a mike in front of the bandstand, which used to broadcast only for white bands. There was a lot of excitement in the air. Fifty thousand colored people were on the levees, close to radios.

"At the last minute the southern radio announcer said, 'I can't announce that nigger man.' My manager rushed over to me with a worried look. 'The announcer refuses to announce you.' I turned to the boys on the bandstand and said, 'Give me a chord.' I got an earsplitting chord and announced the show myself. It was the first time a Negro *spoke* on the radio down there."

Within a year of that day, Louis Armstrong was playing to standing room only at the Palladium in London, the talk of Europe, sought after by royalty, idolized by musicians, given a golden horn by members of the London Philharmonic. And after England and the Continent in 1932, back to the U.S.A. Let Louis tell it again:

"We used to tour the South in a big Packard. Lots of times we wouldn't get a place to sleep. So we'd cross the tracks, pull over to the side of the road and spend the night there. We couldn't get into hotels. Our money wasn't even good. We'd play nightclubs and spots which didn't even have a little boy's room for Negroes. We'd have to go outside, often in the freezing cold and in the dark. When we'd get hungry, my manager, Joe Glaser, who's also my friend, Jewish and white, would buy food along the way in paper bags and bring it to us boys in the bus who couldn't be served. Sometimes even this didn't work. So most of the time while touring the South, we used to stock up in a grocery store. We'd come out with a loaf of bread, a can of sardines, big hunks of bologna, cheese and we'd eat in the car. Sometimes we'd go to the back doors of restaurants where there were Negro chefs. They'd give you what you wanted. Many are the times I've eaten off those big wooden chopping blocks."

Louis Armstrong has seen his face on the cover of both *Time* and *Life*. He was the first jazz musician *Time* did a cover story on (February 2, 1949), and when *Life* had its cover story (April 15, 1966), they ran a huge foldout picture of Louis, eyes popping, blowing his horn at you from a cover that carried a headline "Vietnam — Week of Wild Uncertainty" right over "The Louis Armstrong Story — As Only He Can Tell It."

Edward R. Murrow did a full-hour CBS-TV program on him which was then expanded into a film called *Satchmo the Great*, released in 1957. Four half-hour interviews with him were broadcast on National Educational Television in the early 60s in addition to innumerable other network shows (including one in the R.J.G. series Jazz Casual in 1962). Magazines all over the world have done in-depth interviews and articles with and about him. His second autobiographical book, *Satchmo*, was issued in 1954 and parts of it were printed in several national magazines including *Holiday*. And he has appeared on so many TV variety shows that it is impossible now to tabulate them all.

There is probably only a handful of concert halls in the Western world where he hasn't appeared and the *New York Times* once ran a front-page story on the hysteria at the Zurich airport when Louis arrived. When he played in the Berlin Sportspalaast, fans slipped across the border from East Germany to hear him, and he came close to causing a revolution by his appearance in Yugoslavia and other Iron Curtain countries.

After his appearance in East Berlin, reporters asked him how he felt about the reunification of Germany. "Unify Germany? Why man, we've *already* unified it! We came through Germany blowin' this old happy music and if them Germans ain't unified, this ain't old Satchmo talkin' to ya!" Louis then said he'd like to warm up the Cold War by going to Russia. "They ain't so cold but what we couldn't bruise them with the happy music."

Medals and awards from all over the world grace the walls in his Corona, Long Island, home, but his native country has honored him only with money.

In the late 50s, the *Vancouver Sun* noted that Congress had on occasion honored civilians with a special Congressional Medal and suggested, diplomatically, that Louis Armstrong be given such an award. For instance, Congress gave one to George M. Cohan for writing "Over There" in World War I. President Kennedy instituted a program of similar awards, and although an atomic scientist made the first list, Louis did not. After John Kennedy's murder, early in the presidency of Lyndon Johnson, a campaign was mounted by several writers and elected officials including Senator Javits to get a special award for Louis or, at least, to have him included on the presidential list.

We wrote letters to congressmen and officials. I even got from the U.S. Information Agency the names of people on the President's Commission who were to make the awards and wrote to each of them.

The response was polite but noncommittal. Daniel Moynihan wrote an ominous note saying that sometime when he was in San Francisco he would tell me all about what had happened, but he never did; and only recently, from a source that begs to be unnamed, did I learn that Lyndon Johnson, emulating that now anonymous New Orleans radio announcer, just couldn't bring himself to approve the award. And apparently, rather than give one to Louis, the whole award system was dropped and there has not been, as far as I know, any other such honors for anyone since.

Louis has made, literally, thousands of records. He has tapes of them all, having transferred them from the original discs long ago. "I got it all down on tape," he told me once. "My records, Bessie,

Joe Oliver, my concerts. They're all lined up against the wall. I look forward to going through them and listening to them. That's my hobby. It's all there — my side of the story — and it will keep. Think what it would be to have them transcribed and arranged for a symphony, even. Me blowing them with a symphony orchestra!"

Although his recorded output is probably greater than anyone else's, and certainly greater than any jazz player's, he has had few hits in his fifty years on disc, though dozens of people have themselves made hits out of songs Louis first made famous. A perfect example is Bobby Darin, whose "Mack the Knife," as close a duplicate of the Armstrong version as Bobby's gift for mimicry could make it, sold infinitely more than Louis'. Another is Fats Domino's "Blueberry Hill," cut long after Louis' original version. Louis' only big top-40 hit was "Hello Dolly" which, in 1965, was the first disc by an American artist to break the Beatles' monopoly on the top rung of the Hit Parade ladder.

Louis' version of "Mack the Knife," incidentally, was a victim of censorship. Barred from the radio both in the United States and in England because of so-called bloody lyrics, the disc has nevertheless endured and has become a standard, the only case I know of a single disc becoming any kind of a hit without air play.

It is a fascinating song for Louis to have chosen. George Avakian, then a producer at Columbia Records, had heard it in the off-Broadway production of *Threepenny Opera* and had jazz trombonist Turk Murphy, long an Armstrong admirer, make an arrangement of it for Louis.

The song, you may recall, was a litany of corruption, a musical account of a pimp called Mack "The Knife" McHeath who stabbed a man to death, robbed him, and spent the money on whores. It was written by Kurt Weill and Bertolt Brecht out of the miasma of vice, decadence, corruption and despair that marked the underworld of Berlin in the early 20s. Armstrong sang it with a conviction that made it seem as though it had been written for him. And in a sense it was, because "Mack the Knife" is about all the people Louis Armstrong grew up with, his boyhood a black version of Brecht's song. And his natural affinity for the lyric tells

39

us a great deal about Louis and provides a glimpse behind that mask.

Actually, Louis Armstrong was a juvenile delinquent with a police record. He was arrested twice in New Orleans when he was a teenager and eventually was sentenced to a year in a place called Jones Orphanage, a kind of detention home for black youths. In his autobiography he tells of his early life with the same kind of frankness Charles Evers displayed when he recently announced his candidacy for the governorship of Mississippi and told of his career as a bootlegger, gambler and pimp. Like Evers, Louis offered no excuses. He told it like it was.

After his father disappeared, Louis wrote, "My mother went to a place at Liberty and Perdido Streets in a neighborhood filled with cheap prostitutes who did not make as much money for their time as did the whores in Storyville. Whether my mother did any hustling or not I cannot say."

She would, however, Louis recalled, be gone for days and his childhood was filled with a succession of "stepfathers." "I remember at least six," he wrote.

"When I was about four or five — still wearing dresses — I lived with my mother in a place called Brick Row — a lot of cement, rented rooms. . . . And right in the middle of that on Perdido Street was the Funky Butt Hall. Old, beat up, big cracks in the wall. On Saturday night Mama couldn't find us 'cause we wanted to hear that music. Before the dance the band would play out front for about a half hour and us little kids would all do little dances.

"Then we'd look through the cracks in the wall of Funky Butt. It wasn't no classified place, and to a tune like "The Bucket's Got a Hole In It" [Hank Williams' version of the song, recorded in the 50s, carries Hank's name as composer!], some of them chicks would get way down, shake everything, slapping themselves on the cheek of their behind. . . ."

As a teenager, "the boys I ran with had prostitutes workin' for them. They did not get much money from their gals, but they got a great deal of notoriety. I wanted to be in the swim, so I cut in on a chick. She was not much to look at but she made good money, or what in those days I thought was big money. I was a green inexperienced kid as far as women were concerned, particularly when one of them was walkin' the streets for me. . . ."

Louis' career as a pimp lasted a short time until the girl stabbed him in the shoulder. But he worked as an errand boy and go-fer in and around the brothels of that classic brothelized city and played in them, too. Eventually he married a whore whom he met in a brothel called the Brick House. He tells of this, too, in his autobiography. She named her price and he accepted and later married her.

"Everybody wanted to know was Mama satisfied that her son's marrying a prostitute twenty-one years old. She say 'I can't live his life. He's my boy and if that what he wants to do, that's that.' "

So that's why, when Louis sings of Mack the Knife, of Louie Miller and Sukey Tawdrey and Jennie Diver, he sounds like it is real because it *is* real. Louis' teenage world was filled with true life characters called Dirty Dog, Steel Arm Johnny, Mary Jack the Bear (a tough whore who fought like a bear), One-Eye Bud, Cocaine Buddy and Egg Head Papa. The blood ran in the streets of the ghetto when he was growing up; it was a world of gambling, prostitution, no-holds-barred living in which you didn't press charges against corrupt white cops because you were black. It was a world where blacks were always beaten up, guilty or innocent, when they were arrested. *Threepenny Opera* as true story, in fact.

And when Louis moved out and up to Chicago, he stayed mostly in the ghetto — Chicago's Southside, with the real-life mobster prototypes of *The Untouchables* enforcing contracts with guns.

But New Orleans, when Louis was coming up, was unique. "There was over a hundred bands then," Louis says. "Most of them six pieces, and most of them working. Now, on Sundays, the bands would be out on the wagons, doin' the advertisin'. See, in those days, there were long wagons, pulled by maybe one horse or two mules. They hauled furniture weekdays.

"On Sundays, a dance hall owner would hire a wagon for his band. And the wagon would go around the streets. Bass fiddle player and the trombone man sit on the tailgate, so they won't bump the others. Rest of the boys — drums, guitar, trumpet, and so forth — sit in the wagon.

"So, on Sundays, the musicians who wanted to work, not lay around and drink, went 'on the wagon' and that's maybe where that saying come from.

"You see, they always had the big dances on Monday nights, and you did the advertisin' the day before, Sunday.

"For instance, one gentleman is giving a dance at Economy Hall tomorrow, and another gentleman is giving a dance at the Funky Butt Hall. The hall where — well, everybody, they named this kind of dancing they did there 'funkybuttin',' and the hall was famous by that name.

"Anyhow, these two gentlemen each are giving a dance and they want, each wants to draw a big crowd. So they send out their wagons, paradin' and advertisin'.

"Now finally these two wagons meet at a corner. Their wheels are chained together. Then the two bands blow it out. And the one that gets the big ovation from the crowd, that's the one gets most all the people Monday.

"Musicians used to help each other in those days. I mean, the older ones would help the younger ones. Now, I was just a kid, sixteen, but Joe (King) Oliver, he was a powerful man. *The* top trumpet. I could play a whole lot of horn in my little way, but Joe was the *King!*

"But Joe told me, 'Now, if you ever get on the corner with a wagon, and *my* wagon comes up, you stand up, so I can see you. That'll be our signal, you know. I'll just play ordinary and give you the break.'

"But one Sunday, I didn't stand up and oh, man, he like to blow me out of the business.

"It was good money according to the times. At the better places, like the Economy Hall, we'd get $2.50 a night. Easter Sunday was our big day. We'd make $3 at the Easter Sunday picnic, and then we'd play that night for $2.50.

"Remember, that was Economy Hall, a big place. Now, all of them great musicians down there in the Red Light District, which they called Storyville, they only got a dollar a night. Joe Oliver got $1.50 and that was top money for the leader.

"Thing is, in 1915 I got a dollar a night at Henry Metrango's honky-tonk and I could make a living and still have enough money to buy a suit of clothes.

"I was very young when I first heard Joe Oliver. He was in The Onward Band, a brass band they had down there in New Orleans — a good brass band. About twelve pieces: with three trumpets and three cornets. Joe was playing cornet at the time. Two of them would play lead; there was Joe and Manny Perez. I used to play second line behind them. When Joe would get through playing, I'd carry his horn. I guess I was about fourteen. Joe gave me cornet lessons, and when I was a kid, I ran errands for his wife.

"I could stay at the parade and listen to them blow all day. They just knocked me out. They'd come along with blue serge coats, white pants, and band hats, Joe would have cream-colored pants. I remember those hot days, and the hot sun. Joe would have a handkerchief on his head, and put his cap on top of it, with the handkerchief covering the back of his neck to keep the sun off him while he's blowing. All the cats would be blowing, even the second line. They'd play 'Panama,' or something like that, and the second line would applaud, and Joe was really blowing — he'd go way up there, you know, like on that last chorus of 'High Society.' If you ever heard us play it, that's Joe Oliver up and down, note for note. I wouldn't change that solo; I see to it that I hit those same notes in my mind, because that's the way he'd end up those brass band solos.

"Joe used to come by Liberty and Perdido. I used to play in the honky-tonk and he used to come from down in Storyville and come up there where I played, 'cause he got off at twelve o'clock at night and seein' they threw the key away where I worked, he'd come up there and sit down and listen to me play and then he'd blow a few for me, y'know, and try to show me the right things. At that time I didn't have no idea he would send for me to come to Chicago. I was playin' in the Tuxedo Brass Band with Kid Ory and I just had left the excursion boats and I was playin' with the Tuxedo Brass Band, and that's when King Oliver sent for me to play the second trumpet with him at the Lincoln Gardens. Was I surprised? I was happy, couldn't nobody else get me out of New Orleans but him! I wouldn't take that chance.

43

"I hadn't heard his band 'til I got to Chicago. When I heard it at the door I said, 'I ain't good enough for *this* band, I think I'll go back.' . . . that was one of my life's biggest moments. It was the same set up as New Orleans but, see, we didn't have no pianos in New Orleans, we had git-tars and Lil was on the piano here, see what I mean?

"And they was wailin'! I fit right in there, sitting with Joe, because I admired him so anyway, y'know. I just went to work. No rehearsal. I knew all the guys and I just sit in there and went to work the next night. I played second trumpet to everything he played. Second cornet at that time 'cause we both was usin' cornets.

" 'Snake Rag' was one of the ones he just made up for the record, Gennett Records. When he started makin' records he started bein' a writer ha ha ha. We'd rehearse it on the job and when we got to the studio all we had to do was cut it up and time it. Was no trouble at all to make them records, we'd just make one after the other. They wasn't as particular then as they was today. No drums at all at that time. They was scared it would throw the needle off."

Louis was talking on National Educational Television where I had been playing him some of his first records. I had always wanted to ask him how he and Joe Oliver were able to improvise the fabulous two- and four-bar breaks they played simultaneously. It has always been a feat of astonishing virtuosity.

Louis smiled and told me, interspersed with sly chuckles and demonstrations of Joe Oliver's fingers on an imaginary horn.

"I put notes to his lead, whatever he made, . . . we didn't write it, he'd tell me while the band was playin' what he gonna play on top wa wa wa wa and I'd pick out my notes and that's why all the musicians used to come around to hear us do that, y'know. They thought that was a secret we had heh heh! Bix and Louis Pancio and Paul Whiteman and all the boys used to come around, you know, and they thought that was sumpin'! Whatever he was gonna do, he'd let me know about four, five bars ahead while the band was jumpin' heh heh heh."

Playing with King Oliver was easy, Louis said, and so was making all those incredible records accompanying the classic blues singers of the 20s — Ma Rainey, Bessie Smith, Clara Smith, Maggie Jones. "All we had to do," Louis recalled, "was play the blues and fill in them gaps! Like Bessie Smith. I remember she just stayed in the studio and wrote the blues there. She finish one, she write another.

"I don't know who was first, Ma Rainey'd been singing a long time. But Bessie came a little later and outsang 'em all!"

Making the great Hot Five and Hot Seven records — still classics of jazz — for Okeh was easy, too, Louis recalled. "We'd just make up them things! Make 'em up in the studio. One tune there, where I dropped the paper an' started scattin', we used to do that in the quartets in New Orleans. Sound like an instrument, or somethin'."

And in Chicago Louis doubled from the Oliver band to bigger orchestras. "Playin' for silent pictures. Big old symphony orchestra for siiiiiiiiilent pictures! After the curtain go up, you play an overture. Then a hot number. That's where I came in!"

Louis went to New York in 1924 to join a band at Roseland Ballroom (still the palace of dance in Manhattan). "When I went with Fletcher Henderson's band in 1924, why that was sumpin' else! The minute I got up on the stand, there's a *part* in front of me! Y'know? Well, I wasn't used to *that*."

Louis took up the horn in Jones Orphanage in New Orleans. And all over the world in the years since then he has played "When the Saints Go Marching In," the spiritual that the orphange band played when the boys marched to church on Sunday morning.

When he got out of the orphanage, Louis hung around the New Orleans clubs and dance halls listening to the great players of the first days of jazz. "Louis was always worryin' me and worryin' me to carry my horn," Bunk Johnson, the veteran who played with Buddy Bolden's Original Superior Band, has said as he told how Louis learned — "Anything he could whistle, he could play."

In those days, after the reign of King Buddy Bolden as chief musician in New Orleans, Joseph "King" Oliver was the man. Oliver played so strong he would blow a cornet out of tune in a few months and Bolden could be heard across Lake Pontchartrain, old-timers recall. But Joe was Louis' idol. Oliver went to Chicago

45

while Louis was still in short pants and working the local gigs. Armstrong stayed behind, playing with Kid Ory's band and then on the Mississippi River steamboats with Fate Marable.

The Oliver band was the band which scored the big success in Chicago. It had the legendary Johnny Dodds on clarinet and Johnny's brother, Baby, on drums, and when Joe sent for Louis, the young Armstrong packed his trumpet and took the train to Chicago.

The Oliver records were and remain marvels of collective improvisation. Louis' and Joe's breaks would be thrilling. Armstrong was soon the sensation of Chicago's black community but Oliver, who acknowledged Louis' ability, insisted, "He can't hurt me when he's with me," and they stayed together for a long time. But eventually the virtuosity of Armstrong drew him away from the Oliver band into recording sessions on his own, accompanying blues singers such as Ma Rainey and Bessie Smith, and with the Hot Five and Hot Seven.

These latter groups were studio groups assembled from the Chicago musical cadres and included the best sidemen in the city, with players such as Kid Ory, Earl Hines, and the Dodds brothers, and in a short period in 1926 they made the series of jazz records that included some of the greatest solo instrumental performances ever put on record. Many of the tunes were old New Orleans street songs and blues and musicians' warm-up tunes and others were things the band or Louis made up in the studio. It is hard today to imagine the original impact of those records. There was simply nothing remotely like them at the time. Okeh was a reasonably big record company with national distribution (it later became part of Columbia) and the thick old shellac 78-rpm discs were available in the ghetto record stores all over the country. They were never played on the air then at all, incidentally. Few, if any, records were played on radio at that time, and actually the old discs carried a legend plainly stating "Not licensed for radio broadcast." But all over the country, in that mystical way in which the underground has always worked, musicians, white and black, heard those discs. It was like the Second Coming of Christ. They could not believe their ears. That such sounds could be made!

46

Louis spent some time in New York with Fletcher Henderson's big band — the big band era was just beginning and Henderson was the man whose book of arrangements was to be the basis for Benny Goodman's success a few years later — and then he returned to Chicago.

A man named Joe Glaser, who managed dance halls and nightclubs in Chicago during Prohibition, hired Louis to lead the band at the Sunset Café, a favorite spot for Chicago black and white nightlife. Glaser recognized the importance of Louis and became his lifetime manager and friend. He once told a writer for *Life*, "Louis has always been inclined to feel he's got to go out and blow his brains out. . . . so I used to say, 'Louis, forget all the goddam critics, the musicians. Play for the public. Sing and play and smile.' At first in Chicago, Louis was always very, very shy, very quiet. When I hired him at the Sunset, I used to act like the coach on a football team. I'd say, 'Louis, sing and make faces and smile. Smile, goddamit, smile! Give it to them. Don't be afraid!' "

Glaser really changed Louis' life. From then on Louis smiled and made faces and played and sang, and even years later, when he was asked about his reaction to the way young musicians in the bebop era were breaking away from his style, Louis went right back to the Glaser formula. "I'll play for the old-time people," he said. "They got all the money!"

Glaser, who died in the late 60s, became one of the biggest booking agents in the country as head of Associated Booking Corporation, which he founded. Louis was always his first-line attraction even when he was booking Noel Coward and other stars. Once Glaser, a tempestuous and profane man, was asked by a leading folk group whom he wanted to book to guarantee them he would give them as much attention as he gave Louis. "Goddamit!" he yelled in a hotel lobby when he was telling me the story. "How in hell could I give them as much attention as I could Louis? I'm Louis and Louis' me. We grew up together. We're a part of each other."

Yet Louis (he has always been "Louis" and not "Louie") always called Joe Glaser "Pops" or "Mister Glaser" just as he called the white trombonist Jack Teagarden, himself a jazz virtuoso who

47

played in Louis' band for a number of years, "Pops" or "Mister Jack."

In the mid-30s Armstrong led a big band himself and made scores of records for various companies of current pop tunes. His great thing was to take the lyrics of some silly song, even "Stardust" is a good example, and treat those insipid lyrics in such a fashion that they became a work of put-on art. At the end of "Stardust," where the lyric goes "the memory of love's refrain," Louis would growl out, in a vocal riff, "Oh memory! oh memory! oh memory of love's refrain," breaking down the banal lyrics more and more until they became something else altogether.

His endurance and his power were legendary. His lips were iron and his lungs had the strength of a hurricane. During one of his periods in New York he held down three jobs. He played downtown in the Hudson Theater for a show with the Connie's Inn Hot Chocolates Revue. Then he went uptown at midnight for a late show at the Lafayette Theater in Harlem and then after *that* played a breakfast set at the Connie's Inn Cabaret!

It took strength but Louis always took good care of himself. He catnapped whenever he could and he always slept on his back after heavyweight boxing champ Max Baer told him that was the best way to relax. "He taught me how to relax one muscle at a time."

But it was to the care of his lips that Louis gave the most attention. The lips are crucial to the trumpet player since they control the entire horn-blowing operation and Louis took great pains not to split a lip. Once when he did at a show in a Baltimore theater, he continued to play, blood dripping down his chin, while members of the orchestra literally cried to see him put himself through such agony for the sake of the show.

Years later, Louis talked to a reporter about staying in condition.

"You got to stay in shape, man. To me, it ain't the money in this business; I could have been a millionaire four times. I just want to blow the horn as long as I can. All those musicians trying to get famous, so they can have yachts and swimming pools and all that. . . . I come through life trying to get more joy out of staying healthy, so I can blow. And so, if I get a million dollars, I don't have to have nobody wheeling me around in a chair.

"You see, most those fellows in the old days in New Orleans, they wouldn't relax ever.

"Around 1916, I'd see those boys play all night, then go to the Eagle Saloon at seven on Sunday morning when they got a parade coming up at nine. Instead of taking a two-hour nap to break their tiredness so they could tough the day out — no, they'd stay up and drink!

"And at two o'clock in the afternoon, when that sun beat down on them, I've seen them drop dead in the parade.

"So I learned my lesson early. Some of them didn't believe in going to the dentist every so often, for a checkup on their chops. Joe Oliver, that great trumpet player, played till his teeth got so loose you could pull them out with your fingers. Take Buddy Bolden. He was a great trumpet 'way back in 1910 to 1915, but he blew too hard.

"You take a cat who's blowing, and he's got a tough high note coming up. He don't figure he can make that note no more, so he'll make a hundred notes, just to get around that one.

"But Buddy Bolden, he would *try*. He would blow sooooo hard . . . well, you could see the veins. Finally, he just blew his brains out.

"Not long ago, I sat in with Count Basie's band in Florida one night, just havin' fun. Count says, 'DAMN! I ain't never heard that much strong horn played in all my life!'

"Now, Count Basie's trumpet players are all good musicians, but they run away from their notes. Why? Because they don't keep their chops fortified; their lips are sore.

"Everybody wants to know why I play stronger than any other trumpets. Well, it ain't nothin' mysterious. Ain't no witch doctor, two-head stuff. If you can take the soreness out of your lips, you can put pressure on that horn.

"How to do it? I bathe my lips every night, soon as I leave the stand, with witch hazel and lip salve and sweet spirits of nitre. And I bathe 'em again before I go to bed.

"Sweet spirits of nitre will take the soreness out of anything, man. Oh, it stings! You put it on and then grab a chair for about five minutes, and too many trumpet players ain't got the guts to stand the ache.

"Or they won't use the salve, 'cause it's greasy. It's not bad, smells like strawberry.

"Now, when I get up to go to work, I put witch hazel and sweet spirits of nitre on again, and by the time I get to the club tonight, I'm OK again.

"Sure, my lips are scarred up — I been playing that horn fifty years — but they're *relaxed* at all times, and that's it. If your lips swell up a fraction on the mouthpiece, you're in trouble with your notes."

Louis has always used a special salve from a special factory in Holland, and even during World War II, musicians conspired to break the wartime blockade and get the salve to Armstrong. For years he has been a devout believer in the efficacy of a laxative called Swiss Kriss, even giving out samples of it to friends and preparing a special instruction sheet on how to stay healthy and lose weight "The Satchmo Way."

So on through the 30s and the 40s, and yes, the 50s and the 60s, Louis made those one-nighters, those concerts and nightclubs and shows all the way from Korea, where they booked him to open some gambling house in Seoul, to the opera houses of Europe.

Wherever he went he was always good copy for all the media because he kept saying things in that personal, colorful style in which he always spoke.

When he played for England's King George V, he dedicated the number thus: "Here's one for you, Rex." And thirty years later, when he played for King George's granddaughter Princess Margaret, Louis blew "Mahogany Hall Stomp," a rousing number named after the raunchy old dance hall in New Orleans. "We really gonna lay this one on the princess," he growled.

People always asked him to define jazz. What is it? they would ask, and Louis' standard answer has become one of the legends of the music world. "Lady," he is reported to have once told a bejeweled dowager, "if you got to ask what it is, you'll never know." Pure Zen, even if Louis never heard of Dr. Suzuki.

Over and over, down through the years, he has blown the fuses of jazz critics and fans by giving unexpected answers. What records did he listen to when he was a kid? The Original Dixieland Jazz Band, that's who, and the disc of "Tiger Rag" by that group of young white New Orleanians, Louis insists, is the all-time best performance of that classic.

What's his favorite band? He has determinedly insisted for decades that it is Guy Lombardo and there's no trace of put-on in his statement.

"I haven't heard no band that plays more perfect music than Guy Lombardo *yet*. That's the way I feel and I don't let my mouth say nuthin' my head can't stand," he told *Life*. "Any time I walk up on the stage with Guy Lombardo, I'm relaxed. That's the music I've played all my life." Those of us who have listened in vain for some clue to what Louis hears in The Sweetest Music This Side of Heaven (as Lombardo has always billed his work) have just had to accept the fact that he digs them and to hell with it.

He even put down the big anti–rock 'n' roll crusade back in 1957 when they thought they could get the Old Master to put rock down. "It's all right," he surprised everyone by saying. "Ain't nuthin' wrong with rock 'n' roll. The cats have fun with it. It's nuthin' new. I been doin' it for years."

He even dug folk music, but again he wasn't surprised by it. Louis said something profound when he uttered his famous comment about folk music in the Peter, Paul & Mary–Kingston Trio era. "Folk music?" Satch said. "Why daddy, I don't know no other kind of music BUT folk music. I ain't never heard a hoss sing a song."

His bitterest words about music were directed against the late-40s, early-50s bebop or so-called modern jazz. Chuck Berry sang, "I got nuthin' against modern jazz," but Louis wasn't so benign.

What bothered Louis about modern jazz was its disrespect for the old-timers and the implication that nothing important had happened before the young beboppers came on the scene. "I remember every note I ever played," he said, "I got some respect for the old folks who played trumpet before me. Then," he added murkily, "the trumpet is an instrument that's full of temptation." Then he brightened and told anthropologist Ernest Borneman, "I'm doing something different all the time, but I always think of them fine old cats way down in New Orleans — Joe and Bunk and Tio and Buddy Bolden — and when I play music, that's what I'm listening to. The way they phrased so pretty and always on the melody, and none of that out-of-the-world music, that pipe-dream music, that whole modern malice. I mean, all them young cats along the street with their horns wrapped in a stocking and they say, 'Pay me first, pops, then I'll play a note for you,' and you know that's not the way any good music ever got made!

"You got to like playing pretty things if you're ever going to be any good blowing your horn. These young cats now, they want to make money first and the hell with the music. And they want to carve everyone else because they're full of malice, and all they want to do is show you up and any old way will do as long as it's different from the way you played it before.

"So you get all them weird chords which don't mean nothin', and first people get tired of it because it's really no good and you got no melody to remember and no beat to dance to. So they're all poor again and nobody is working and that's what that modern malice done for you."

Louis, of course, is a very philosophical cat. For instance, there is his attitude towards "Sister Kate," a song which has been recorded and performed for decades, most recently by the Olympics, Taj Mahal and the Kweskin Jug Band.

"Once I was promised fifty dollars — more money than I'd ever seen all at once — for a tune I wrote called 'Get Off Katie's Head.' I sold it to A. J. Piron and Clarence Williams [two early black songwriters, musicians, and publishers]. . . . They wrote some words and called it 'I Wish I Could Shimmy Like My Sister Kate.' They never did pay me for it, never even put my name on it. I didn't holler about it. You can't get everything that's coming to you in life."

"I fell in love with that horn and it fell in love with me," he once said. "Man, I ain't leavin' this old horn *nowhere*, not even when I go to heaven, because I guess them angels up there are waitin' to hear old Satchmo's music, too. I'm my own audience. They put a stop sign up on my head, I take it right down. Me and my horn ain't never gonna stop."

"I'm not the ambassador, the music is," he said on TV apropos his effect upon jazz fans in the Iron Curtain countries. "They hear a lot of things, some good, some bad, but I know one thing — this ain't no cannon!"

In Yugoslavia they called him "Satchmovic" and in Africa "Okuka Lokole." In New Orleans they called him "Satchel-mouth" (a reference to his huge mouth) and usage shortened it universally to "Satch" or "Satchmo." But Louis says, "Call me anything at all. Just don't call me too late to eat! I been blowing that horn for fifty years and I never looked back once.

"You can live on this earth without pouting all the time. I bet I made a million dollars, but I don't know. I just blow my horn and let my manager count the money. When a man's in love, what else can he want?"

Louis has been married four times and, as far as we know, has no children. "I'm a Baptist, married to a Catholic, and I wear a Jewish star all the time for good luck. I'm a good friend of the pope's," he added. Louis visited the pope once and one of the great legends about him concerns their exchange on that occasion. The pope reportedly asked Louis if he had any children and Satch replied, "No father, but I sure had a lot of fun tryin'."

Louis' fourth (and current) wife is Lucille "Brown Sugar" Wilson, a chorus girl from the old Cotton Club in New York. They have been married over twenty-five years. A handsome, dark woman, she was the first to break the "high yaller" color standard maintained by the Cotton Club chorus line for years (Lena Horne is also a graduate of that chorus line). "I like my women beautiful, dark and tender — the blacker the berry the sweeter the juice," Satch says. "But I love my trumpet, too. I always made it plain to all my wives that that trumpet must come first before anybody or anything. That horn is my real boss, because it's my life!"

Always a sharp dresser by show business standards, Louis sometimes has had as many as sixteen suits in his road tour luggage and he always carries his trumpet mouthpiece in his coat pocket.

Since he uses up so much energy playing and singing, Louis sweats profusely, and one of his road manager's chores is to have sixty clean white linen handkerchiefs ready for every working day. During his heavy road touring days, Louis had "Satchmo" embroidered on his handkerchiefs and used a cologne of the same name.

For years, on the road he spent his time in the dressing room between shows pecking out letters on the typewriter to friends all over the world in his own inimitable style replete with "heh hehs" as asides for laughter and always signing off "Red beans and ricely yours."

Louis Armstrong's dressing rooms over the years have changed only in one respect — he plays a better class of place now. There are always the old friends from New Orleans. Musicians, people he knew when he was a kid (New Orleans must have had millions of black jazz fans; they show up everywhere he works). The people associated with whatever show he's playing, fans from all over, young and old, and his musicians and personal staff. Louis frequently receives visitors sitting in his dressing room wearing nothing but his shorts and a handkerchief wrapped around his head, and as he talks or signs autographs, he rubs his lips with his special salve and chuckles.

Louis is dedicated to his fans. That's really true. I remember once seeing a young producer of a concert stopped cold by Louis when he tried to tell a line of autograph hunters Louis was too busy to sign their programs. "No, no," Louis was almost salty. "Them's my people," and he dutifully signed them all, program after program, "Red beans and ricely yours."

I've been going to hear Louis Armstrong at stage shows, concerts, nightclubs and dances since I was a kid in college and dug him at the Apollo Theater, standing there with his gleaming trumpet and the white handkerchief in front of that big band.

I remember him walking into a club one night to hear Kid Ory's band, and as soon as they saw Louis, Ory and Papa Mutt Carey (the trumpeter in the band and a contemporary of Louis') broke into "Mahogany Hall Stomp." Then there was the time at the Monterey Jazz Festival when he was scheduled to appear on a panel discussion with Dizzy Gillespie and arrived late. When Louis walked in, Dizzy stood up applauding and the room was

54

Louis'. Just as Dizzy sat on the stage at another Monterey festival night at Louis' feet while the Master played.

Back in 1962 after the show at a big hotel, Louis told me he had something to announce and then took me to his room and talked about his plans to retire. "I'm tired," he said, and went on to describe how he wanted to travel slowly, and for fun, and to listen to all kinds of other music. "Let them young fellas play for a while," he said, while his wife, echoing his plans, said, "I got twelve big rooms [in their Corona, Long Island, home]. I don't need 'em. What's home without him?"

But Louis didn't retire. His manager, Joe Glaser, told me not to pay any attention to what Louis said. Louis wouldn't *know* how to stop, goddamit. And Joe was right. Louis didn't stop until he was too sick to travel.

Despite all the ironies of his life ("I can have lunch with the president of Brazil," he once said, "in the presidential mansion, but I can't walk into a hotel dining room in the South and order a steak or a glass of water as any ordinary white man can do"), Louis has refused to become bitter or depressed.

It has only been in the years since jazz achieved some acceptance, in the late 50s, that Louis has stayed at a downtown hotel even in such a cosmopolitan city as San Francisco. Before, he stayed out in the ghetto boardinghouses and hotels. When he was making his early pictures in Hollywood (he's been in over thirty flicks including *New Orleans*, that classic of jazz history), he couldn't stay in the downtown hotel in Los Angeles but stayed out on Central Avenue. And at the parties he went to in Hollywood, he quickly tired of people with a couple of drinks in them coming up to him and starting a conversation by saying, "Y'know, I used to have a colored mammy."

As late as 1960, Louis could say he didn't go out with the Hollywood movie crowd. "Even though I've played with a lot of them . . . Danny Kaye, Sinatra. I don't even know where they live. In fact, I've never been invited to the home of a movie star, not even Bing's."

Louis has been called an Uncle Tom. Kenneth Tynan even quoted Billie Holiday once as saying (in admiration and love), "Louis toms from the heart." And he makes jokes about one of his musicians being "Bing Crosby in Technicolor." And he once traumatized network TV bosses when, making a guest appearance on the Dorsey brothers show (the same summer series that presented Elvis Presley for the first time), he gave his instructions to the band: "Don't play too slow or too fast — just half-fast."

But then Louis never was one to hide anything. Take, for instance, his classic record of "You Rascal You." The lyric went like this:

> I'll be standin' on the corner, high
> When they bring your body by,
> I'll be glad when you're dead
> You rascal you.

When Louis made that disc back in 1931, even though grass was still legal, the song swept across the underground of the time like a rumor about Mick Jagger today.

Black people had it on their jukeboxes and in their homes and a handful of white record collectors bought it in the record stores of the ghettos.

Jazz was still an underground music then, in many ways, but curiously enough bands like Louis Armstrong's would broadcast almost nightly, from wherever they were, on the late night radio network shows. And when Louis laid down that one word "high," the aficionados all over the country fell out. White and black. And they used to listen for it. Just as they listened for other special messages, like his line about "smokin' a Louis Armstrong special see-gar." They had the kind of impact in the underground then that "everybody must get stoned" had forty years later.

Louis has always been one of the mythological heroes of the grass culture. ("Stoned in Rome," Louis once scrawled on a postcard of the Colosseum.) He figures heavily in Mezz Mezzrow's autobiography, *Really the Blues*, just as he figured in the lives of all the jazz musicians of the 30s and 40s. Mezzrow was a big dope dealer, an early Owsley, with the same quality control and, like Owsley, he gave his name to his product, the "mezzerole," made with the golden grass he specialized in. The Mezz. Alberta Hunter, the blues singer, sang, "Dreamed about a reefer, five foot long, the mighty mezz, but not too strong." Mezz sold his grass by the shoebox coast to coast, mail order, as well as standing on 125th Street underneath the Tree of Life, dealing with all who came by.

Louis even got himself busted when grass was brought under the Harrison Narcotic Act by that prince of hypocrites Harry J. Anslinger, and he did a short stretch for possession. Some twenty years later, en route from Honolulu to the mainland there was another possession bust, but this time it was Louis' wife the narcs claimed was holding.

But Mezzrow is cautious about linking Louis to grass, though the implication runs throughout the book. And Louis himself has put grass down in recent years. Still, it is an interesting point that censorious officials never picked up on the drug references in the early Armstrong songs.

I never saw Louis light up a joint (though Mezz writes about the motto in his circle being "Light up and be somebody"), but I sure watched some of his sidemen blow some gage. Louis had a pianist once who used to lean back from the piano and take a long toke from a friend standing behind the curtain and keep right on playing. And Big Sid Catlett, the drummer who played with the Armstrong All Stars, once had a San Francisco club so stashed with grass that all he had to do, wherever he was in the joint, was run his hand along the top of the paneling near the ceiling and grab a roach.

Louis, though, was always Louis no matter where the gig and no matter who the audience. In the Oakland Auditorium the week he was on the cover of *Time*, when there were less than five hundred people in the place, or in the Fairmont Hotel before a crowded room of bankers, it was still Louis. And he gave them all "Mack the Knife" and "Coal Cart Blues" and the rest, and they never — at least the audiences in the Fairmont never did — picked up for even a second on what a slice of reality he was laying out before them. Louis' "Coal Cart Blues" was a folk song. No "hoss" could sing it, true, but it came right out of Louis' own childhood, picking up coal along the railroad tracks coming into New Orleans to feed the thin fire in his mother's shack. He made 15 cents a load doing that, and when he sang about it to the Fairmont Hotel audience they thought he was charming.

I don't know how many times I've seen Louis Armstrong perform. I've lost count. But I do know what his most moving performance was for me and that was the night he appeared at the Monterey Jazz Festival in Dave Brubeck's *The Real Ambassador*, the musical Dave had written for Louis. It was a cold night, but the stage and the audience were warm with love. Louis stood there in his ambassadorial costume, high hat and all, and he sang, "All I do is play the blues/ and meet the people face to face . . . in my humble way/ I'm the USA . . . though I represent the government, the government don't represent some policies I'm for. . . ."

It was a thrilling night in the fullest sense of that overused word. And when Louis ended the show with the lines "They say I look like God. . . . could God be black?" *that* audience, at least, was ready and willing to believe it just might be.

Gene Krupa once described what it felt like to play with Louis: "It was like somebody turned the current on." It was like that on that Monterey evening and it was like that every time the stars were right for Louis because he did a truly original thing in art.

From the time he came on the scene at the beginning of the 20s until the first level of the modern jazz revolution (led by Charlie Parker, Thelonious Monk and Dizzy Gillespie) in the late 40s, Louis Armstrong's concept of improvising and of playing was the basis of almost all of jazz.

He took the tools of European musical organization — chords, notation, bars and the rest — and added to them the rhythms of the church and of New Orleans and (by definition) Africa, brought into the music the blue notes, the tricks of bending and twisting notes, and played it all with his unexcelled technique. He went as far with it as he could by using the blues and popular songs of the time as skeletons for his structural improvisation. He would take the thirty-two-bar chorus of a song and build upon it, like a carpenter with scaffolding, building on upward and upward until the original thirty-two bars were (at least in his ears and hopefully in the audience's) supporting an incredible superstructure which could, theoretically, be divided down until individual elements all related directly to the original bar structure.

Louis as a trumpet player (and cornet player before he took up trumpet) had astonishing speed of execution and he had a range that extended the possibilities of the trumpet beyond the concept of the time. Brass players from the Royal Philharmonic heard him in London and were awed by his range. He was said to be capable of hitting three hundred consecutive Gs above high C.

But he could and did play simply, too. His sparse use of notes (listen to him on the sides he recorded with Bessie Smith, Ma Rainey, Clara Smith, and Maggie Jones, for instance) became an extraordinarily effective device to transmit emotion because of two things: his intonation and his phrasing.

Leading the final choruses of a number by his big seventeen-piece swing band, Louis' horn would sail on up above the sections of the band not unlike the way B. B. King leads the ensemble on his guitar today. Louis would swing the band in the old and truest meaning of the term, using his horn like a long leash to pull them one way and then another, but never losing sight of the original chord pattern, melody and harmony.

It was not until the bebop era of Parker and Gillespie that the use of passing chords, classical dissonances and irregular rhythmic patterns added another dimension to jazz playing which was to bring it to the end of the path defined by European musical rules. After that, Coltrane and Ornette Coleman broke through and made music on those same instruments in an entirely different, non-European way for a New Morning in jazz.

As a singer, Louis' style was as original as his trumpet playing. Nat "King" Cole told me once Louis had a style rather than a voice in the formal sense. But in his way, Louis was the first singer in popular music in America to include as a part of his language sounds made by the human voice which were not merely the reproduction of notes on the scale. Louis growled and grated, grunted and wheezed, for special effects. He bent notes as he sang, just as he would bend them when he played. His singing was his own reflection of his trumpet playing.

Just as Ray Charles was later to make the phrase "All right" into an almost universal ritual in vocal performances, Louis made the phrase "Oh yeah" into the same kind of thing as a tag at the end of his songs and as a signature expression within them, as "Amen" sung over two notes is the preacher's signoff.

59

Along with Bessie Smith, he was the seminal influence on many of the popular singers of the 30s and 40s.

Not only Billie Holiday, but almost every other singer, directly or indirectly, who performed during the Swing Era and who was at all influenced by jazz (and most of them were) bore the mark of Louis' style.

George Bernard Shaw once wrote that "anybody, almost, can make a beginning; the difficulty is to make an end . . . to do what cannot be bettered." And that is precisely what Louis Armstrong did. He did his thing so well that no one else has been able to equal his achievement within his style and what he did was so good in and of itself that it has survived generations. Whole tunes and countless arrangements have been based on parts of an Armstrong solo. At least one band of the 30s, the Glen Gray Casa Loma Band, made up instrumental compositions which were simply phrases from Armstrong solos played by horn sections, trumpets or saxophones and strung together into a full number.

Any night, the studio bands on the TV shows can be heard still, fifty years after Louis arrived in Chicago to join King Oliver's Creole Jazz Band, playing little bits of Louis' music in their charts.

An entire generation, no, two generations of trumpet players were ruined and frustrated by Louis' brilliance. What he did was so right, there seemed to be no other way. Musicians abandoned the trumpet and took up other instruments. Others became alcoholics or junkies trying to ape his style, his tone and his phrasing. Some of them did it so well that on early records collectors thought they were, indeed, Louis.

Young black musicians copied his gestures, his clothes and his manners as well as his vocal sound both in singing and in talking. Young white musicians got so far into his bag that they tried to do the same thing. Young Italians from Chicago and New York growled and grated away when they talked, trying to sound like the gravel-voiced original from New Orleans.

His style was impressive enough as an original contribution so that people who played other instruments were deeply influenced by it. Earl "Fatha" Hines, himself a classic jazz player, adapted it to the piano, playing what was termed "trumpet style," with octave runs in the right hand that would sound, if one took the top or bottom line, like an Armstrong solo.

Even such an original musician as Duke Ellington borrowed from Armstrong. Early Ellington records show his trumpet players, when they were not utilizing the growl trumpet "jungle" sounds, tended to play like the rest of the jazz trumpet players — straight out of Louis Armstrong. They still do, for that matter. And the big successful (financially) swing bands of Tommy Dorsey, Benny Goodman and Glenn Miller always had trumpet players whose main virtue was their ability to play in the Armstrong manner.

His was an overwhelming achievement and it made him known and loved throughout the world. He invented no labor-saving devices, designed no terrible weapons of destruction and did not break the barriers into outer space. Yet Louis Armstrong will be remembered perhaps longer than those who did these things, for his achievement was for all people.

"I'll explain and make it plain," he sang in *The Real Ambassador*. "I represent the human race."

And that is precisely what he has done.

1973

Jimmie Lunceford

# 3.
# Jimmie Lunceford

THEY USED TO APPEAR on blue-label 35-cent discs every couple of weeks at the bookstore on the Columbia campus — two sides, 78 rpm, and you had to be there right on time or the small allotment would be gone and you would have missed the new Jimmie Lunceford record.

If you were lucky you got one, ran back to your room in John Jay or Hartley Hall, sharpened your cactus needle on a Red Top needle sharpener, the little sandpaper disc buzzing as you spun it, and then sat back in ecstasy to listen to the sound coming out over your raunchy, beat-up Magnavox.

True big band freaks, of whom I was one, were absolutely dedicated to the Lunceford band. It had — and still has — a very special place in the memories of those who date back to the Era of Good Feeling of the 30s, when the big bands symbolized a kind of romance and glamour and exotic beauty long gone from the world of entertainment.

You savored those records and, since this was long before the economy of abundance and the discs came one at a time, weeks apart, and albums (packages of 78-rpm singles or, a bit later, Long Play discs) were absolutely unknown, you had time to absorb the records.

There must have been hundreds of vocal trios in the colleges who tried to sing like the Lunceford band's trio and who spent countless hours memorizing the words and the phrasing of "My Blue Heaven."

I first heard them on the radio. A remote broadcast from some long-forgotten ballroom somewhere in the Middle West, a wild, throbbing sound in the night by people I never heard of, absolutely killing me with its subtlety and its insinuating rhythms.

And when I got to the Big Apple and found that you could actually get to see a band like this in person at the Apollo or the Savoy Ballroom or the Renaissance or the Strand or Paramount theaters, I simply couldn't believe it. It was just too good to be true.

The guy who showed me that this nighttime radio music came fully processed on platters was a tall, rangy, premed student named Keery Merwin, who shared busboy chores with me from eight to ten mornings at the John Jay Hall dining room. We got into a conversation early on as we wiped up the spilt maple syrup from breakfast and I found he not only had a phonograph but a box of records. We went straight up to his room at ten, cut classes and played records all day long. When we met, he had all the early Luncefords — "Sophisticated Lady," (that was Decca 129!) "Rose Room," "Black and Tan Fantasy," "Dream of You" and "Rhythm Is Our Business," with that line that haunts me yet: "Mose plays the bass in the band. . . ." We dug them deeply in an era before the verb "to dig" had emerged into the general slang. What I mean is, we hardly listened to anything else.

We went out and found other people to play them to. A chance conversation in the corridor outside Irwin Edman's philosophy class and the lunch hour was spent up in Keery's room with the turntable spinning away.

Two things became immediately apparent. I had to have a phonograph and I had to have the records. I got them both as fast as I could. Later, I conned the editor of *Columbia Spectator* into letting me take over the record column from the departing previous tenant and I was in business.

Now the Lunceford discs came to the door gloriously free, sometimes even before they were available at the bookshop.

It ruined me, of course. I never felt the same about the classroom. I spent more time at the Apollo Theater when Lunceford was there than I did at school. I used to see two shows a day. Then a week or so later I'd repeat the performance at the Strand Theater downtown in mid-Manhattan.

That summer and on until the war interfered (Hitler's war, that is), I raced hundreds of miles at night in my father's car to hear the band at the Roton Point Casino, at the Armory in Saratoga, anywhere I could find it; and finding it, in those days before jazz disc jockeys and *down beat* listings, was no small task in itself. Sometimes we'd even call the number listed in the Manhattan phone book for the band and get Harold Oxley's office, where the switchboard gal always acted as if we wanted to serve a summons.

Then there was the wonderful summer of 1939 when the band played for two weeks at a nightclub on the Boston Post Road — the Larchmont Casino — and I worked at Playland nearby, and every night after I closed up the joint at eleven or midnight, I ran over to the club and heard the band till the club closed. One fall they showed up suddenly on Fifty-second Street for a two-week booking — was it at the Bandbox? — and opening night there was no one there but me, my girl and her two roommates. It was a beautiful private concert. The absolute end.

Going back now, after thirty years, to hear these discs, it all comes back. The incredible dynamics of the band, the way it could whisper, and the great roar it got from the brasses and the amazing cohesion of that sax section on "I'm Walking Through Heaven With You" and the whole mystique. Usually we can't return again, but this music, like certain other things, brings back an era and a feeling and an emotion like an instant replay. There was never anything like it.

It's impossible to believe now, after all these years, that this band numbered only fifteen and sometimes sixteen members, plus the leader.

In the mental flashback it seems like many more. And I think the reason is that so much went on there that an illusion of great numbers was created.

It wasn't just "For Dancers Only." It was for listeners and for viewers and for lovers, too. With Jimmie taking that little soprano up sometimes to play lead on a song and the rest of the time standing there — white-suited in summer — waving the baton like a magic wand over the heads of the dancers and smiling, the band produced a variety and volume and an ever-changing tapestry of sound that was really unique.

To begin with, it had character, just as Duke Ellington's band has always had character. It *sounded* like Jimmie Lunceford. You didn't have to wait for the individual voice of some musician, for a particular familiar arrangement or for a well-known number. You coasted down the dial on the car radio late at night and when you hit Lunceford, you *knew* it was Lunceford. Who else could it be? Later, of course, there were little Luncefords, now and then, but in the beginning there was only the one sound and of course that was the way it really stayed because the imitators never made it.

Visually, it was the greatest. No other band put on as much showmanship before or since. They looked good all the time and they made music sound like making it was fun, and they enhanced it with all the tricks, from Russell Bowles or Elmer Crumbley putting the trombone wa-wa mutes on their heads to the flaring sideways and up-and-down motion of the sections in unison.

They would have been great on television. The back row visually going one way, the front row visually going the other, and in the middle of it all, hunched behind that great battery of equipment (drummers in those days looked like the center of all things; Jimmy Crawford and Sonny Greer and Chick Webb and Jo Jones had so much equipment you were devastated just by seeing it), the long-jawed James Crawford pounding out that pulse.

The ballroom usually wouldn't let you stand in front of the band. You had to keep dancing (no chore to *that* band), but sometimes you could cluster at the edge of the bandstand or, at Roton

66

Point, stand behind it, outside on the balcony looking at Long Island Sound in the moonlight and feeling the music just the same.

The best place, though, was in front of the band, where you could see and hear it all as you danced along *very* slowly and watch the trumpets twirl and the trombones wave and see those eyes of Earl Carruthers look to his section mates as he rocked backwards in the chair, anchoring the sax section. And where you could see the wisp of mustache on Willie Smith and the sly look in his eyes as he leaned forward to sing and get a good view. Eddie Wilcox, sitting at the piano, extending relaxation to new dimensions. No one else ever equaled the way he could put his legs at an angle to the piano, slump back in his chair and still play! And his only rival for looking blasé was Johnny Hodges!

Lunceford had the quality of projecting excitement instantly. Not in the way he looked, because Jimmie Lunceford looked positively placid. What always puzzled us was how he could *look* so placid standing there in front of all that magic. And sometimes it even seemed as if he listened to a different drummer, from the way that long baton waved.

But the band itself, the totality of it, looked every instant as if it was about to do something you had better not miss. And it usually did. How it could is still a mystery to me. Probably only the Casa Loma band (twelve years of one-nighters, legend has it) spent more time on the road. That was what was so remarkable about the two weeks at the Larchmont Casino. Later, of course, just before the wartime pressure began to get bad, there were other location jobs, but in those days there was a terrible fact of life which none of us even thought of. Where would a Negro band work, aside from the Howard and the Royal and the Apollo, if it didn't have the Cotton Club or some other special place? No hotel hired Negro bands in those days. It was as simple as that. And we never thought then about the rest of it, the lack of everything from a place to sleep to a hamburger, that marked even those one-nighters and the bus rides.

I think now those men were heroes. Then I only knew they were magicians. What a terrible thing I thought it was for Sy Oliver to even want to leave the band! The miracle, of course, now that hindsight clears the view, is that they stood it as long as they did.

It was a young world then, an unsophisticated one by today's standards, and glitter and tinsel and flash could add up to glamour. But I still think the Lunceford band had much more than that. They had class as well. They walked and they talked and they played like men who had been touched with a very special thing. Duke's men had it and, later, Basie's. They looked regal. That's the only word.

And of course, they were.

The Lunceford band didn't play the blues very often. Its repertoire leaned towards ballads and novelties and certain other kinds of original material, such as "Yard Dog Mazurka."

They played the sentimental songs and the cute ones and the tricky ones. And the thing that was so impressive then and remains so now, hearing the music again, is the way in which they could take the most trivial material, the most banal of pop songs in an era when a pop song was by definition banal, and make something of it.

They did it by the arrangements of Sy Oliver and Eddie Wilcox, basically, and then of Eddie Durham, Jesse Stone, Gerald Wilson, Roger Segure, Don Redman and Chappie Willet. You had to have a band that remained the same, month in and month out — and Lunceford's band remained basically the same unit for many years — in order to develop the kind of group skill that made it possible to play complicated things.

But it wasn't the complicated arrangements that did it. What made the Lunceford band was its wonderful way with ballads. The slow, sleepy "Charmaine" and the delightful "My Blue Heaven," and then the novelties, the insinuating "Organ Grinder's Swing" and "Sleepy Time Gal" and "Hittin' the Bottle."

Those tunes became part of the culture of their time, imbedded in the consciousness of all who heard them. In a way, Lunceford made them into folk music. Certainly in "I'll Take the South," to be specific, there was and is social comment.

The songs were all played, regardless of their simplicity or complexity, for dancers, basically. And they were programmed in the sets to serve that function. After all, these *were* dance bands and, except for its one brief tour of Europe just before World War II broke out, I doubt if the Lunceford band ever played a concert. They played dances and they played stage shows; the concert era for big bands came a good deal later.

The dance, of course, was the fox-trot and its acrobatic extension, the Lindy Hop. Lunceford programmed those sets to take care of the dancers. They began with the slow, dreamy ones and they ended with the up-tempo stomps, and periodically towards the end of the night the whole house would be rocking and rolling to "Running Wild" or "White Heat," after an interim period of the middle-tempo groovers like "Pigeon Walk."

They would set up the whole evening with swinging versions of "Annie Laurie" or "Four or Five Times" and then cut loose with a screaming version of one of their flag-wavers. Or maybe they would do "For Dancers Only" for half an hour, grinding down the blues-ish sound and feeling in the growls and the riffs and making the whole audience meld together into one homogenous mass extension of the music.

Dance tempos are themselves an extension of basic body tempos, of the rhythm and speed of walking, and tempos and beats that fit with them work into easy dance music. Everything the Lunceford band did fitted into half-time or double-time and so was a perfect base for dancing.

The era of the Lunceford band was the era of the silly pop song, of "Organ Grinder's Swing," of "I'm Nuts About Screwy Music" and "The Merry Go Round Broke Down." What these artists did — and the Lunceford band was not alone in this; Louis Armstrong's great discs of that period have the same thing and, of course, Fats Waller was the prototype — was to take the silliest song and transform it. Over and over, the Lunceford band proved, as a later Lunceford song was to make famous, that "Tain't What You Do" ("it's the way hotcha do it!"). Style, in a pre-McLuhan world, was it.

The dreadful syrupy ballads of the time, sung endlessly by male and female vocalists in special quarter-hour radio shows on the Saturday night Hit Parade and with innumerable silly hotel bands, were all that the foes of pop or Mickey Mouse music said they were. Until Lunceford's band got hold of them — and then "The Love Nest," "Honest and Truly," "The Best Things in Life Are Free" and the others became music, interesting, as well as danceable, music.

Henry Wells and Dan Grissom could sing the sentimental songs and Sy Oliver and Willie Smith and later Trummy Young could handle the novelties. It worked. It worked so very well that a whole generation of America loved their music and will, I think, find it just as delightful today as in those lost but well-remembered years when it all began.

Jimmie Lunceford died on August 13, 1947, on a tour of one-nighters in the Pacific Northwest at the beginning of the postwar boom.

The band had barely survived the war years. The draft took key men, and inflation and the high cost of operating on the road made it difficult to keep going. With Lunceford gone, the band struggled on for a while and then died.

The question, of course, is whether if Lunceford had lived the band would have kept abreast of music and remained, as Ellington and Basie have, a constant verité in a musical world of flux.

The answer, I think, is unequivocally yes.

In the beginning, the Lunceford band synthesized the influences of Ellington and Armstrong and soloists such as Chu Berry into a style of its own. Then, as Sy Oliver and Gerald Wilson developed as arrangers, it began to offer music that was much more original in concept. There are passages in "Yard Dog Mazurka" and in "Hi Spook" and other later Lunceford numbers that really presaged the musical revolution that transformed jazz in the 50s.

Proof, if you need it, of the way in which Lunceford's music — and by that I mean the music played by the band and arranged by the arrangers; I'll pass by the question of how much Lunceford himself was responsible for, but at the very least he hired the men and bought the arrangements — influenced the course of jazz can be found in several things.

Stan Kenton, for one, is deeply indebted to Lunceford. It is generally forgotten now, but Kenton's first trip to the East Coast in the mid-40s was with a band that did its best to be a white Lunceford, and at one time Kenton even hired James Crawford away from Lunceford.

Then there is, of course, the almost classic case of Sy Oliver and Tommy Dorsey. Much of the success of the later Dorsey period dates to Sy Oliver's joining the Dorsey band to write its book.

The Lunceford trumpet section opened up the sky for the screamers, making Armstrong's earlier high notes seem modest indeed. And the deft employment of dynamics and the strength of the descending chord at the end of a tune were unusual then, though commonplace now.

Of the bandleaders who were strong then and who remain on the scene today, only Goodman has failed to keep abreast of the times.

To be a successful bandleader in the 30s, it seems to me, it was necessary to be acutely responsive to the changes of the times. Lunceford obviously was. He was not afraid of new names and new blood. Paul Webster, a highly important man in the early days of modern jazz, was an early recruit to the band. My intuition tells me there would have been more and more over the years, and had Lunceford lived, the band would have developed into another breeding ground for young talent with a bent for experimentation. Lunceford was certainly not averse to it.

Also, I think the Lunceford band could have been easily the biggest thing to hit television. It was such a visual band and so entertaining that it's hard to see how it could have failed in a medium that has rewarded so well so many with so little visual talent.

Technical brilliance, humor, entertainment, perfect dance tempos and a variety of excellent soloists (Eddie Tompkins, Eddie Durham, Willie Smith and Joe Thomas were just four of the first-class soloists in the original band) gave the Lunceford band all the necessary equipment. The arranging talents of Wilcox, Durham and Sy Oliver, and later Gerald Wilson, would have provided the framework.

The speculation is idle, of course. The war came, the men left,

Lunceford died, and the strange, living but impersonal organism that is a band disappeared. We don't know and can't know what would have happened.

But the music is still there. The nostalgia, of course, but more than that. The invigorating sound, the special feeling, the fresh ideas and, above all, the vitality.

It was a band to have a good time to, to love to, to dance to, to enjoy. It still is and I'm so glad these sides can once again be set out there for the world to hear.

If you missed Jimmie Lunceford, you missed something great, and the opportunity to catch up is present with this set, luckily. They were part of my life and I want them to be part of everyone's.

1968

Billie Holiday

# 4.
# Billie Holiday–
# Lady Day

"I GOT MY MANNER from Bessie Smith and Louis Armstrong, honey. Wanted her feeling and Louis' style."

That was the way Billie Holiday once described her singing and she kept saying it over and over in one way or another whenever they asked her, and they asked her a lot. For Billie Holiday's singing style is one of the most unique and personal in all of jazz music.

That's what history will remember of her, solidly supported by the undebatable evidence of the records. She was a singer of jazz, the greatest female jazz voice of all time, a great interpreter, a great actress and the creator of a style that, in its own way, is as unique and important to jazz as the styles of Louis Armstrong, Charlie Parker and Lester Young. The fact remains that after all the lurid stories of her star-crossed, self-destructive life, she did something no other woman has ever done in jazz. Today, if you sing jazz and you're a woman, you sing some of Billie Holiday. There's no other way to do it. No vocalist is without her influence.

All girl singers sing some of Billie, like all trumpet players play some of Louis. She wrote the text.

The first time anyone was asked to describe her style, it was disc jockey Ralph Cooper, then emcee at the Apollo Theater in New York, and he said, "It ain't the blues. I don't know what it is, but you got to hear her."

That description hasn't been topped yet. It ain't the blues, but the blues is in it. In some strange, arcane, witchlike way, Billie made blues out of everything she sang. But Billie's forte was the ballad, the pop tune. That she could take these frequently banal and generally trivial numbers and make them into something lasting, something artistic (most singers at best are *artful*), is a tribute to the way she was, for her time, the voice of Woman.

"I've been told that nobody sings the word 'hunger' like I do. Or the word 'love,' " Billie remarked in her autobiography, *Lady Sings the Blues* (a story made all the more tragic and poignant by the little-girl-turned-hip-kitty style in which it was told), and this may be true. But it is the way Billie pronounced another word that always symbolized, for me, the role in which she was, for better or for worse, cast in her life: the idealized sex symbol for an American generation just starting to recognize what jazz was all about, four letters and all.

You can hear her do it numerous times in this collection,* but nowhere does she achieve quite the promise, the assumption and the wild longing that she does in "Them There Eyes" when she lets out that deep-throated, magnificently sexual cry, "Ahhh, baby." For in Billie's world, which represents the introduction to the twentieth century's social upheaval if we look at it sociologically, "baby" had become the word for "lover" in the most intimate, perhaps even Freudian, sense. And Billie, born in the city and raised in town, was the symbol of a sexual reality that transcended all the celluloid make-believe of the glamour queens of Hollywood. She was real and she was alive and you could *hear* her and she spoke to *you* in that sulfur-and-molasses voice — the epitome of sex.

* *Billie Holiday — The Golden Years*, © Columbia Records 1962.

76

The story of her life, in all the grisly, tawdry, Sunday-supplement detail, from illegitimate birth, through prostitution, jailhouse, junk, jailhouse again and the final deathbed scene — under arrest in a hospital room for narcotics, gasping out her final breaths, $750 in $50 bills strapped to her shrunken leg — has been told over and over and over. Please God, let her rest in peace at last; she was tortured enough in life in her own all-too-public hell.

Let us deal here with what will live on as long as there is anything left alive in this culture — her music — and forget for now the rest of it, which even carried over into graveyard quarrels as to who paid for her tombstone. Billie needs no tombstone, ever. These records — and her others — are a monument to her that no stone can ever equal. She is in this album, just as surely as in life, all of her, the good and the bad and the beautiful. It's here in her voice, in the songs and in the titles and in the lyrics. You can't miss it.

I heard her say "baby" once, offstage and not in song. It was twelve years ago as these notes are being written, but I hear it yet. She had opened at a San Francisco nightclub and she was with her then manager John Levy. She was wearing a brown turban, a full-lenth blue mink coat, a green wool suit, a brown crepe shirt with a Barrymore collar, pearl earrings and a Tiffany diamond and platinum watch. She had waited for Levy to come out of the club and had finally gotten into a car with a group of us. Then he arrived, slipped into the front seat, and she leaned forward and said, "Baaaaaaby, why did you *leave* me?" In that line was all the pathos of "My Man," "Billie's Blues" and the rest. Nobody could say a word for minutes and she didn't even know what she had done.

It's very possible Billie never knew what she did to people with her voice when she sang. Carmen McRae in Nat Hentoff's and Nat Shapiro's book *Hear Me Talkin' to Ya* spoke vividly of Billie the singer. "I'll say this about her — she sings the way she is. That's really Lady when you listen to her on a record . . . singing is the only place she can express herself the way she'd like to be all the time. Only way she's happy is through a song . . . the only time she's at ease and at rest with herself is when she sings."

And Bobby Tucker, her long-time accompanist, gave us a terrifying hint of Billie the woman. "There's one thing about Lady you won't believe. She has the *most* terrible inferiority complex. She actually doesn't believe she can sing . . ."

Musically, Billie herself had the most illuminating things to say of her own style. First its origin in Bessie Smith and Louis Armstrong, and then, "I don't think I'm singing. I feel like I'm playing a horn. I try to improvise like Les Young, like Louis Armstrong or someone else I admire. What comes out is what I feel. I hate straight singing. I have to change a tune to my own way of doing it. That's all I know."

Listening to the performances on these albums, which is like living over again the best years of our lives for those of us who were lucky enough to have heard her then, the memories are so strong, one is struck by several things. First, how little, in terms of departure from the melody, Billie actually changes the tune. What she does, as Miles Davis was later to work out for himself, is to take a limited canvas and paint exquisitely upon it. She had no tricks, no vocal gymnastics. She may have hated straight singing, but her way was to sing it *almost* straight but with a special accent on articulation, phrasing and rhythm that made each of the lines and each of the lyrics mean something. Phrased as she phrased them, the words mean something. Many lines in drama are banal on their own but in context and in performance take on a meaning. She did this with pop songs because they held meaning for her of a world she never made and never knew except when she sang.

The samples here are overwhelming. The way she says "This year's crop just misses" on her very first record with Lester Young ("This Year's Kisses," Volume I, Side 2), for instance. They become not lyrics, but Billie's own expression.

The other thing is how, in retrospect, she really did sing like Lester Young played. Just listen to the way she comes in on "Them There Eyes." You hear it again and again as she starts a number, as she comes back in for the second chorus or the bridge and in the way she phrases multisyllable words. It's no wonder that after she made her first record date with Pres, in January of 1937

("This Year's Kisses" is from it), there is an entirely new feeling. Billie was home, musically, at last. . . .

For me, at any rate, aside from the intense and very personal memories evoked by all of these numbers, it was a delight of the highest order to hear the three tracks, previously unreleased, which are included here. They are airchecks of Billie Holiday singing with the Count Basie orchestra. For my money they rate not only as three of the very best Billie Holiday performances but as three of the great jazz vocals of all time. I am particularly attracted, for numerous reasons, to "I Can't Get Started." Not only does Billie here, as in her other two sides with the Basie band, have a sound of pure, unadulterated joy in her voice, but she and Pres in the second chorus indulge in what can only be described as an unsurpassed duet. With Billie singing and Pres talking to her on his horn, this must be ranked as one of the most exquisite jazz moments preserved for us on a recording, and we may thank John Hammond for it.

The sides with Basie and the ones from the studio dates around that time are the end of a period of Billie's sound, if not development. Afterwards she had many things, but never again, or hardly ever, that joyous thrust to her voice.

So in a strange, twisted way, symbolic perhaps of her strange, twisted life, it was an anticlimax when Billie Holiday died.

She had been dying by inches for years. You could hear it in her voice — the ugly sound of death — all the way back to her early days at Cafe Society. It was, perversely, part of her charm, like that of Pres and Bird.

Drink, dope and dissipation were really only the superficial aspects of what was wrong with her. She suffered from an incurable disease — being born black in a white society wherein she could never be but partially accepted.

"You've got to have something to eat and a little love in your life before you can hold still for anybody's damn sermon," she wrote in her autobiography.

There was plenty to eat in the later years, though in her childhood as a classic juvenile delinquent she was hungry for more than food. But money never helped Billie, nor did men. She had plenty of both and she died alone and thin, her great body wasted by disease and deliberate starvation, with a police guard at her door.

She was ridden by devils all her life. In the beginning she was in control most of the time. Those were the days when she made the great records, the classic jazz vocals that comprise this collection.

But Billie was more than a singer. She was a social message, a jazz instrumentalist, a creator whose performance could never be duplicated. It's been tried by a whole generation of singers whose inspiration she was. None of them came any closer to it than sounding like Billie on a bad night.

There were plenty of bad nights, too. In the later years her voice and her sense of time would desert her. At nightclub performances, listeners who remembered her when she was not only the greatest singer jazz had produced, but also one of the most beautiful and impressive women of her generation, choked up and cried to see and hear her so helplessly bad.

Billie Holiday, when she was in her prime, in the years covered by these performances, was simply the most magnetic and beautiful woman I have ever seen as well as the most emotionally moving singer I have ever heard.

I remember when she opened at Cafe Society, in December 1939, for her first big nightclub break. She was simply shocking in her impact. Standing there with a spotlight on her great, sad, beautiful face, a white gardenia in her hair, she sang her songs, and the singers were never the same thereafter.

She really was happy only when she sang, it seemed. The rest of the time she was a sort of living lyric to the song "Strange Fruit," hanging, not on a poplar tree, but on the limbs of life itself.

Just as Chaplin never won an Oscar, Billie Holiday never won a *down beat* poll while she was living, but for jazz and its fans her music is unequaled and as indispensable as Louis' and Duke's.

The fall before she died, I saw her sitting stiffly in the lobby of the San Carlos Hotel in Monterey, the morning after the festival finale. The jazz musicians tried to ignore her. Finally, in that hoarse whisper that could still (after thirty years of terrifying abuse) send shivers down your spine, she asked, "Where you boys goin'?" And when no one answered, she answered herself. "They got *me* openin' in Vegas tonight."

"They" always had Billie opening somewhere she didn't want to be. That's over now and all that's left are memories and the records and the poor, misguided singers trying to sound like her, God save them.

There's really too much and too little to say of someone like her. We have the memories and we have the records. As for myself, I feel like the young man in Colin MacInnes' novel *Absolute Beginners*, who says, "Lady Day has suffered so much in her life she carries it all for you." It was a long, long road from "Your Mother's Son-in-Law" to "Gloomy Sunday," but Billie traveled it for all of us. We owe her a great deal.

It is sad beyond words that she never knew how many people loved her.

1961

Lester Young

# 5.
# Pres:
# Lester Young

PRES DIED LAST SUNDAY morning in a hotel room in New York, and if you don't know who Pres was, you've missed a great part of the native music of America in the past thirty years.

The jazz fans knew him, all right. Everywhere in the world. And last Sunday night when Ed Walker made the sad announcement at the Sands Ballroom, the audience went "Ooooooooh!" in shock.

For Pres was the President, Lester Young, one of the real giants of jazz music, whose tenor saxophone playing created sounds and phrases and melodies that are inextricably wound up in almost all of jazz music today. He was one of the three great instrumental soloists of jazz who changed the course of this music; the other two: Louis Armstrong and Charlie Parker.

If they built statues to jazz musicians in this country instead of to politicians, there would be one of Pres in Kansas City. For Lester Young of New Orleans and Count Basie of Red Bank, New Jersey, put Kansas City on the musical map. They did it together

83

in the 30s when the slight, limp figure of Pres, his horn held out sideways, his eyes shut and his head back, was a familiar sight to the thousands of jazz fans all over the country.

Pres was Kansas City jazz incarnate.

He was only a tenor saxophone player, you say. Oh no, he was much more than that. Much more. To begin with, he was a poet, sad-eyed and mystical, hurt that the world was not in actuality as beautiful as he dreamed of it. So he made it the way he wanted it with his art — his own beautiful world into which all the paradox and misery of the real one could not enter except to be cleansed. He let us share it with him, and when he died, every jazz fan in the world and every jazz musician lost a member of his family.

Had his natural inclination been painting or sculpture, his masterpieces would be hung on the walls of the great galleries of the world and mounted in the courtyards of palaces. As it was, he etched a tiny portion of his art into the grooves of phonograph records, where it will remain, a treasure for the listener, as long as we can play them. The rest of his precious music he gave away as freely as the wind, in countless jam sessions in after-hours clubs and hotel rooms and basements all over the world, in thousands of choruses of the blues with Count Basie, in ballrooms and theaters and in years of nightclubs working with his own band and on countless stages with Jazz at the Philharmonic. That is the music we'll never hear again. That is the lost art of Lester Young.

But there are memories of those times. I never knew him, except most casually, but I have vivid memories. Let me tell you of two. One night in a basement club that used to be a Chinese restaurant in downtown Oakland, Pres gave me a cigarette out of a case that was a foot long and then went on the stand and blew the most beautiful, light and feathery blues I ever heard. Another night, twenty years ago in The Famous Door on Fifty-second Street, the Basie band was stacked up at the rear of the room with the trumpets knocking on the ceiling. The sound was so great, so intense, that it became almost solid enough to walk through. Out of this acoustical wave Pres, with long and wavy hair and a thin wisp of mustache, rose and whispered, "How d'you *do* there!" It cut

84

through the brass like a bullet, soft as it was, and hit me right in the pit of my stomach. I almost cried. I can almost cry now thinking of it and the fact that in reality his recognition is still only from a few.

Yes, Pres' memory will outlast sports heroes, scientists and generals who have been *Time*'s Men of the Year. Because his music set up the ringing of chords in the minds of men that will last as long as the human race.

1959

Charlie Parker

# 6.
# Charlie
# "Bird" Parker

The first of these two pieces was written in 1958 as an
introduction to Charlie Parker's work for what was then
*Hi-Fi Stereo Review*. Ornette Coleman and the jazz avant-
garde of the late 60s had not yet appeared and so Parker's
achievement was at that time the most advanced step in the
progression of the music.
 The second piece is from 1971.

## 1.

A SHORT WHILE AGO a distinguished classical music critic, who is
interested in jazz as an American folk art, confessed to me that he
was unaware of any further evolution in jazz music since Louis
Armstrong.

What has happened to jazz since Louis is, by and large, contained in the career and style of one man — Charlie Parker, an
alto saxophone player from Kansas City whose concept of jazz,
style of playing and personal influence was as revolutionary as that
of Armstrong himself a generation earlier.

Parker returned jazz to the small group where, by and large, it
has stayed ever since. He allowed long solos by individual horns,
occasional duets or ensemble passages with two or more horns.
And he freed the rhythm section from the 4/4 straitjacket. Today
the drummer is free to use his bass drum for punctuation (the
"bomb" one sees referred to in technical discussions), while switch-

ing the sticks from cymbals to tom-toms to snare drum for coloration and sound, rather than rhythm alone.

In addition, Parker and his followers expanded the concept of a line of improvisation. This was formerly limited, in units of construction, to the framework of the popular song, i.e., thirty-two bars, or the eight-bar unit out of which the thirty-two-bar popular song is constructed.

With Parker, the jazzman began stretching his improvisational line past this thirty-two-bar, one-chorus limit as far as his sense of design allowed him and his inspiration would support it. Today a lyric statement by a jazz soloist can be almost any number of bars in length.

Although a number of others, such as Dizzy Gillespie and Thelonious Monk, were also original contributors to the post-swing school of modern jazz, it was Parker — who was and remains even after his death its main influence — who expanded the harmonic concepts of jazz as far as the limits of modern classical music. Before, jazz improvisation had been largely restricted to the basic chords of whatever popular song the band was playing (swing style) or to its melody (New Orleans style). Since Charlie Parker, the jazz musician has been free to explore all the passing changes, the suggested harmonies and the dissonances of modern music in his solos, improvising at will on both the chord structure and the melodic line.

It is quite true that historically the time was ripe for such an innovator — where else could jazz have gone? — but nevertheless a musician of extraordinary and compelling talent and personality was required to wreak such extensive changes in jazz — an art that bows to none in individuality and in the strength of its personalities.

Charlie Parker was such a man.

Bird was an apt name for him; in his hands, at the touch of his fingers, the alto saxophone literally flew. His lyricism was so exalted at times that no bad recording, no indifferent accompaniment and no technical faults of tone or embouchure could keep him earthbound.

Parker died in New York City on March 12, 1955. He was

88

thirty-five. Born in Kansas City, he had played briefly (and almost anonymously) in clubs and orchestras there in the 30s and then joined the Jay McShann band, one of the swing bands from K.C. that went out to make records and tour the country after Count Basie had shown the way. With McShann, Parker recorded his first solos on alto and began attracting the attention of other musicians.

With McShann, too, Parker came to New York on a quick visit and later, in 1939, returned alone, lost in a world of illusion (he was already a victim of narcotics at an age when most white youngsters are just getting their drivers' licenses and thinking about a summer job before entering college for their freshman year), to wander in and out of Harlem jam sessions, evolving the style which was to revolutionize jazz.

By 1942, Parker began playing more or less regularly with other young jazzmen at a late night spot called Minton's, and it was here that the combination of his talents and those of Kenny Clarke (a drummer), Dizzy Gillespie (a trumpeter) and Thelonious Monk (a pianist) merged into the new, modern jazz style. That they were all experimenting with the possibilities of expanding jazz beyond the swing band, small group, jam session format is obvious now. It wasn't obvious then. All that seemed important to them was that they had found fellow musicians who "thought" the way they did.

In the early 40s, Parker played first with the Earl Hines band and then with the Billy Eckstine band which grew out of it before beginning a series of small band engagements in New York which brought him to the attention of the jazz public. These appearances, and his first records made for various small independent jazz labels, made Bird into a figure of prominence in the shimmering nightlife world of jazz.

Plus the legends. As an emotionally unstable man fighting the terrifying addiction to narcotics, Parker's career had the same attraction for the public that automobile races and bullfights have — what Jung has called "the ceremonial death of initiation." People came from sheer curiosity just to look at him, to see what would happen next, to be in on some hair-raising episode with which to spice their conversation ever after. A short while before he died, Parker was playing in Chicago. He was on the verge of collapse, unable to bring himself to get on the stand and play. To a friend who urged him not to disappoint the crowd, Parker said bitterly, "They just came out here to see the world's most famous junkie."

Yet Parker was not basically a bitter man. Eloquent testimony has been paid to his sweetness of character by writers in *down beat, Metronome,* the other jazz journals and in the chapter devoted to him in *Jazzmakers,* edited by Shapiro and Hentoff. As Leonard Feather has observed, Parker was engaged in a lifelong love-hate battle with himself, and despite the adulation heaped upon his work by fans and musicians, he disappointed himself as an artist. He could never bring himself to recommend one of his records to a purchaser. On what was to be his deathbed, he finally selected one of his sides, *April in Paris,* from Verve's *The Genius of Charlie Parker* eight-LP series, played with a string orchestra, as a present for the doctor who was treating him.

Just as was the case with the lost child of early jazz Bix Beiderbecke, Parker has been idolized and the fire of legend fed until now one can hardly see the real person who must have existed behind it all. Beiderbecke died young, too, a victim of his own death urge. With Parker the choice seemed less free — the difference between liquor and narcotics. Parker's was a sentence of death from youth, waiting to be consummated, like the racing driver out to see how many times he can get away with it, knowing that in the end the odds will catch up with him.

Today, in the fever of legend, musicians who walked away from him when he was alive, knowing that greeting him would mean a touch for money, speak of him as a god. And the reason for this, of course, is the giant contribution he made to jazz. It has proven almost literally impossible for a young musician today to play the alto saxophone any other way than Charlie Parker's way. With rare exceptions, they are all "little Birds." In fact, his influence has been so great that even pianists have utilized his ideas (Hampton Hawes, a young West Coast pianist of considerable stature, says that his main influence has been Parker). And an entirely new school of tenor saxophone playing has been built around the work of two New York youngsters, John Coltrane and Sonny Rollins, who have been heavily influenced by Parker's concept.

Make no mistake; Charlie Parker is an important figure in the history of American music. His tragic death in 1955, under mysterious circumstances and of causes never fully explained, added to the bittersweet legend of the young hero bent on self-destruction. But his music is carrying his name wherever jazz is played — and that's almost everywhere.

1958

## 2.

He had a round face and a smile that could beam, yet he could be evil and nasty when he wished as well as sweet as a child. In later years, his weight made him look like Buddha.

But no matter what he did, no matter how many times he disappointed them, hit on them for bread, blew gigs, missed planes, passed out, or otherwise punished them for liking him, Charlie "Bird" Parker remained until the day he died loved and admired and venerated by jazz musicians.

And he is still loved and venerated, his image joining that of Lester "Pres" Young and Billie "Lady Day" Holiday as the three dead saints of jazz's middle period.

Like Pres, Charlie Parker has yet to be discovered by the young jazz listeners of the 60s and 70s. But he will be. It is inevitable. His music was so drenched in the blues (even when he played a ballad it sounded like a blues, in a way) that it comes easy to the ear of a jazz neophyte of the 70s educated in the blues idiom from rock 'n' roll. And why shouldn't it? One of the earliest hits of the rock era was "The Hucklebuck," a rhythmic instrumental taken faithfully (and without credit) from Bird's "Now's the Time."

And today's audience is being prepared for the resurrection of Bird by the numerous solos of his musical offspring sprinkled among the jazz/rock albums and incorporated in the instrumentals of the soul records which they dig. Blood, Sweat & Tears, for instance, has in Fred Lipsius an alto saxophone player whose first solo on an LP with that band was such a faithful reproduction of a Charlie Parker improvisation that it was eerie. And as this is being written Grover Washington, a fine saxophone soloist in his own right, has reached the radio play lists and the best-seller charts with an instrumental of "Ain't No Sunshine," on which the long saxophone improvisation is a pure emulation of the Parker style, sound and feeling.

Just as Bob Dylan unconsciously has paved the way for Jimmy Rushing, George E. Lee, and Count Basie with his line (from "It Takes a Lot to Laugh/It Takes a Train to Cry") "Don't the moon look lonesome shinin' through the trees," so have the Parker descendants paved the way for Bird, even though the imperative of "Now's the Time" (with Jon Hendricks' additional line "Not later, but right now") did not prove feasible. The time *is* coming, though. Believe me, it is coming.

They named a nightclub after Charlie Parker — Birdland — and in its time it was as famous as Fillmore East or West. And the cult that emerged after his death spread his name throughout the land as part of an unorganized but effective campaign of graffiti — "Bird Lives" — scrawled on the walls of nightclub johns and abandoned buildings. ("The words of the prophet are written on the subway walls. . . .")

It got so bad — the legend's pervasiveness — at one point that Lenny Bruce even had a bit worked out, the concept of which was to satirize that legion of pretenders who claimed to have been close friends with Parker. "I got Bird's ax," one of them would remark, "we were real tight." Max Roach, who *was* close to Bird and who played with him in innumerable sessions and on innumerable records, went into helpless laughter when he first heard that.

The only thing consistent about Charlie Parker was his music. It always flew like a bird and it always swung and it always, with the same kind of otherworldly logic of inevitability that Johnny Hodges had, seemed to be exactly right. I think it was because

Bird lived in the music in a way he never did as a person. They couldn't make Bird conform to the real world even though there was a time, in between his bouts with dissipation, in which he was pictured in a food advertisement, sitting at the table like any other middle-class success story, scarfing up the goodies.

Like Louis Armstrong and Pres and Dizzy and Miles, Bird carved out a style of playing that was so big and so deep and so broad that countless others rode on it successfully. They still do. When he died, musicians from all over remarked on how much everyone took from Bird, and they are still taking from him. They probably always will. Mingus put it better than anyone when he told *down beat*, "Most of the soloists at Birdland had to wait for Parker's next record in order to find out what to play next. What will they do now?"

Mingus' tribute was the reality of Parker the musician. He was the wellspring of an entire way of playing and it was not only imitators who learned from him. All of jazz learned from Charlie Parker after he made his initial appearance on the Jay McShann record of "Hootie Blues" playing the quote from the Saturday afternoon radio* broadcasts by "the Reverend Elder Lightfoot Michaux and his Happy Am I Congregation from the banks of the Potomac in Washington, D.C." And it is an important point about his playing, which was so simple and yet so complex, that his first recorded solo was that quote from "Happy Am I, I'm Always Happy," which in later years became the phrase he was to repeat the rest of his life, a classic bebop phrase. Parker's concept was complete when he emerged. Fascinating.

The stories about Bird are just as much a part of the jazz culture as his music. He went on the road with Jazz at the Philharmonic and Norman Granz hired a detective to watch him so that Bird would get to the shows on time and not get hung up along the way trying to score. Bird promptly got the private cop to score for him.

When Jazz at the Philharmonic played a concert in Canada once, crossing the Canada-U.S. border on the way to Vancouver the border guards asked for Bird's identification. He just stood

* Mutual Broadcasting System in the 30s.

there repeating, "My name is Charlie Parker. I play the alto saxo-phone," over and over as if that should have been enough. And indeed it should have been.

Sometimes when he was introduced, he would smile benignly and say, "People call me Bird"; and he could recite from the *Rubaiyat* ("The Bird of Time has but a little way to flutter — and the Bird is on the Wing") and poets were his friends. He loved music. All of music. And he would raid a record store, buy-ing anything from bebop to country and western as well as clas-sical and Broadway show original cast recordings. He'd lie back on the bed in a hotel room and listen to them, smiling.

He wore chalk-striped suits sometimes and he never pressed the pants. Some musicians copied the suit style and even rumpled the pants just to think they looked like Bird. A musician from Susanville, California, named Dean Benedetti (who died a short time after Bird) followed Charlie Parker all around the country with an old wire recorder faithfully permanentizing, in nightclubs and concert halls, huddled in a basement or crouched in a corner, every Golden Note that Bird played. I have known people to buy an LP with Bird on it, tape the Bird solos by themselves, and only play that. The rest of the music was of no interest to them.

Bird loved to play. That was obvious. In fact he really couldn't keep from playing. He walked into a dance hall in Kansas City one night where Woody Herman and the Herd were playing and blew with the band for hours. Bird loved to play with the big bands when they hit New York but sometimes his life-style just couldn't accommodate it. Musicians remember nights when they would come up to the street after the last set only to find Bird chugging up to the club toting his ax, asking if he was too late again.

Countless nightclub owners and small concert promoters from New York to California hired Bird to play and then found him working for free on the other side of town. He meant no harm, really. He just wanted to play and the club was there and the band was willing. The band was always willing for Bird. He could sit in with anybody.

He hung around San Francisco once for over a month. It began with a gig at the Say When during which he fired the band the

94

first night and then broke in a new one. Chet Baker,* a private in the Sixth Army at the Presidio at the time, played his first real jazz gig as Bird's trumpet player on that one. Half the time Bird never got to the Say When at all but blew at the Blackhawk across town, and he always made the late sessions at Jackson's Nook, Jimbo's Bop City, or any other spot that was open. He even got involved in a Jerry Lewis Muscular Dystrophy telethon on television in which he played for more than an hour to the astonishment of the producers.

He inspired fiction writers as well as musicians. But reading about him is no good at all. What the world needs is to hear him. Hear his lovely singing music with its life pulse throbbing like the pulse beat, hear his marvelous flights of lyricism and pick up on the fascinating free flow of ideas. The art is what counts. True, he was a doper's doper and the junkies made him into a cult hero in addition to his jazz stature, but Bird always said smack was bad and that nobody played better when he was high. The junkies didn't believe Bird any more than they ever believed anybody else. They never believe anybody but the horse. Not even themselves.

Like I say, listen to the music, it's all there; and if you need some words to help, then think of King Pleasure's lyric to "Parker's Mood":

> Sing a little song for me and let the world know
>   I'm really free. . . .
> Don't cry for me, 'cause I'm goin' to Kansas City.

1971

* Later with the Gerry Mulligan Quartet.

Dizzy Gillespie

# 7.
# John Birks
# "Dizzy" Gillespie

The first of these two pieces is made up of extracts from the liner notes to a 1961 Verve album and a 1963 Phillips album by Gillespie. The second was written in 1974 when Prestige reissued the classic Gillespie big band and small group recordings from Musicraft made in the 40s.

## 1.

IT IS NOW almost twenty years since Dizzy Gillespie assisted in the musical revolution by which the Young Turks of jazz overthrew their predecessors. Time has softened the struggle and allowed the once bitter enmity to die down.

But that revolution changed the basis of jazz completely and it has never been the same. It makes no difference if it started with Pres or Bird or Monk or out of a combination of all. The important thing is that it happened and Dizzy — among the others — made his mark with such strength that those who came after, no matter who they are, or who they ever will be, must take him into account.

You do not make a contribution like that with any shallow intent. That takes depth and what André Gide called "density." Thus today you can hear Dizzy play the Old Ones (old only in time lapsed, not in content) and hear echoes of big bands, references to people, places, things and times which make up a stream-of-consciousness history of modern jazz. You can hear him quote himself. Certainly. And what artist, what poet has not? The art consists in making it new each time — and he does. Hemingway, as Nelson Algren has put it, took chances in his art and in his life. Dizzy, consciously or unconsciously, applies this to music.

For certainly Gillespie is one of the great musicians in jazz history, a trumpet virtuoso without peer and an experimenter and innovator who, after twenty years at the picket point of jazz's development, still is searching and exploring. "What knocks me out about him," a fellow trumpet player once told me, "is that there he is, night after night, after all these years, when he *could* play it safe and he doesn't. Not for one chorus. He has the courage to be adventuresome and I have never heard him but what he didn't try something new."

To be an individual in an age of conformity, if one may twist the old proverb, is harder than getting a camel through the eye of a needle. And if any of us jazz fans ever meets a human being more individual than John Birks "Dizzy" Gillespie, we have every right to be thoroughly surprised. It is not only in the way he has dressed all of his public life, with the series of jackets from leopard-skin through leather, Chinese silk, bleeding Madras and flowing Nigerian robes. Or the hats — the berets, the caps, the fezzes. It is, in a very real sense, in every word he utters, in every step he takes, as well as in every note he blows that Dizzy is a true individual.

He is the greatest put-on artist in life. He dressed in all his regal robes to fly from Seattle to San Francisco once, rehearsed James Moody and Chris White as attendants, and let everyone think he was a United Nations delegate, a visiting dignitary from an African state, as he strode around the airport, examining everything and peering at everybody.

Of course, that is the essence of Gillespiana — curiosity. You find this in walking a city block with him. You don't just *walk* a city block, you take excursions into every doorway, peer into every window, talk to every person you meet on the way. Part of this is Dizzy's beautifully innocent approach to the world. Like the Yellow Kid Weil's antidote for con men, Dizzy assumes "You can't cheat an honest man." Since he is without guile and above reproach, he can do anything.

Dizzy is one of the very few completely *free* men I have ever known. Most people, of whatever color, are prisoners of their own image or of their own worry about someone else's view of that image. Gillespie, like very, very few, is simply himself at all times and under all circumstances. One afternoon outside the Blackhawk in San Francisco we were talking and a woman walked by, middle-aged, obviously European. Dizzy walked right after her, engaged her in conversation, found out where she was from and that he had played there once, and the two of them had a fine twenty-minute talk. I could no more do that than stand on my head in Macy's window.

When Dizzy played the Jazz Workshop in San Francisco last summer [1961] and set the house record, he reigned nightly in his Nigerian tribal robes and beaded cap. He got on the job early just to answer the telephone with "Birdland" or anything else he could think of to bug the caller and/or the owner. And when I say he reigned, I mean it literally. He was host as well as leader. He walked the guests to the door and got out on the sidewalk and brought new ones in. During the intermission one night, the crowd was stacked ten deep behind the rope at the door. In the first row was a tall, beautiful, Oriental girl. Dizzy spotted her from the other end of the bar, stormed down the aisle and lifted the rope and pulled her in. "They keeping *you* out of here?" he hollered, and proceeded to find out if she was Korean, Eurasian or what. "You're the tallest Korean I ever saw," he told the girl. Now the interesting thing to me about this was the fact that everybody dug it right — the girl, her escort and the whole crowd. *You* try it sometime and you'll get a left in the chops.

Just because his nickname is Dizzy ("*You* may call me John," he told a lady fan one night, as he bent down to kiss her hand), the impression prevails among some that this indicates unreliability. The owners of the Blackhawk and the Jazz Workshop, the two clubs in San Francisco where he has played in recent years, were amazed and grateful to find that he was anything but dizzy when it came to business. And his musicians have found this, too. Dizzy is absolutely and unquestionably the one leader of whom I have never heard a former sideman say a bad word. Even those who sometimes regret his antics love him. And anyone who has ever seen him in operation knows that the Gillespie antics can thoroughly hang up any operation.

I watched him scare a TV station within an inch of its collective life once. In the early days of TV, he did a guest shot and turned knobs, poked at lenses and pulled levers, inquiring innocently all the while, "What's this?" while the engineers became gray and shaken. Another time, at the Monterey Jazz Festival, I watched him in the early hours of a Sunday morning absolutely and totally disrupt a Chinese restaurant just by carefully insisting on the accuracy of each item of a complicated order.

This makes some people think he is some kind of nut. But watch Dizzy answering questions at a press conference or speaking before the Foreign Affairs Council (which he does now and then without the publicity fanfare some musicians arrange every time they talk to four hippies on the corner) and you will see how far he is from this stereotype.

And from all others, I might add. If you want to play chess, he's your man; if you want to discuss international affairs, he's a walking encyclopedia (from personal knowledge and acquaintance with the leading characters) of the complicated political situation in Africa. The list is endless. " 'Kush,' " Dizzy announced one night, "is a number we wrote on our recent trip to Africa, where we were busy making apologies for the State Department." He said it for laughs, but he was telling the truth.

All of this involvement, this jumping wholeheartedly into everything that comes along, makes Dizzy the most thoroughly alive person I have ever known. His energy is fantastic and it is all devoted to the unlimited business of living every single second of the day. When Dizzy walks into a room, the voltage meter rises. I have heard him play trumpet with a collection of youngsters just out of the amateur class and by the end of the first tune, suggesting, directing, actually playing parts for them to follow, have the group so organized that it sounded way over its head. Total concentration. The same thing happens when you introduce him to children.

A couple of years ago, when Dizzy played the Blackhawk one Sunday afternoon matinee, there were a dozen or more children, ranging in age from toddlers to preteeners, *out of their minds* about him. We were — all of us parents — in strictly legal terms violating the California state law by bringing our children into a saloon. But for my money, my kids have seldom been in better surroundings than they were that afternoon with Dizzy. Better, I might add, than in the chamber of the state assembly. At least there were fewer drunks. And Dizzy made those kids instantly at home. A one-man circus, seventeen clowns rolled into one.

What is he like offstage? How can anyone ask? The man is the music and the music is the man. He is just as complex, delightful, exciting and unpredictable as his music. And yet he has simplicity and humility, for all his bravado. Talk to him about Duke Ellington, for instance, and you discover that Dizzy admits he literally gets goose pimples in the presence of the Master.

Does he see his own place in jazz history? I asked him once if he ever listened to his records or to tapes of his bands and he said he didn't, much, because he had played with the greatest musicians of his time and what experience could have been equal to that?

Would you think that only those days, on the stand with Bird, were the pinnacles of his musical life? That same afternoon he told me offhand that the previous night he had played so well that it was the equal of the two or three times in his life he felt absolutely unimprovable.

At one festival opening night there was one hell of an argument over which of several groups would go on first. Dizzy settled it. "I'll go on," he announced, and then proceeded to perform with such impact that nothing short of World War III could have topped it.

You think that makes him arrogant? You're wrong. It just makes him a man who knows what he can do. At Monterey one year he introduced the All-Stars like a youngster in the presence of the greats. Because, beneath his knowledge and his certainty, he is still a fan with a fan's reverence plus a professional's respect.

At the Monterey Jazz Festival, when he played the compositions of J. J. Johnson and Lalo Schifrin on a hot afternoon, he glowed afterward in the Hunt Room with the knowledge that he had fulfilled himself. And he prayed and gave thanks for his strength and his ability to get through that terrifying musical confrontation. The trick is to know when to save yourself for the difficult moments in music and in life. And Dizzy knows.

Dealing from such a position of strength, there is no need for equivocation, and Dizzy has never dodged the issue. At a university conference, a young student asked him if it wasn't true that only Negroes could play jazz. "Negroes are the best," Dizzy said flatly, but added, "We ain't the only ones that swing, baby." And later he was adamant that he was not protesting anything with his music. Which brought up the question of another musician who, it was claimed, had a definite program of musical protest. "He has not communicated it to me," Dizzy insisted.

At a press conference once, some nut asked him to compare himself to Miles Davis. Dizzy intelligently refused. Then the questioner, entrapment in mind, insisted, "Do you think you can do things Miles can't do on the trumpet?" And Dizzy, exasperated at the musical ignorance, snapped "I *know* I can." Which only goes to show how incongruous any such comparison must be.

John Birks Gillespie: bon vivant, comic, satirist, composer, dancer, instrumentalist, vocalist, stylist, student; list what you will, it all adds up to a great human being. I have a button one of his booking agents sent out once as a gag. DIZZY GILLESPIE FOR PRESIDENT, it says. I'm not kidding when I tell you he's got my vote any time he runs.

1961, 1963

2.

When these records were made, the U.S.A. and the world were in the midst of a tremendous social upheaval which was disguised by the turmoil, chaos and joy of the end of World War II. It was not obvious, but the world was changing so drastically that things would never be the same again.

The clues were in music, of course; art always precedes history and the musical revolution which was led by the troika of Dizzy Gillespie, Charlie Parker and Thelonious Monk had, by the time Dizzy made the first two sides herein reissued (his first session under his own name as a leader), thoroughly shaken up the musical establishment as represented by the big swing bands and by the Dixieland and traditional jazz players.

It was just a few months short of twenty years since Louis Armstrong had had the same kind of effect with his first records as a leader. Musicians were literally forced to reconsider all their assumptions about playing once they heard Dizzy and Bird on these records. Unlike the time when Armstrong's first discs were issued, by 1945 there were at least a few jazz programs on the radio. In New York, for instance, you could hear Symphony Sid and Fred Robbins (both named for history by musicians' compositions, "Jumpin' with Symphony Sid" and "Robbins' Nest"), and the new music of Gillespie and Parker was brought instantly, if only occasionally, to the huge New York metropolitan audience. It took a little while for it to spread around the country, but it caught on in New York with the young jazzmen like a flu virus in midwinter.

Just as Armstrong's music had been greeted originally by classical musicians and the hotel dance band heroes of that time as noise, bebop, as the music of Parker and Gillespie was called, drove already established critics and musicians into fits. Tommy Dorsey attacked it; so did Louis. Newspaper nightclub columnists alternately plugged it or kicked it. The two trade papers of the music business, *down beat* and *Metronome*, publicized it but only *Metronome* really supported it.

Personally I was just coming out of a romance with blues, gospel music and traditional jazz and couldn't hear the first sounds of bop I encountered in New York. It was not until the following year when I was in San Francisco and heard Dizzy Gillespie's big band that I got into it. But that's another story.

Many of the Swing Era musicians, however, even though they thought it was a fad and not a revolution, were able to work with the Young Turks of jazz, and it is interesting to note that on three of the first tracks the drummer was Cosy Cole, one of the great drummers of the Swing Era who was later to be one of the few jazzmen to have a genuine pop music hit in "Topsy, Parts I & II." You hear it still on the Oldies but Goodies shows.

The Dizzy Gillespie big band was the natural child of Billy Eckstine's big band which was itself the child of the Earl Hines big band of the very early 40s. Hines had Gillespie, Parker and Sarah Vaughan and Eckstine in his band and they, along with several others, left to form the Eckstine band. Eckstine's big band and the Gillespie big band which followed it were the last black big bands to have any kind of chance. Several others tried in later years, but Eckstine almost made it, and Gillespie made it to the extent of these historic records and a renaissance in the late 50s which took him around the world with his big band in its later version.

Out of the Gillespie big band came the Modern Jazz Quartet. It came naturally, almost organically in the sense of growth. Gillespie's big band had what John Lewis called the hardest music for trumpet players to play. You can hear it on this collection. The bands would play in those days in a dance hall or nightclub (in the East) until four in the morning sometimes and without any alternate band. In some halls the band played forty-five-minute sets with a fifteen-minute break four times a night. Do that for a while and the trumpet players' lips start falling off.

It was necessary to devise something to let the trumpet players rest after they had wailed away at a couple of things like "One Bass Hit" and "Things to Come." So the pianist, the drummer, the bass player, and Milt Jackson (then with the band) playing the vibraphone would do a set of their own while the high note specialists let their aching chops rest. Thus the MJQ — which, in its original form (just before it took the name) was pianist John Lewis, drummer Kenny Clarke, bassist Ray Brown and vibist Milt Jackson — Dizzy's rhythm section plus Milt.

This band and all the musicians in it, including Dizzy, individually and collectively were deeply and irrevocably influenced by Charlie Parker.

Parker had come to New York with the Jay McShann band from Kansas City. It was a blues and swing band, like a less flexible version of Count Basie, with Walter Brown (who was Chuck Berry's first inspiration) as the blues singer. Bird and John Brown, another saxophone player, went to the Earl Hines band and there began that association with Gillespie which was to change musical history.

Parker, however, after McShann and then Hines and then the Eckstine band, really had had his fill of big bands. He was not programmed for that kind of structure, and although he made seven of the tracks in this package, he did not become a working member of the Gillespie big band. However, the music that he and Dizzy produced here is absolutely incredible in its inspiration, its energy and its freshness, even today. I think it is reasonable to say that every night on television, in the big bands on the talk shows and in the studio bands for the other variety shows, the influence of these seven tracks is heard. I say these seven tracks rather than the other records Bird made during that period because I think that these, which were originally cut for Guild and then transferred to Musicraft, actually got out all over the country and into every musician's collection of current inspirations quickly.

There are, I think, several examples of the kind of influence these musical pioneers had. Armstrong had it in his day. B. B. King had it with guitar players. And Bob Dylan and the Beatles had it. They all literally changed the sounds of America.

The Jay McShann band and the Earl Hines band were really swing bands in the same matrix as Count Basie and Benny Goodman and the others. Their music was music designed to be danced to by people who danced a basic step called the fox-trot. Everybody learned it in school. (I remember being taught it in the auditorium during lunchtime to music coming in over the radio from WNEW, which was the only station playing records at the time.) Phonographs were not in everybody's home then; a big hit record in the Goodman/Basie era was less than 100,000, for instance. The fox-trot went with the 4/4 rhythm of the swing bands like ham and eggs. First the Eckstine band and then the Gillespie band played a music that was designed to be danced to, all right, but equally designed to be listened to. And if you danced to it, you had to be a virtuoso dancer like the Lindy specialists at the Savoy or like Gillespie himself.

Because they did not direct their music to the fox-trot dances, the beboppers could let the drummer out of the straitjacket he had been in for a generation, serving as a guide to dancers, and permit him to swing on the top cymbal while using his left hand and his bass drum, and sometimes the high hat played with his left foot, for punctuation, embellishment and coloration. The timekeeper was the bassist and a free drummer became a thing of beauty.

In addition to what it did rhythmically, the bebop revolution worked out in small group playing the exploration of all the musical devices of classical music, the use of intervals as surprise, the harmonies and tempos which were excluded almost totally from the big band style. They still utilized a good deal of the swing band structure, the basic instrumentation, the whole orchestral idea and the set tempo and standard bar lengths. Yet everything was recycled through a different language so that "Good Dues Blues" or "Hand Fulla Gimme," which are straight-ahead blues songs right out of the blues tradition, sound quite definitely different from any of the Count Basie classic blues of two or three years earlier. But the blues is still there and a solid link. Taj Mahal uses lines from these songs today.

There's great humor in this music. Quotations of pop songs are used as jokes, and there is a kind of intellectual game involved in creating an entirely new melody on the basic chords of a familiar one and then arranging that new melody with all the trappings of the new style. Thus "Whispering," a standard song for over twenty years when these records were made, becomes "Groovin' High" (with its double entendre reference to both playing and being), and then at the end, the last four trumpet measures become, a short time later, the main theme of "If You Could See Me Now," one of Sarah Vaughan's most memorable numbers. If you know "Whispering," you might try whistling it while Dizzy and Bird play "Groovin' High." There's at least one direct reference to the original and several that are close in the performance but it taxes one's concentration to do it and not goof.

Aside from the blazing creativity which poured out in the choruses by Parker and Gillespie in the small groups, the sound of

Dizzy's big band was one of joyous exultation. I don't suppose they ever did it exactly as they wanted to. Even though John Lewis credits the trumpeters with being the best, the whole band suffered from a lack of the vital money substance. They never really made a dime and you can go only so far on kicks. But they were as exciting a musical group as anything I have ever heard, before or since.

Dizzy, of course, was and is a master showman/performer/ entertainer. He, like all who clown successfully, knows exactly what he is doing even if he did say one night on the radio in answer to Jimmy Lyon's question, "Why do they call you Dizzy?" "You don't know me very well!" Dizzy led the band dancing and jumping around and playing like a man possessed. The energy that blasted out from that band was sensational. They had only a microphone for the vocalist to sing into and be heard over the house public address system. They had no amplification for the band itself and no electrical instruments at all, not even a guitar with a pickup and amplifier. But they had as much volume as Cream or The Who, and with that band I discovered a truth about loud music. If it's good, it turns you on and makes you feel good, and the volume does not hurt and you can stand there all night and listen to it and go away after five or six hours feeling better than when you came in. But if it does not make it musically, then it is sheer physical torture and you leave exhausted and aching. I never left a performance of that band anything but sky high on its sound and feelin' no pain. At all.

In San Francisco they played a cramped ballroom on Fillmore Street one night that doubled as a roller rink and they drove the listeners wild. Dizzy ended up playing "Second Balcony Jump" (the Hines band used to do it) and then leaped on top of the piano and yelled, "All the men go home and all the women stay right here!" Another night in an armory in Brooklyn (it took us hours to find the place) they played to a small crowd of dedicated boppers, alternating with Lester Young's Sextet, while the maddest assortment of early hippies you could hallucinate danced alone or in couples around the floor in front of the National Guard vehicles which were covered with green tarps and parked along the back.

They played a mad engagement at the Edgewater Ballroom in San Francisco which ended its life a couple of years ago as the last home of the Family Dog, and they did two weeks once in a nightclub on the old Barbary Coast, a converted strip joint. I couldn't stay away. Their basic repertoire was the compositions in this package and it really doesn't suffice to say that they played the hell out of them just as they do here. It was something else involved with the musical liberation they represented and the sociological change they heralded.

Ever since those days, these have been some of my favorite records. I have never failed to be turned on by them whenever I have played them and I have worn out the original 78s and all the subsequent pressings.

There was a cartoon once of a goateed musician with a beret peering into a window of a record store which had a sign in it saying BEBOP SPOKEN HERE. We knew what it meant. I'd liked to turn on the world to this music so everyone could have the kicks I've had listening to it. Bebop spoken here.

1974

# 8.
# John Lewis and the Modern Jazz Quartet

It was my special privilege to be able to hear the Modern Jazz Quartet almost from its very first engagement right up to the group's final U.S. appearance in May of 1974.

The MJQ's career, which has included many appearances with symphonies and on special programs with various string quartets, made them a unique group in the jazz world. John Lewis, their pianist, served as the group's chief arranger and composer, but Milt Jackson, the vibraphonist, also occasionally wrote and arranged.

These two essays were done in 1961 and 1972 as album notes. The first is intended to give a personal glimpse of John Lewis, the second an appreciation of what the group has meant to jazz and to me.

## 1.

ONE NIGHT at the Blackhawk, that combination nightclub and shrine for jazz worshipers in San Francisco, the audience was relatively amazed (they *are* used to almost anything) when the last set of the Modern Jazz Quartet began and Milt Jackson was not on the stand. He was at the bar, instead, and remained there listening — and obviously enjoying — the set as played by the John Lewis Trio.

Later that same week, similar sets were played by the Milt Jackson Trio with John Lewis in the audience listening with equal pleasure. It was all part of a deliberate move by Lewis to afford different contexts in which to play (both for the sheer pleasure of playing and for the audience's pleasure as well).

And, of course, the audience was entranced at the opportunity to hear Jackson (and later, Lewis) carrying the solo load alone. The things they played were not the difficult music usually associated with the Modern Jazz Quartet, but relatively easy and casual interpretations of ballads and blues.

Again, at the 1960 Monterey Jazz Festival, when it came time for Helen Humes to appear there was confusion concerning her accompanist, and John Lewis (who serves as musical director of the Monterey Festival) took charge, pointing out that he used to accompany her on concerts. It took a while for the audience to realize just who the pianist was, since again it was a facet of the Lewis musical personality not usually exposed. But it was — again — thoroughly delightful.

Make no mistake about it, John Lewis is a very complicated personality despite the seeming simplicity of his compositions for the MJQ and of his piano playing there and elsewhere.

To begin with, there have been very few musicians, in jazz or in any other music, who have devoted themselves so completely to their art as has John Lewis. He is, I think, the only jazz musician I have ever known with whom it is possible to schedule a nine A.M. appointment and know that he will make it. Stories of the intensive rehearsals of the MJQ are legendary now, but Lewis applies the same discipline to everything else he does.

Functioning as musical director of the Monterey Festival — and it is no small part of its success that he *is* the musical director — Lewis has paid personal attention to every detail possible. During a rehearsal one year that the Woody Herman Orchestra was there, Lewis had to be stopped — almost physically — from going out after extra chairs himself. He came to rehearsals carrying his famous large leather bag from which he extracted, when needed, pencils, sharpeners, erasers, notepaper and almost anything else that could possibly be required at the rehearsal except substitute musicians.

When he prepared his *Original Sin* ballet score for the San Francisco Ballet, he devoted the same sort of ceaseless attention to rehearsals and to planning. He spent a week in San Francisco prior to the opening performance and ninety-nine percent of that time was spent working with the ballet company and the orchestra on the music.

Even though the Modern Jazz Quartet is not really a nightclub performing group, Lewis has, when the group has played the Blackhawk in San Francisco, devoted this same incredible concentration of effort to what it did there. Not only would the group rehearse every afternoon — or almost every afternoon — but before the engagement started he would personally arrange the lighting, moving the spotlights around for maximum value, set the piano the way he wanted it, *tune* it personally, and with a special little portable vacuum cleaner thoroughly clean it.

The object of all this, of course, is to have the music of the group presented with a minimum of distraction and a maximum of quiet dignity, under the best working conditions. And he has succeeded; those who maintain that he has succeeded too well seem to me to be confusing the entertainment business with the presentation of concert jazz.

Music dominates John Lewis' life. His evenings off he spends at concerts (at least this is what he does in San Francisco) and they may include the Budapest String Quartet at the Opera House or a sixty-mile drive to San Jose to hear Erroll Garner. ("I once spent a thousand dollars in a week listening to Art Tatum on Fifty-second Street," he has said, indicating the seriousness with which he regards the great artists of jazz piano.)

Discipline and elegance are the key words in describing both his music and his personality. And there's a third word: wit. As should be obvious from listening to him play, Lewis has a quiet but thorough sense of humor. As the subject for an interview he sounds, especially on the radio, as though he were noncommittal. But this is only when the interviewer insists on talking about things John is not interested in or in asking questions which are really irrelevant. On subjects in which he is deeply interested, such as the Lenox School,* he can be positively eloquent.

Lewis' high musical standards reflect a highly aesthetic attitude toward life in general. He is the only musician I have ever known who has made sure to tell me that whatever personal relationship

* A short-lived summer jazz school in Lenox, Massachusetts.

we may have, it is not to interfere with what I say about his work (or that of the MJQ), that if I don't like it, I must say so.

And whatever the jazz public — musician and layman alike — may think of that music, even if there are those who dissent, John Lewis himself has the universal respect of all who have known him.

The best illustration of this I know comes from J. J. Johnson. When J. J. found out that John Lewis would be in charge at Monterey, he turned to his band in their dressing room at the Jazz Workshop and said, "You know what that means! Work! Work! Work! Fifteen rehearsals a week!"

1961


2.

The Modern Jazz Quartet grew out of the Dizzy Gillespie big band of the 40s as naturally as any other child grows from its parents.

The Gillespie big band (possibly the most exciting big band in jazz's Golden Era) was led by a trumpet player and so the band was a showcase for brass players. It just happened to have the world's greatest modern jazz rhythm section, and because that rhythm section was composed of special people like Milt Jackson, Kenny Clarke, Ray Brown and John Lewis, it was no problem at all for them to relieve the brass for an hour at a time, improvising endless and intricate music while the trumpet and trombone players' chops recovered from the chore of playing the difficult arrangements the band had. Necessity, as Duke Ellington remarked in another context, is the mother.

Milt "Bags" Jackson was the star of that rhythm section because he is a natural soloist and also because his was such a blindingly unique style of playing. It would have been hard to have made the bass the star in a four-man group, though Ray Brown was right there with Oscar Pettiford, following Jimmy Blanton's lead in taking the bass down front for solo time. Kenny "Klook" Clarke, great drummer though he was and is (and he is certainly among the handful of percussionists who changed jazz), faced the problem all drummers face: It is hard to carry a solo load past a certain point without melody. And John Lewis was a brilliant pianist, but even more shy then than now.

So it was Bags' groove, so to speak, and thus it was natural that when the chance came to offer that rhythm section a record date, it emerged as the Milt Jackson Quartet on Dee Gee.

But they are really Dizzy Gillespie's children, just as Dizzy and Bird and Sarah were Earl Hines', and the moment, twenty years later, when the MJQ played with Dizzy again at the Monterey Jazz Festival and acknowledged that relationship was one of those rare and touching moments only jazz seems to provide.

The Modern Jazz Quartet didn't manifest itself under that name on records until it made the two albums for Prestige which comprise this package. By that time, Ray Brown had left to become Ella Fitzgerald's musical director (and husband for a time) and had been replaced (both in the Gillespie band and then as the fourth member of the quartet) by Percy Heath, the bass-playing member of that remarkable Philadelphia musical family.

When the MJQ became a working and recording unit, its impact on the jazz world was immediate and important. It was the right response from the Big Apple to the intellectualism of the emerging Dave Brubeck Quartet and the West Coast "cool" school and, above all, it swung like mad, getting off behind Milt Jackson's glorious solos and cooking like demons.

The MJQ took itself and jazz seriously. They were the complete answer to the funny hat bands and the clowning of entertainers. They modeled themselves on classical chamber music groups in their sober, sometimes somber, but always musical stage appearance. They devoted more time to practice than any other small group in jazz that I've ever heard of. They spent time and money on dress and on taking care of themselves. They were ebullient and could even be carefree off the stand, but they set out to and in fact did earn the respect of the entire musical profession for their sheer professionalism. The MJQ always took care of business, both on and off the stand. They made promptness and professional, responsible behavior almost into a fetish. And in a world where the "hang loose" term had yet to be invented but was being defined by great jazzmen, they stood out.

But the MJQ would have stood out in any case. They were superior musicians, including in the beginning (in Klook and Bags) two of the outstanding players in jazz history and in John Lewis one of the best musical minds ever involved with improvisation. Percy Heath had to work to build himself up into the solid player he became, and there were moments, we know now, when it looked as if the job might be too much for him, since he had started late. But he made it and in doing so accomplished a most fantastic feat.

The MJQ deliberately and with malice aforethought arranged things so that only their fellow musicians could tell how much was written music and how much was ad-libbed differently night after night. And even their peers couldn't always be sure. In that sleight of hand they followed the path of Duke Ellington, who not only confounded his audience in that particular fashion for decades, but for many years delighted in refusing to state clearly who had written what — Strayhorn or Ellington.

The MJQ practiced and practiced until their minds were interwoven with their music, and then they were able on the stand to make it all seem so easy no one could ever be sure. It came as a shock years later to know that, for instance, on one particular composition, less than twelve bars was actually written down. But most jazz audiences (like most other musical audiences, in fact), for all their devotion, never did listen closely enough to know that Milt Jackson could play anything from a scale to a concerto a thousand times and each time do it differently, even while making the overall impression appear to be the same.

I for one will never forget their West Coast debut. When they opened at the Blackhawk it was like a religious service. We were afraid to breathe for fear we would disturb them. And yet they had fire and a deeply swinging groove that was undeniable. And they always, in everything they ever did, had class.

Just when the MJQ got off the ground and out into the forefront of jazz, they suffered what everyone thought would be a fatal loss. Kenny Clarke, that great drummer with whom they had all worked in the Dizzy Gillespie band and who was acknowledged (with Max

114

Roach and Art Blakey) to be definitive in modern jazz drumming, left. He was irreplaceable and that was a fact. That the MJQ was able to go on to the heights it did without him is due to three things, I believe. The first is that what they were doing was such a correct concept that it depended on the sum of the parts more than on any one of them. The second factor in my eyes (ears?) is that John Lewis was so possessed by a vision of what could be done with the quartet that it was a demon riding on his back and he could not have given up even if he had tried. I am sure he felt discouraged, even hopeless, when Klook left. But he had to go on.

The third factor may be the most important of all. With the same kind of inevitable logic that makes an unexpected note become absolutely the right one when everything is jelling and a band is truly together, the drummer they found for a two-week fill-in for Klook was the right man for the spot. His two weeks have, like Harry Carney's temporary job with Duke Ellington, extended themselves into a lifetime career. Connie Kaye had precisely the right combination of technique, taste, style and adaptability to make it work. And exactly the right kind of secure personality to sit in the chair of one of the great masters of jazz drumming and not be traumatized by doing so. He is a subtle man. His rightness for the role has been more and more obvious over the years, just as Percy Heath's development had made his position all his own. It was, if you wish, a miracle. But art always brings forth those miracles. That's one of the things that makes it art.

Looking back now, it is obvious that the MJQ's music is all of one piece in a way, the combined product of all their talents and their minds. John Lewis shaped it, of course, but in the very act of shaping it he was governed, to some degree impossible to assess, by the diverse personalities (musical and otherwise) of the men themselves. And the view that they had, not only of themselves as musicians but of their music as music, itself shaped that music as well as how they presented it.

And the music stands up. That is clearly true. Despite the changes in styles and fads, the emergence of first funk and then gospel and then rock and free-form jazz, what the MJQ has done has lasted. It is unique and a complete world unto itself. Traces of other styles and influences appear from time to time to be added to the original influences of Pres and Bird and Monk. But the totality of the MJQ's music is by itself original.

Articulate, urbane and catholic in their tastes in music as in everything else, the MJQ has always been in the company of the vanguard of American art. It is no accident that it was the MJQ which first found Ornette Coleman, recorded with him and sponsored his appearance at the Monterey Jazz Festival.

By its nature, a quartet without horns and with only the twin sounds of piano and vibes in addition to string bass and drums cannot roar like a seventeen-piece band nor can it scream like an electrically amplified solid body guitar group. In spite of that, and in the age of volume (from airfield to Fillmore stage), the MJQ has made its presence known, for the index of art lies not in decibels but in some other measure of the fire of creativity. And creativity is exactly what the Modern Jazz Quartet has always been about, from its first moments relieving Dizzy's brass section to wherever it played last night.

1972

Carmen McRae

# 9.
# Carmen McRae

SHE STOOD THERE on the stage, a vision; Georgia Rose in the flesh, the burning eyes reaching right out across the rows of seats, the spotlight shining on her cheekbones, her head thrust back a little as she sang "When Sunny Gets Blue."

There were over eight thousand people in that packed, open-air arena at the Monterey Jazz Festival. They froze, or I'd better say they melted, for the emotion she put into that song was the direct enemy of ice. They swayed, when she moved her hand, as though each person in that audience was connected by some invisible silken thread to her hand and to her heart as well as through the sound of that magic voice.

And when she finished there was a moment of total, absolute silence in which no one even moved. And then they applauded.

Maybe it was "When Sunny Gets Blue" again; if not, it was another of her special sad songs. I no longer remember the song, only the effect. It was a big club and it was all but empty. Nobody there to hear the magic. Just the band and the bartender and over in the corner the waitress, almost weeping. "How can she know so much?" she said to me when it was over and Carmen had opened up her heart to that most sacred audience of one.

The contrasts are delightful. On the afternoon of that Monterey nighttime triumph, Carmen sat around the backstage area, hair in curlers, wearing raunchy, faded blue jeans, carrying on like one of the funkiest musicians in jazz. But out on that stage she was The Grand Lady, the Queen, possessed of the power with her voice to move people as no one else in her time.

Another night in a San Francisco club, some member of the audience interrupted her, shattering the mood like a crumbling icicle. Carmen stopped short, leaned into the microphone, and said with that edge her voice assumes when she gets salty, "Either you're coming up here or I'm goin' down there!" She glared for a moment at the cringing customer, and then resumed her song. But I mean she not only started singing it, but she stitched back the mood, put it all together again in an instant as if the interruption had never happened.

That's magic. You can call it showmanship, you can call it stage presence, you can call it anything you want to call it, but I know it's magic, so don't tell me anything else. You see, I'd actually quarrel with the title of this collection of songs. To me it's not *The Art of Carmen McRae*, but the Magic of Carmen McRae.

Very, very few singers in any genre are able to  go out there on that lonely stage, take off all the shells of pretense and convention, and stand there emotionally naked. Listen to her do this on Jim Webb's "Didn't We?" with no accompaniment save Alexander Gafa's sympathetic guitar. It is an incredible performance — simple, unadorned, not stark but revealed and vulnerable. And warm. Listen to it again, in a different mode, but with the same openness and vulnerability when she sings "Satin Doll" with only Chuck Domanico's bass behind her for the first half of the song. She can get a quality of intimacy into a public performance that is almost embarrassing, it's so real.

Let me tell you about another thing she can do. I remember a cold April night in the Greek Theater at the University of California in Berkeley. A huge amphitheater, close to sixteen thousand people packed there, huddled on concrete benches and jammed on the grass behind the top row. It was another jazz festival, the U.C. Jazz Festival, and while it had a solid house of jazz fans, it also had thousands of college students there for the novelty of the occasion rather than for the specific artists.

Carmen sang a couple of songs. Did well with them and then began Bob Lind's lovely "Elusive Butterfly." This was the students' language. They went wild, interrupting her with applause just for singing the song and then, like their elders at countless Carmen McRae appearances, getting hit with that electric shock she can produce, and going silently into themselves and her until the end when they literally screamed for more.

Songs, you see, have words and they have music and then there is the performance which ought to be, but seldom is, greater than the sum of the parts. With Carmen, you get it all. For the melody of the song itself, you get a jazz musician interpolating, bringing variations of phrasing, melodic line and rhythm and sometimes adding completely spontaneous improvisations. It's the human voice, but Carmen makes it sound sometimes like a cello, sometimes like a saxophone, sometimes like a violin and sometimes, for brief little passages — and this is exquisitely difficult to do — like a trumpet.

Then you get the words. Carmen McRae sings the lyrics of a song like Sir Laurence Olivier delivering a Shakespearean speech. She gives lessons in elocution. There are songs — and the first one on this collection, "I Only Have Eyes for You," is one — which take on multiple additional meanings by the manner in which Carmen McRae delivers the lines. You can hear a song for years — I've been through this and believe me, I know — and then hear Carmen sing it and all of a sudden the lyrics become a story, they literally come to life.

That's part of Carmen, the actress. And her performance of every song she sings, sad or happy, love song or dirge, saucy comment or heavy emotional binge, is a playlet, a short one-woman exercise in dramatic art. She lives those songs when she is singing them and thus she brings them live and direct to you.

In all my life I have found only four persons who could do that out of all the great singers I have heard. One was Billie Holiday, and she's dead, and only Carmen has a moral right to sing her songs; I heard Judy Garland do "God Bless the Child" once and was almost moved to violence. Edith Piaf could do it, and oddly the language was no barrier. You knew what she was saying even if you could not understand literally a word of French. The "broken sparrow" is dead now, too. And there was another, also no longer with us. Her name was La Niña de Los Peines, "The Lady of the Combs," and she was a flamenco singer, perhaps the greatest singer of that high-voltage music who ever lived. She could do it, too, and again, the language barrier was no barrier at all. She spoke, as Carmen speaks, in pure international emotion.

Were this society as open and as free as it pretends it is, Carmen McRae would be a national heroine as Edith Piaf was and as La Niña de Los Peines was. But Carmen comes from the world of jazz, as pure a jazz musician as Charlie Parker or Thelonious Monk, and this country has still to mature to a point where it can take jazz seriously.

Some years ago I did a television show with Carmen McRae. Half an hour long. Just Carmen and her trio. She sat on a stool in the middle of the set and talked and sang and mesmerized the technicians just as, when the show was aired, she mesmerized the audiences. It was a remarkable demonstration of improvisation. We didn't know what she planned to sing. I'm not sure yet that she knew until she sang. Television is ordinarily not done that way. They have rehearsals and sound checks and they mark off camera angles and go through a whole ritual. Carmen just came in, got the musicians in place, and sang. Just like that. It was so good I was scared to death something would spoil it. As a television program basically concerned with music it had great humor, because Carmen is a woman with a salty tongue and the brassy guts of a second-story man. She is afraid of nothing on this earth, man, beast or inanimate object. After those audiences in nightclubs and concerts all those years, a television studio was just another stage. We did the show right through from top to bottom with no stops, no retakes. Just straight. It should be shown to every performer on television as a model of how to do it. I really had very little at all to do with it. I just walked on and asked a couple of questions. Carmen was in charge, and Carmen wove the magic web for all of us.

You see, she truly has the magic touch for songs. She picks the right ones. Then she gets inside them, puts them on like costumes. They become Carmen and she becomes the song. But since each song is a different role, a different personality, a different story, it becomes necessary, for a successful program of these performances, to understand a deep and, again, a magical thing about songs. They must be done in the proper order so that, just like the lyric and the melody and the performance add up to more than the sum of its parts, the show, whether it be a half hour or longer, ends up being more than the sum of its parts no matter how powerful each of those parts may be.

And Carmen can do this. She can take a dozen numbers and knit them together into a whole thing. You can back away and realize that there are individual songs and they are naturally different. But when Carmen sings them, she catches you in her web and brings you along with her into a spell so powerful that while it lasts — and it lasts at her discretion — you just take them all for part of the whole and never think of them as individual songs at all. Even though, when all is over, you realize they were each the product of different writers' inspirations at different times. But in Carmen's hands they become one, because she has lent her magic to them.

I could go down the list of songs in this collection and say things about each of them, how Oliver Nelson gets a marvelous bebop feeling of the 50s into the introduction of "Day by Day," how Anthony Newley's "There's No Such Thing as Love" comes alive for the first time with Carmen singing it, how Al Kooper's Blood, Sweat & Tears ballad "I Love You More Than You'll Ever Know" is utterly transformed, how Tommy Wolf's "I'm Always Drunk in San Francisco" becomes a special kind of tribute, how Buffy Sainte-Marie's "Until It's Time for You to Go" takes on such an added dimension when Carmen sings it that it is hardly the familiar song at all.

But I don't want to do that. If you are already familiar with Carmen McRae you know it anyway, and if you are not, well, all I want to do is to move you to listen. Actually, just to move you to listen to any part of the collection because *The Art of Carmen McRae* will get to you once you open your ears and your heart even a little bit.

There's one more thing. Carmen occupies a place in the hearts of jazz musicians that is a very special place, and its special quality means no criticism of the other great singers of her time but only that Carmen is very, very special. If Ella Fitzgerald will forgive me, I'd like to quote Miles Davis on the subject because it sums up the way they feel, the way we all feel. Miles was looking up at a billboard in San Francisco one night which announced Ella was playing at the Fairmont's Venetian Room and it called her "The Queen of Jazz." Miles grunted and then growled, "If Ella Fitzgerald is the Queen of jazz, what the fuck is Carmen?"

What indeed.

1973

# 10.
# John Coltrane

WHEN ERNEST HEMINGWAY DIED, Nelson Algren, in a moving tribute, assessed Hemingway's importance, saying, "No American writer since Walt Whitman has assumed such risks in forging a style . . . they were the kind of chances by which, should they fail, the taker fails alone; yet, should they succeed, succeed for everyone."

That is — from where I stand — a perfect description of precisely what is going on with the young tenor saxophonist John Coltrane.

Coltrane personifies the young jazz musician who, in searching for a personal style, in striving to establish his art as valid and individual and real, takes chances in forging a style which, by definition, challenges the form of tradition while remaining loyal to the essence, and assaults the conventional and the orthodox.

Jazz musicians like Coltrane are linked inexorably with those creative artists such as Joseph Heller, Ken Kesey, Lenny Bruce and others who are searching for what Kesey refers to as "a new way to look at the world, an attempt to locate a better reality."

And it ought to be noted about such jazzmen that they not only represent the improvisatory nature of our society, but by the very nature of what they do they take more chances, even, than Hemingway. For the jazz musician such as John Coltrane is *improvising*, making it up right now, creating instant art in the supermarket of the jazz club, which is like writing poetry in the men's room at Grand Central Station.

And they perform this improvisation without the chance of revision. With the knowledge beforehand that what comes out may be good or may be bad. It depends. But in any case they can't change it; it must rest where it is and be judged as it came out.

In the process of this striving, a creative jazzman such as John Coltrane may very well annoy and antagonize in exactly the same way that Joyce and Stravinsky and Bartok, in their times, have annoyed and antagonized.

Coltrane plays long solos in which he frequently eschews the melody of the tune and embarks on a long, volatile series of flashing improvisations. He plays with a hard tone in a rushing, dynamically aggressive style that sounds as if he might be angry.

For this he has been critized as "an angry young tenor." Coltrane's reply is interesting. "The only one I'm angry at is myself," he says, "when I don't make what I'm trying to play."

"What is he trying to do?" is the question frequently asked about Coltrane and constantly hurled at musicians and critics by irritated listeners who feel their goodwill towards jazz frustrated by what they find to be the inexplicability of Coltrane's playing.

He has a simple answer. "The main thing a musician would like to do is to give a picture to the listener of the many wonderful things he knows of and senses in the universe. That's what music is to me — it's just another way of saying this is a big, beautiful universe we live in, that has been given to us, and here's an example of just how magnificent and encompassing it is. That's what I would like to do. I think that's one of the greatest things you can do in life, and we all try to do it in some way. The musician's is through his music . . ."

That the language and the means by which John Coltrane chooses to express this universal artistic message should be unorthodox, and being unorthodox dismay some critics, merely makes him a member of an artistic hierarchy that runs from Wagner to Joyce to Picasso to Albee.

John William Coltrane was born in Hamlet, North Carolina, on September 23, 1926. His father, a tailor, played several instruments and Coltrane studied clarinet and E-flat alto in high school. Later, briefly, he attended music schools in Philadelphia. He played these for a short time before entering the navy, where he worked with a band in Hawaii in 1945–1946. After discharge from the service, he worked with the big bands of King Kolax and Dizzy Gillespie, the blues groups of Eddie Vinson and Earl Bostic and Johnny Hodges' Ellington-oriented small band.

He joined Miles Davis in 1955 and with this group first came to the attention of the jazz public. In 1957 he worked with Thelonious Monk and credits Dizzy, Hodges, Monk and Miles as important influences in his life. Since 1960 he has led his own group.

One of the fascinating things about Coltrane is not only the immediacy of his creative art, but the variety of moods and feelings with which he plays. His recent album, for instance, *John Coltrane and Johnny Hartman* (Impulse A-40), is a quiet, reflective, fiercely lyric collection of beautiful ballads in which Coltrane is completely subordinated to the vocal performance of Hartman. In *Coltrane "Live" at the Village Vanguard* (Impulse A-10), you have Coltrane at his most turbulent, extending his playing into the "cries" and "strange noises" which carry the saxophone beyond its original limits. In an album called merely *Coltrane* (Impulse A-21), he improvises on such a melodic number as "The Inch Worm," a favorite of the bittersweet supper club ballad set.

At times he plays the soprano saxophone (he is a fan of both Sidney Bechet and Johnny Hodges on that instrument) and his tenor saxophone playing (which sometimes includes playing notes in clusters, or in such a swift sequence that they have been called "sheets of sound") can become soft and supremely melodic, as on the Prestige LP (Prestige 7188) *Lush Life*.

An early admirer of Lester Young (who epitomized the soft

sound on tenor), Coltrane has also been a devotee of the music of Charlie Parker, Coleman Hawkins, Thelonious Monk and Miles Davis, but he has never faltered in his respect for the elder statesmen of the tenor saxophone. He once said of Ben Webster, in admiration, "The sound of that tenor! I wish he'd show *me* how to make a sound like that!"

On a Miles Davis album, *Kind of Blue* (Columbia CL-1355), Coltrane takes a solo on a track called "Flamenco Sketches" in which he sounds exactly as if he were imitating the timbre of the voice of La Niña de los Peines, but until he made that record he had never heard *any* flamenco music except casually on the radio.

Once he remarked on his fascination with harmony, "When I was with Miles, I didn't have anything to think about but myself so I stayed at the piano and chords! chords! chords! I ended up playing them on my horn!"

From his association with some of the most famous and most individual performers in jazz, such as Miles and Monk and Dizzy, Coltrane finds a similarity underlying their work. There's just "one thing . . . remains constant," he says. "That's the tension of it, that electricity, that kind of feeling. It's a *lift* sort of feeling. No matter where it happens, you get that feeling and you know. It's a happy feeling," he adds.

Coltrane, who is a mild, modest, soft-spoken man who is also highly introspective, says of his own music, "Sometimes I let technical things surround me so often and so much that I kind of lose sight . . . basically all I want to do would be to play music that would make people happy."

The long solos, the unorthodox "cries" and sheets of sound, the hard tone, the swift changes of mood from the lyric to the turbulent urgency of his modal improvisations, indicate a restless nature. And Coltrane is still unsatisfied with his own playing. He is searching. "I don't know what I'm looking for," he has said, "something that hasn't been played before. I don't know what it is. I know I'll have that feeling when I get it and I'll just keep on searching.

There's a story in jazz told by Cannonball Adderley, who worked with Coltrane in the Miles Davis group. "Once in a while,"

Cannonball says, "Miles might say, 'Why you play so long, man?' and John would say, 'It took that long to get it all in.' "

That's a pretty good summary of what motivates and inspires and directs the life of this jazzman. His music is all-encompassing; his vision of life is so full, that he does, indeed, sometimes have trouble "getting it all in."

1963

Miles Davis

# 11.
# Miles Davis

These pieces on Miles Davis begin with a description of
Miles during the weekend in 1961 when Columbia made
the historic *Friday and Saturday Night at the Blackhawk*
double LP. The two assessments of Miles' career that
follow come from a 1961 pamphlet written for Broadcast
Music Inc., the publishing representatives, and from a
double LP package of his work in the 50s which was
rereleased in the early 70s. The following pieces are concerned with the Miles Davis of the 70s and include the liner
notes to two of his important Columbia albums, *Filles
de Kilmanjaro* (1968) and *Bitches' Brew* (1970), which
were seminal in their influence in modern jazz.

Miles is unique in jazz except for Ellington in that he
is not only a superb instrumentalist (trumpet), but a
composer/arranger/leader and a figure who sets personal
style with his followers as well as in music.

## 1.

IT HAS BECOME as fashionable to write of Miles Davis as a social
symbol and as one of the charismatic personalities in the religious
symbolism of jazz as it is to write of him as a jazz musician. And
these things are true, even if now commonplace. Miles does occupy
a position in the jazz culture far beyond that of a jazz soloist
(even though based on that). His mode of dress sets styles ("Pin-
stripes are coming back," a hipster remarked when Miles appeared
opening night at the Blackhawk in San Francisco in a pinstriped
suit. "I got to get me one"), his language and his attitudes are aped
by thousands for whom he has the status of a social leader. Long
before Eva Marie Saint brought a four-letter expletive to the
attention of the country in her impromptu remarks after a lauda-

tory introduction at a motion picture industry dinner, Miles Davis had made acceptance of liberal use of that same word a prerequisite for conversation in most jazz circles, though with characteristic individuality he had transformed it from one syllable to two.

The debate over his onstage attitude has raged wherever he has appeared: Is it pretense? Is it real? His refusal to make announcements, his habit of leaving the stage when others are soloing, his occasional turning of his back to the audience, are either vigorously defended or attacked depending on one's point of view. Do we get announcements from the Budapest String Quartet? Or do jazz musicians owe their public more? But one thing Miles Davis is and that superbly: He is controversial. He is never dull. His basic attitude, from which all the rest springs, is realism and antipretense. That he is aware of what is said and argued about him, he occasionally implies in one aside or another. "They're all worried about making records with me," he said at the Blackhawk on one of the nights this album was being made. He paused and looked up, deadpan, with his eyes gleaming. "An' I'm just standing here, minding my own business, being my own sweet self." Miles' own sweet way has been to do exactly as he pleased with his own music throughout his entire career. The fact that he is now, like Picasso and a very few other artists, a great commercial success in his own lifetime is a tribute to his courage and his sanity and his basic good sense. It is also, whether or not he wills it, a rare symbol to all artists everywhere of the complete triumph of uncompromising art. At the Blackhawk, for instance, he almost never played the last set at night and never played the Sunday afternoon session. "I should complain," Guido Cacienti, the owner, said, "as long as the people come." And, of course, what makes Miles right is that they *do* come.

Despite his legendary intransigence, he mingles with the audience at the Blackhawk, signs autographs and answers questions, idiotic as they may be, with surprising patience if not exactly a loquacious manner. He will leave the stand when the other men solo and walk back by the entrance and stand with the cashier, Elynore Cacienti, Guido's wife, the center of a small crowd of admirers too awed, usually, to speak to him. He is capable of devastating bluntness on occasion. Once he told me he had been past my house that afternoon en route to Dave Brubeck's. "Why didn't you stop in?" I asked in a stereotyped social response. "What for?" he answered with shattering frankness.

The nights this album was being made were tense ones, whether Miles wanted it that way or not. Everyone *was* worried about whether or not the idea would come off. Photographers, imported especially for the occasion, were ordered not to use flash and everyone walked on tiptoes for the first part of the evening. Miles, imperturbably smoking and sipping champagne, exchanged anecdotes with singer Bill Rennault, a fellow veteran of the Howard McGhee band, and with trumpeter Benny Harris, then working in town. At one point, almost as if seeking to get his mind off recording, he gave a vivid lecture, with illustrations, on the theory and practice of the art of picking pockets. A tape recording of this would have been useful to any sociologist examining the mores of "whiz mobs." Right in the middle, he turned to Wynton Kelly and asked him to go next door to the 211 Bar, where the recording equipment was set up, to check on the sound, and then continued his lecture to a fascinated group at the bar.

Miles likes to shock reporters with his statements. "I'm going to retire and go to Europe. I can't stand this, it's too much work," he's said every time he's played the Blackhawk for the past three years. And if it looks like you are taking him seriously, he will go into it at length. When a case-hardened cynical newspaper photographer asked him to pose for a picture at the club, Miles completely stopped him with the statement: "I wouldn't go in where you're working and take *your* picture." Neither Nikita Khrushchev nor any other visiting VIP had ever thwarted that particular photographer before.

But none of these things for one moment means that Miles isn't totally concerned with his music. Of course, this is obvious if you think about it. But many people refuse to go beneath the surface and think his attitude means he doesn't care. How could he play the way he does if he wasn't totally concerned? For all the improvisation that is inherent in jazz, I have a deep conviction that Miles does nothing in his playing that isn't deliberate. He may make surprising turns and twists, by accident or design, but it is all part of a deliberate plan of approach, a definite conception of music. And of course the history of his career proves this. What other artist in jazz, with the sole exception of Louis Armstrong, has been so consistently the leader of highly influential groups from which a whole host of players, themselves influences in turn, have come? Bunk Johnson once put it this way: "Playin' jazz is from the heart. You don't lie." That applies with equal force to Miles Davis and is, really, the best summation.

The recording of this album, the first recording of his group in performance in a club that Miles has ever made, was treated with exactly the same concentration and pains that mark everything he has ever done. "When they make records with all the mistakes in, as well as the rest," he said, "then they'll really make jazz records. If the mistakes aren't there, too, it ain't none of you." After the album was completed, I asked Miles if he had anything he wanted to say about it for the notes. "I've been trying to get Irving [Irving Townsend, the Columbia A&R man] for years to put out these albums with *no* notes," Miles said. "There's nothing to say about the music. Don't write about the music. The music speaks for itself." And so it does, and what it says — here and in everything else he has ever recorded, whether or not he now admires the records — is a celebration of the human truth of the creative artist telling his story of the world as he sees it.

1961

## 2.

The immediacy of communication that marks all good jazz has never been more highly developed than in the work of Miles Dewey Davis.

An intense, dapper (*Esquire* once included him in a list of the best-dressed men), hoarse-voiced man, Davis has played the role in his generation that Louis Armstrong played in his. He has been the supreme influence and motivating force within his peer group.

134

Not only has Davis had an almost messianic hold upon contemporary jazzmen, but he has reached a lay audience of greater proportion than any pure, undiluted, jazz-for-its-own-sake player has up to now. Armstrong's mass audience came long after his influence as a jazz musician among jazz musicians had faded; Parker and Gillespie never approached Davis' appeal. Only Miles has managed to play his individual, iconoclastic style of music with absolutely no consideration of commercial or show business values and make it acceptable on its own terms to a mass audience. It has made him a relatively rich man.

The core of the Davis style is the intense concentration of emotion he packs into his playing and the relatively small framework in which he operates. His playing at times seems slow and even labored; actually, it is careful and deliberate and highly charged. "I play music more for pleasure than for work," he has said.

If contemporary society really is, as David Riesman holds, a lonely crowd, then the artist (and what artist is more representative of today than the jazz artist?) is the personification of that loneliness. We may think of it more often in terms of writers and painters, but it is even more true from the aspect of a jazz musician.

At best his is a casual life, improvisatory like his music: a succession of hotel rooms, motels and transient apartments separated by jet flights, bus rides, or eight hours in an auto roaring from one city to another. Once at his destination, he is plunged again into the center of a private hurricane with the faces flashing swiftly by, the familiar voices saying "hello," and all the terrible impermanent audience of casual friends and fans constantly surrounding him. Other artists can work in isolation; the jazz artist must create in a crowd.

The tension and turmoil these people work under reflects dramatically the tension and turmoil of our time. It is no wonder, then, that what they do has the flash of inspiration; there's little time for anything else.

As part of the reaction in the years following World War II, jazz seemed to be lost in the ethereal clouds of intellectualism, its roots no longer in the blues, shaped instead by the specter of European orthodoxy. With one record, "Walkin'," Miles Davis changed all that and brought back lyricism and melody (and the blues) to jazz. In the same motion he reaffirmed that one could play pretty and still play jazz. It seems unlikely that jazz will ever forget the lessons it has learned from Miles Davis. With the single exception of Louis Armstrong and the classic discs he made with his Hot Five and Hot Seven, there has been no series of recordings in jazz history that has had the impact of the Miles Davis Quintet and Sextet records, nor the later albums with Gil Evans and the large band.

Miles Davis was born in Alton, Illinois, on May 5, 1926, but moved to East St. Louis the following year. His father was a dentist. Miles played trumpet in his high school band and in other units in St. Louis and met Dizzy Gillespie and Charlie Parker when they came through town with the Billy Eckstine band.

He attended Juilliard School of Music in New York for a period in the mid-40s and also worked on Fifty-second Street with Charlie Parker, then he traveled with Billy Eckstine. In 1948 he had his own band in New York and shortly after that made the first of the historic series with Capitol with a nine-piece group. These records made Miles' reputation in jazz. He played at various festivals and with concert tours for several years and then in the mid-50s organized his Quintet with John Coltrane, Red Garland, Philly Joe Jones and Paul Chambers. That group, and its successor which included Julian "Cannonball" Adderley, Wynton Kelly and Jimmy Cobb, set the pattern for small band jazz in the late 50s and early 60s. Simultaneously, he recorded a series of LPs for Columbia with a band conducted by composer-arranger Gil Evans that was a logical outgrowth of his work with Evans in 1948 and which has become among the most popular big band recordings of the past two decades.

Musically, Miles Davis has led an entire generation of trumpet players into the use of mutes, a wispy tone, experiments with over-blowing into a microphone, and the quiet use of spatial elements and lyricism in playing. He has been a social symbol, not only to his generation of his race (to whom he represents a strong and

136

uncompromising attitude), but to the entire post–Korean War, H-bomb generation.

If contemporary jazzmen, as Gunther Schuller says, reflect our strange, troubled and uncertain world with a strange, troubled and uncertain series of musical sounds, Miles Davis certainly represents the longing of contemporary man, locked within the terrible loneliness that only a crowd can bring, for beauty and tenderness and lyric celebration of joy. Seen against the backdrop of all of jazz, it is a great achievement; seen against the backdrop of contemporary music as a whole, it is even greater; and against the backdrop of all contemporary art, it is perhaps more significant than we yet realize.

1961

## 3.

Only once before in the history of the music that has been called jazz has a small group made the kind of universal impression that the Miles Davis Quintet of the late 50s did. The other time, of course, was when the historic Louis Armstrong Hot Five records were made.

But the Davis Quintet was a working group, playing night after night in the jazz clubs and on the tours across the United States, amazing musicians with their inventiveness and above all with the blinding speed with which their musical/mental interaction took place. It wasn't that the group always played at a fast tempo, though they certainly did do that sometimes. It was that the slightest move of an eyelid, the slightest shrug of a shoulder, became instant nonverbal communication and changed the course of the number being played as much as a note of music did.

The intricacy of the linkage between the minds of these musicians has never been equaled in any group, in my opinion. They were attached to some kind of invisible system by virtue of which they really did think as one. Philly Joe Jones, the remarkable drummer, once remarked to me that his and Miles' minds were so attuned that he could go 'way out beyond easily countable time' in a drum solo and come right back in with Miles, because they each *knew* where the other was.

Jazz had submarined into one of its periodic depressions when the Davis Quintet emerged. West Coast "cool" had run its course and, for better or worse, established jazz as a potential box office draw in academia, but the active world of music itself was torpid. Miles called all the children home at Newport with "Walkin' " and then the Quintet appeared, in which a set of virtuoso players melded their talents into a common sound.

A group like the Quintet, which lasts for years, develops its own rhetorical world with what might be called musical versions of family jokes, references, allusions and mythology, the net effect of which is to give the language they develop a highly personalized style. So if one individual person leaves the group and is replaced by another, there is a change in the group's character, even though the basic style and sound remain. One of the most remarkable things about the Davis Quintet was how, over the years, a series of changes in personnel occurred, yet the group retained its distinctive voice, and, above all, retained the incredibly fierce flame of inspiration which marked everything it did, slow or fast, original or standard, ensemble or solo, by day or by night.

Miles, of course, has always had style. Pure simple style. You see it in the photographs of the old groups back to Billy Eckstine's big band. Miles always *looked* distinctive. And like all the great instrumentalists, when he held his horn to his lips and blew, that horn became part of his flesh and blood, the whole looking as though it had been painted by one brush. Even when he was blowing his hardest, and the strain was obvious in terms of pure physical effort, Miles has never looked awkward any more than a master athlete can look awkward. The physical part of playing, which involves different kinds of effort with different people, brings to the playing of a note all of the strength, either in effort or in control, that the body has. Done right, it is a kind of ballet, and Miles has always done it right.

The original Quintet — which is heard on these two albums — comprised the best musical minds of their generation: John Coltrane, Philly Joe Jones, Paul Chambers, Red Garland. I don't mean to imply they were better than others, but only that they were the best for this purpose, and an indication of their quality is the impact they had as individuals as well as the impact of the group.

In this version of the Quintet, the axis stretched from Miles to 'Trane, and from Miles and 'Trane to Philly Joe. The interplay between these personalities made the group. It was characteristic of Miles' gifts as a leader that he, like Duke Ellington, could let his men have their way and end up making it *his* way. The band could become, by Miles laying out, a quartet, by Miles and 'Trane laying out, a trio. And even though the driver was Philly Joe, the concept and the style were Miles'.

There were times when the Davis Quintet seemed like an exercise in rythmic dialogue between Philly Joe and Miles as an individual or Miles and the group as a unit. "I could read his mind," Joe said once of Red Garland, and in no group before or since have I ever heard the kind of rhythmic interaction that went on between Garland and Philly Joe.

I heard this band many nights at the Blackhawk in San Francisco, for which I am grateful. When I missed even one night of their two weeks I was angry. They were such an entity unto themselves that it really didn't matter if the club was empty or full. They wailed. And they didn't need to warm up. They started playing at nine at night like it was three in the morning, and the sheer intensity of it was thrilling. Fast or slow, they made every bar sound like it had been born in an atom-splitting burst of energy.

Years later, after 'Trane was dead, I said to Miles one night that he really needed five tenor players, his music was so complicated. He shot those eyes at me and growled, "I *had* five tenor players once." I knew what he meant. John Coltrane was an utterly remarkable musician even in a group of remarkable musicians such as this. He came into his own with Miles, he was given his full opportunity to find his way and develop as an individual, and in the course of it he contributed some of the greatest tenor playing in the history of that instrument. Like Louis and like Bird, what he did influenced not only those who played his instrument but those who played other instruments as well. Miles has that effect, too, and it is because they always dealt in the kind of ideas that could open the door for everyone.

The music on the Miles Davis Quintet sessions for Prestige was almost all of the repertoire of the band. They had been playing it night after night on the job, refining each number with little touches, turning ideas around, inside out, and changing the ideas, not in a random fashion, but according to some intuitive creative dynamic that resulted in an ostensible form that was actually ever changing. The versions that are preserved were cut in all-night sessions just as though they were playing a set in a club. I doubt there were many retakes. That band didn't have to do anything over. All a second take would have been was different; they were so deep into what they were doing that they couldn't do it any other way but beautifully even if they had tried.

They knew they were good. How could they not have known? When they came off the stand they were smiling. Music like this represents the ultimate in pleasure to those who make it, no matter how hard they must strain in order to do it.

And my God, how they blazed across the world of music! Like a meteor in the August sky, burning, burning, burning, and in its wake a long trail of light. They left behind them innumerable imitations, innumerable individuals and groups who, having heard this sound, stopped whatever they were doing and tried themselves to do the same thing.

And that is the sad part of such magnificent creativity. It can only work when the masters do it. Oh, sure, others can play the notes. And even borrow some of the elements or even the players for their own records. But the thing itself can't be copied. It is past that into some kind of magic which requires the original gift. Ellington has shown that; Armstrong showed it for decades. Miles shows it right up to today. And this Quintet showed it all through its existence.

These are classic records in the best sense of that word, meaning that they will stand as art. Styles and stylists come and go. Something like this, born of this special kind of artistic intensity, just simply goes on forever. There's no point in adding "Accept no substitute." There isn't any. This is it.

1972

4.

Throughout the history of jazz the problem has been to get the music onto the disc without losing the special quality of excitement it has when you are there while the artist is creating. This is the thing about improvisational music. When it is right, it takes great strength to leave because you have the overwhelming feeling at each moment that more surprises and delights are coming. This is the quality which caused Danny Rifkin, a long-time student of improvisational music as well as long-time listener to Miles Davis, to say that such music should not be recorded but only heard once — when it is played.

But the special quality of Miles Davis is to overcome the very real thing Rifkin was talking about and to give to his music the kind of magic that lets you hear it anew every time. We may listen to this album long enough to memorize every nuance but it will still sound fresh. I don't know what does this, I don't know how Miles Davis achieves it (it is quite possible that he does not know, either, incisive thinker about music though he is; but this is different, this is mystical). All I do know is that the quality is there.

This album, "Filles de Kilmanjaro," strikes me as being particularly impressive in that fashion. Each time I hear it, it becomes a new sound track to a new movie in my mind. Sometimes I see the group on a stage, Miles standing there shaking the horn as he waits to take his place at the mike or finishing a burning run, wiping his lips and walking off the stand. Sometimes I see it on a concert stage in a huge hall, everyone in formal concert dress, and sometimes I see it as accompanying a long march to some dedicated goal, the line of marchers, reminiscent of New Orleans parades, dancing and skipping along to the music as block by block the mood and the pulse shift, but not to separate, just to evolve out of what went before and lead naturally into what follows. Once when I listened to this album all the way through, I saw it inside my head as a concert for drums with the band surrounding Tony Williams and Miles in front of it, leading by slight gestures and playing his part in the dialogue.

"An artist is never ahead of his time but most people are far behind theirs," Edgar Varese once said. Miles Davis has been an example of this for a very long time. He is connected to the basic artistic drive of his time in a way which puts him in the vanguard of music. His use of space and time, his breaking through the barriers of structure and formalization, his construction of improvised music in layers of sound on this album indicate the direction in which he is traveling. The organization of sound into music can set off all kinds of responses through the human ear far beyond the mathematics of the music itself. David LaFlamme, the San Francisco electronic violinist, once described this as "light shows for the blind." Miles Davis does this all the time. The consistency is really amazing.

1968

5.

There is so much to say about this music. I don't mean so much to explain about it because that's stupid, the music speaks for itself. What I mean is that so much flashes through my mind when I hear the tapes of this album that if I could I would write a novel about it full of life and scenes and people and blood and sweat and love.

And sometimes I think maybe what we need is to tell people that this is here because somehow in this plasticized world they have the automatic reflex that if something is labeled one way, then that is all there is in it, and we are always finding out to our surprise that there is more to Blake or more to Ginsberg or more to 'Trane or more to Stravinsky than whatever it was we thought was there in the first place.

So be it with the music we have called jazz and which I never knew precisely what it was because it was so many different things to so many different people, each apparently contradicting the other, and one day I flashed that it was music, that's all, and when it was great, it was great art and it didn't have anything at all to do with labels and who says Mozart is by definition better than Sonny Rollins and to whom.

So Lenny Bruce said, there is only what is and that's a pretty good basis for a start. This music is. This music is new. This music is new music and it hits me like an electric shock, and the word "electric" is interesting because the music is to some degree electric music either by virtue of what you can do with tapes and by the process by which it is preserved on tape or by the use of electricity in the actual making of the sounds themselves.

Electric music is the music of this culture and in the breaking away (not the breaking down) from previously assumed forms a new kind of music is emerging. The whole society is like that. The old forms are inadequate. Not the old eternal verities but the old structures. And new music isn't new in that sense either; it is still creation which is life itself and it is only done in a new way with new materials.

So we have to reach out to the new world with new ideas and new forms, and in music this has meant leaving the traditional forms of bars and scales, keys and chords, and playing something else altogether which maybe you can't identify and classify yet but which you recognize when you hear it and which when it makes it, *really* makes it — is the true artistic turn-on.

Sometimes it comes by accident, serendipity, with the ones who are truly valuable, the real artists. It comes because that is what they are here to do even if they can say as Miles says of this music, I don't know what it is, what is it? They make this music like they make those poems and those pictures and the rest because if they do not they cannot sleep nor rest nor, really, live at all. *This* is how they live, the true ones, by making the art which is creation.

Sometimes we are lucky enough to have one of these people like Miles, like Dylan, like Duke, like Lenny, here in the same world at the same time we are and we can live this thing and feel it and love it and be moved by it and it is a wonderful and rare experience and we should be grateful for it

I started to ask Teo* how the horn echo was made and then I

* Teo Macero, Davis' producer.

thought, how silly, what difference does it make? And it doesn't make any difference what kind of brush Picasso uses, and if the art makes it we don't need to know and if the art doesn't make it knowing is the most useless thing in life.

Look. Miles changed the world. More than once. That's true you know. *Out of the Cool* was first. Then, when it all went wrong, Miles called all the children home with "Walkin'." He just got up there and blew it and put it on an LP and all over the world they stopped in their tracks when they heard it. They stopped what they were doing and they listened and it was never the same after that. Just never the same.

It will never be the same again now, after *In a Silent Way* and after *Bitches Brew*. Listen to this. How can it ever be the same? I don't mean you can't listen to Ben.* How silly. We can always listen to Ben play "Funny Valentine" — until the end of the world it will be beautiful — and how can anything be more beautiful than Hodges playing "Passion Flower"? He never made a mistake in forty years. It's not *more* beautiful. Just different. A new beauty. This is new and right now [1970] it has the edge of newness and that snapping fire you sense when you go out there from the spaceship where nobody has ever been before.

What a thing to do! What a great thing to do! What an honest thing to do there in the studio, to take what you know to be true, to hear it, use it and put it in the right place. When they are concerned only with the art that's when it really makes it. Miles hears and what he hears he paints with. When he sees he hears; eyes are just an aid to hearing if you think of it that way. It's all in there, the beauty, the terror and the love, the sheer humanity of life in this incredible electric world which is so full of distortion that it can be beautiful and frightening in the same instant.

Listen to this. This music will change the world like *The Cool* and "Walkin'" did, and now that communication is faster and more complete it may change it more deeply and more quickly. What is so incredible about what Miles does is whoever comes after him, whenever, wherever, they have to take him into consideration. They have to pass him to get in front. He laid it out there

* Ben Webster, the tenor saxophonist of the 30s and 40s (see page 250).

and you can't avoid it. It's not just the horn. It's a concept. It's a life support system for a whole world. And it's complete in itself like all the treasures have always been.

Music is the greatest of the arts for me because it cuts through everything, needs no aids. It is. It simply is. And in contemporary music Miles defines the terms. That's all. It's his turf.

1970

## 6.

The kind of music Miles Davis plays now [1974] stretches the capability of stereo sound to the limit and finds it failing. There is more sound here than stereo can handle on record.

It is not a new situation; mono sound was first threatened, strained and stretched by artists from Louis Armstrong to Duke Ellington — who finally, in stereo, found a context suitable to what they created.

But today's stereo, no matter how good, is inadequate to Miles Davis' music, as listening to a live performance can tell you in a hot minute. Perhaps quadraphonic will do it, but we don't know yet.

I mention all this because I have just heard Miles' band with its huge Yamaha amps and all his electronics, his multiple guitarists and drummers, and the effect was overwhelming. So overwhelming that in retrospect the stereo records he has made sound pallid by comparison, even granting the ordinary distance between live and recorded performances.

Miles' music now is difficult to describe with words. We do not yet have a proper vocabulary to handle the intricacies of its rhythmic construction, the way melody passes from what are ordinarily considered melodic instruments to percussion instruments, or instruments played at a given moment in a percussive manner.

This is simply music of another sphere. It has deliberately abandoned all traditional concepts of melody and harmony and accepted the challenge to create beautiful sounds outside the structures the conservatories and the music teachers operate in. This is the purest music I have ever heard in that sense.

Miles, like Duke Ellington, understands the elements of drama in music. His band can be loud. At top level its volume equals The Who. But Miles does not stay at that level. He uses the top volume as a position against which to contrast musical whispers of incredibly fragile beauty.

When I first heard Miles' group I thought the music was completely free form, that everything was without any direction or restraint or concept — except for the emotions of the moment. Then, as I listened, I began to realize that within this tremendous maelstrom of sound there were melodies on the bass, melodies on the guitars, melodies on the various drums, and sometimes even melodies which went from one to another of those instruments, defying definition.

There are no "songs" or "tunes" in the ordinary meaning. The rhythm (three conga drums, a standard drummer plus a rhythm guitarist) builds a pyramid of sound over a pulse that allows the bassist to contribute both melodically and rhythmically.

On top of all that, Miles' own trumpet and his occasional keyboard sounds plus the infrequent solos of the soprano or tenor saxophone add a whole spectrum of coloration to the totality of the sound.

None of this is random or undisciplined. It is certainly plotted, controlled, anticipated and quite possibly written in one form of notation or another. Miles conducts with his hand, his trumpet or a nod of his head and on signal, tempos shift, rhythmic patterns alter, keys change and volume rises or falls.

In a nightclub (I heard the group at Keystone Korner in San Francisco, a room dedicated to sauna bath temperatures and standing and seating accommodations designed by medieval torturers) the sound completely surrounds you. The bass produces tones you can feel in the air around you and in the pit of your stomach. The synthesizer, the guitars, the wah-wah effects on Miles' trumpet — all combine to deluge you in sound from all corners of the room. But that bottom pulse, which is really at the same time a kind of melody of different tones, keeps the emotional feeling building and carrying you along so that at the end of a set you are emotionally exhausted but exhilarated, out of breath but not tired.

Miles sings with this group on his horn in a kind of combination of trumpet phrases and spurts of sounds which are rather like the human voice.

And he plays duets with the drummer, the conga drummer, the bass player, the guitarists, and now and then with the whole rhythmic base of the band. In years gone by, Miles and his drummers (Philly Joe Jones in particular) used to function like two players linked in a rehearsed ballet, always in motion together, but doing different things.

Now Miles has, on one level, an entire rhythm orchestra against which to lay his trumpet sounds. It is an amazing performance, and it is impossible not to be affected by it.

The greatest single thing about Miles Davis is that he does not stand still. He is forever being born. And like all his other artistic kin, as he changes, leaves behind one style or mode and enters another, he gains new adherents and loses old ones. The public cannot stand being surprised and so some of them petition for the "old" Miles as some of them cried for the "old" Lenny Bruce and, as we have just experienced, some of them mourned for the "old" Bob Dylan. Their resentment of the artists' progress blinds (or deafens) them to the value of what they do now. It is a tribute to artists like that when the pages of publications steam from the anger of thwarted fans. It is a measure of their artistic value and integrity.

Miles won't quit and thank God for that. As long as he lives he will create music, and the music he creates at any given moment will be different from the music he created before that moment. And just as valid.

Miss him at your loss. He is amazing.

1974

# 12.
# The Death
# of Albert Ayler

In the musical revolution of the late 60s and early 70s, in
which jazz players abandoned chord structure, keys and
bars for what they call "free form" improvisation, saxophonist Albert Ayler was one of the orginators. His compositions, like those of most jazz players, were improvised and
not written down, but were nonetheless important for
that. His death was a great loss and it symbolized for me
the way in which American culture ignores its true contributors.

WHEN I HEARD THE NEWS that Albert Ayler had died and was then
shocked to discover that his death was not mentioned in the *New
York Times* or the *San Francisco Chronicle*, much less on the wire
services, I thought of Anton Webern.

Webern was one of the men who revitalized so-called classical
music (along with Schoenberg and Alban Berg). In the period right
after World War II, while U.S. troops were still occupying parts
of Austria, he was shot and killed in a terrifying episode. The
American soldier who ended the life of one of the foremost composers of the world did not know whom he had killed and went to
his own death some ten years later still ignorant. And the first
stories of Webern's end did not appear in English publications
until some months after his death.

Albert Ayler was dead an undetermined period before his body
was found in the Hudson River, and it was not until his funeral
almost two weeks later that the news appeared in the *Times,* and

then it was embodied in a story on the funeral. The *Chronicle*, which at one time pioneered in coverage of modern musicians, never did mention it, at least in the regular edition.

That's how it is with artists, I'm afraid. If they are lucky enough to have their period of artistic creativity coincide with an equal receptivity on the part of the public, the press or the opinion makers, then they assume an importance in the society. Sometimes, like Picasso and Miles and the Beatles, they make money as well. But Albert Ayler was one of those geniuses and artistic innovators whose fate it was unfortunately to die before his time. And so his passing was lacking in public notice, as his artistic contributions have been.

Albert Ayler, in a group that included John Coltrane, Archie Shepp and Cecil Taylor, moved through the gap opened by Ornette Coleman to create an entirely new concept of how music might be played in this society. Individualistic, reverent of roots, committed to personal expression above all, the music that resulted was inhibited by many factors, sometimes rejected and still has had the vitality and creative energy to survive. Its influence will eventually parallel that of Jimi Hendrix in the coming together of all music which is ahead of us.

Until these men, of whom Ayler was one, made their statement in the 60s, contemporary music was really defined in terms that were archaic. There was a "right" way and there was a "wrong" way and the definitions of both were rooted in concepts that were basically pejorative. As always, music was ahead of other things, sometimes even of other arts, and we are now finding out that the absolutes of right and wrong do not hold, especially in areas of art and culture, and not as much as we thought they did in other areas either.

Jazz has had a peculiar history, another peculiar institution, if you will. At just the moment when it assumed the mantle of the most creative music in this society, the whole electronic world erupted, rock and radio gave birth to the amazing amalgam of poetry and music with which we have been blessed these past few years, and jazz seemed to diminish, somehow.

But, as might have been expected, that was only an ostensible

149

diminishing. What was really happening was that the centers of gravity, the major forces of thrust in jazz, were changing. The concepts were shifting around and the very purpose of jazz's existence was being redefined.

It did not then and it does not now make older forms and styles of jazz any less important or any less creative, any more then the existence of Jimi Hendrix was a denial of Bessie Smith. Rather, the opposite. But it did take from in front of jazz the mass audience it almost had and made it again a truly underground art form in its best and most creative sense.

And that is where Albert Ayler flourished. His music, Ayler once told Ira Gitler, was more about "feelin's" than about notes. And at the same time the Russian poets behind Yevtushenko were talking about a "conspiracy of feelings."

What it was all about was revolution in the arts, the taking away of the standard of creativity from control of an official or unofficial academy and placing it in the hands of the people. Ayler and his circle went out and made music that broke all the rules except that art must be true to beauty and to the creative spark and to truth. Other musicians who in their own time had been called revolutionaries put them down. Critics who thought they were being avant-garde when they praised music fifteen years old were repulsed by the music that was more about feelin's than about notes.

But art is very difficult to kill. Artists are not, unfortunately, and whatever it was that put Albert Ayler in that cold, cold river stilled an important voice. In this society we rarely reward our true artists with prestige and respect. Sometimes we give them money instead, and sometimes when they think they are getting the prestige and respect, the benches in the halls of academe are stained with tears and perspiration. And the prestige and respect do not follow the symbols which are handed out in their place.

Albert Ayler couldn't get a job at the Monterey Jazz Festival. Neither can Cecil Taylor or Archie Shepp. The music they play, and the music he played, is all about the fact that such decisions are reached by people in control who are actually not interested in art at all. Power to the people, if it has more than the meaning of a slogan, is about just this.

They took Albert Ayler's body home to Cleveland and they buried him, and we will never know if he fell or was thrown into the river and it doesn't matter. What does matter is that he is dead and the others live on, faced every day of their lives with the same kind of demoniac frustrations in the practice of their art that he was faced with. It's not that the only beauty's ugly, man, it's that even ugly may be beauty and that brings us to where there is no ugly and that's what art is about, and the music of the Aylers and the Shepps and the Taylors is music of beauty. That we may not at some point in our lives be open enough to see and to hear that it is, indeed, beautiful is our loss.

It is tragic that Albert Ayler is gone. Let us remember at least those who were with him and are still with us. Both the Newport and the Monterey jazz festivals should institute an Albert Ayler program each year and on it present the most adventuresome, experimental and daring young jazz musicians they can find. There is no shortage of them and they deserve a hearing. It would be a decent tribute to an artist who, no matter what the official report might say, died because he was not loved enough.

1971

# III
# The Duke

Duke Ellington

# 1.
# Farewell
# to the Duke

EDWARD KENNEDY "DUKE" ELLINGTON was three weeks and three days past his seventy-fifth birthday when he died last month (May 1974) in a New York City hospital.

He had played his music in almost every city in the world outside of China and Siberia. He had dined with presidents and kings, had a Prince of Wales accompany him on drums, played piano duets with a U.S. President, been presented on TV performing his music in Japan, Sweden, England and in the United States. He wrote Broadway musicals, a ballet with Alvin Ailey, conducted symphonies in various countries, wrote for Toscanini and the Paris Symphony, and film music for Otto Preminger and special shows for television.

His series of Sacred Concerts, among his most important works in his own estimation, were presented in cathedrals from Coventry and London and Barcelona to New York and San Francisco.

He composed approximately three thousand original works, many

155

of them portraits of leading black artists, members of his own orchestra, friends and lovers and many others, and tonal histories of black people in America. His accomplishments defy cataloguing and his honors are so impressive, diverse and extensive that they are almost bizarre. He received honorary degrees from at least fifteen colleges and universities including Yale, Columbia, Brown, Harvard and Wisconsin. Nixon awarded him the Presidential Medal of Freedom (the highest civilian award of the United States), Lyndon Johnson gave him the President's Gold Medal, and Paris honored him with a special medal. Musicians' organizations around the world gave him special awards; he was made a member of the Royal Swedish Academy of Music and the National Institute of Arts and Letters in America. In 1964 the Poultry and Egg National Board elected him a member of the ·National Good Egg Club and two countries, Chad and Republique Togolaise, have issued stamps in his honor.

The list of prizes for him and his band (in magazine polls) comes to seventy-seven. Seven U.S. states gave him special recognition and he won nine separate awards from the National Academy of Recording Arts and Sciences.

The April 1974 issue of the Schwann Catalog, the reference guide to recorded music, lists seventy-two Ellington albums in a special section.

But in the "Composer Section" immediately following there is only *one* Ellington listing, a recording of three of his longer works with the Cincinnati Symphony.

Ironically, in 1965 the Pulitzer Prize committee, rather than give him a special award in music, decided instead not to give any award at all in that category. Two members of the committee quit in protest. Ellington, in a typical mocking, wry comment, said, "Fate is being kind to me. Fate doesn't want me to be too famous too young."

Something seems wrong here. America's greatest composer, in the opinion of so many musicians, never got the acceptance his art deserved from American intellectuals. It's as simple as that.

Until the day he died, Duke Ellington's appearances with his orchestra were governed by the American Federation of Musicians rules that apply, not to so-called classical concerts, but to dance bands and entertainment.

Ellington early in his remarkable career knew he was more than a piano player, more than a songwriter and more than a bandleader. He knew he was a composer and an artist of the first rank, and the first time he took his orchestra into the studio in 1926 to record orchestrally, not just as an accompaniment to singers or as a blues or a novelty group, he did two original compositions that have become classics: "East St. Louis Toodle-oo" and "Birmingham Breakdown."

In the years that followed, Ellington recorded more than three hundred times, putting down on disc a history of pop music of the 20s, 30s, 40s, 50s and 60s from funky down-home blues to "Blowin' in the Wind" and his own serious compositions. One of the most consistent things about his original works is that they were a continuing reflection of the black culture from which he came and in which he lived, celebrating life in the ghettos of New Orleans, Birmingham, Washington and New York. They evolved only in the past ten years into the extended religious works of his Sacred Concerts. And even there he incorporated adaptations or revisions of other, ostensibly secular, material.

By the time Ellington went into the hospital early this year at the beginning of his terminal illness, the recognition black artists were achieving in other fields seemed somehow to be superfluous for him. He had won all the polls, his popular songs from "Mood Indigo" and "Sophisticated Lady" to "Satin Doll" were standards in the catalogues of record companies and in the libraries of performers, and his serious music stands on its own as a body apart from the rest of American music, so individual as to be almost a protest.

Ellington knew what league he was really competing in ("Bach and myself both write with the individual performer in mind"), even when the critics and the impresarios and the managers denied it. After his first Carnegie Hall concert in the early 40s, one manager dismissed his extended compositions as valueless (as did some critics) and is supposed to have told him to get back to "nigger music." He even had to fight at first to get his membership in

ASCAP, the American Society of Composers, Authors and Publishers.

So Duke early on reached a decision. Let the symphonies and philharmonic orchestras be supported by civic organizations and foundations. He had to have his music played and since he wrote for a special group of virtuoso players he would pay for his own orchestra and he would do so by writing pop songs and playing in nightclubs. He did it for decades. He carried the most expensive payroll of musicians in the popular music or symphonic field. He wrote hit songs that earned him a guaranteed six-figure income for years, and he toured night after night. His was the only band that always worked fifty-two weeks a year and never disbanded. Some of his people played with him long enough to have earned retirement pensions from General Motors. Harry Carney joined him in 1927 and was with him till the end. Johnny Hodges, Ray Nance, Cootie Williams, Lawrence Brown, Russell Procope, Jimmy Hamilton — all of them spent upwards of twenty years playing the Ellington music. "I let them have all the money and I have the fun," he once explained.

He became so successful as a nightclub performer, as a songwriter, as a *personality*, that his serious musical efforts never got the attention they deserved. He mesmerized everybody with his elegance, his charm and his melodies, and then went ahead and wrote important music behind that screen.

He called it "skilapooping" and defined it as "the art of making what you're doing look better than what you're supposed to be doing."

And so, in nightclubs, he would introduce Johnny Hodges, the alto saxophonist, and, under the guise of having Hodges play some lacy, luxurious, bluesy melody, the band proceeded to perform a five- or ten-minute composition inspired by a Shakespeare play, a mountain in the Near East, a city in Japan or his memories of life in Harlem.

Duke was addicted to his own music — a prisoner of it, in truth — and some of his most casual efforts were so successful that audiences demanded them twenty years and more after Duke thought he had finished with them. The same was true of his

158

musicians. Ten years after one of them had left people would still ask for him, and critics would compare Duke's immediate program with his early compositions and his current band with his original one. Duke was philosophical about it all.

"This nostalgia for the old days and our music is really a great compliment. To think that twenty-five years ago I had the good taste to select Barney Bigard, Juan Tizol, Wellman Braud, Harry Carney and all the rest! I'm just a victim of my own good taste."

The problem with Ellington was always that he was so much more than he seemed, so many things at once. He confessed never to be able to resist a challenge and deplored his own drive to move on to different things. Yet he was, beneath it all, always consistent in the quality of his music, and no matter what bows he made to fads, from the bossa nova to the twist, he was serious under the suave smile because, as he once said, "There has never been a serious musician who is as serious about his music as a serious jazz musician."

Duke lived well. He came from a family that lived well. He was never in want and never scuffled except for his first period in New York when, as he recalled, he and his band (then a small group) used to "split a hot dog five ways." He traveled in the 30s on his tours of the United States not on a bus, but in two railroad cars. "That was the way the President traveled." The band lived and ate and loved and partied in those cars throughout the most prejudiced areas of the South. In fact, as Ellington once remarked when a TV reporter tried to trap him into putting down the civil rights movement, he had his own freedom march in the 30s. "We went down in the South without federal troops."

The public saw Duke on TV or in concert or in nightclubs as a man who dressed his speech in all sorts of verbal circumlocutions, who changed clothes two or three times during a show or concert, who eternally smiled and blew kisses at the audience and accepted their applause with his standard line, "We love you madly," that he would sometimes deliver in a variety of foreign languages to accentuate his sophistication.

But backstage Ellington could be as funky and down home as any human being alive. I remember standing with him one afternoon in the wings at the Paramount Theatre in San Francisco while his band played. Duke listened, his legs spread apart, gently rocking from side to side, chewing gum (Juicy Fruit) and hitching up his belt from time to time. In the band at that period were two saxophonists who were dedicated to achieving nirvana through chemicals. While a long trumpet solo was in progress the two sat in their chairs, heads drooping, nodding on the job. Duke shook his head and, out of the side of his mouth, said to me, "I don't understand it at all. I'm a cunt man myself."

And so he was. Ellington nightclub engagements were especially notable for the appearance of ladies of all ages, colors and conditions. And Duke treated them all as though they were queens. I remember when two young high school girls showed up to interview him at a ballroom in Oakland, just before the band started to play. After delaying the start of the dance, thoroughly charming them, Duke asked what they would like to hear. They named one of his compositions which required special instruments. Ellington turned to the band and yelled the name of the song and waited almost five minutes more while the musicians slowly got up and walked across the stage to drag the instrument cases out from under the piano where they had been stashed by the band boy, who'd expected, since it was a dance and not a concert, that they would not be used. Nothing was too much trouble, he told the girls, for such beautiful ladies.

When we were filming the documentary *Love You Madly* [nominated for an Emmy in 1967], Duke turned to the script girl the second night of the shooting. "Sweetie," he said, "I don't know your name. You must tell me right away because last night when I dreamed about you I could only call you 'baby.'" She almost fainted.

Another time I introduced a young lady to Duke, saying, "She's in a class I'm teaching." Duke took her by the hand, smiled, and said to both of us, "And have you told her I'm giving classes every night in my hotel suite?" Duke's delicacy about romantic matters was legendary. Once when he called to ask if I could make a hotel reservation for him, he added, almost as an afterthought, "and a separate room for the young lady who is traveling parallel to me."

In his autobiography, *Music Is My Mistress*, Duke tells about the time at the White House when Nixon presented him with the Presidential Medal. Duke gave the President double kisses on each cheek in return. "Four kisses?" he asked. "Why four?" "One for each cheek," Duke responded smoothly, and Nixon said, "Oh." I've seen that bit of choreography done with an aging society matron who then walked away dreamily after Duke's answer only to stop suddenly, turn around and blush, as she finally understood the implications of his statement.

Old lady friends, one-night stands or longer engagements — never forgot. One night at a San Francisco club, a tall older woman who looked like the ghost of an all-American beauty of twenty-five years before came up to him. She was wearing a mink coat that dripped money and was bejeweled like an oil baron's wife. "Duke," she said, "can you play 'Birmingham Breakdown' for me?" He smiled and turned away. She tugged his coat and added, "Don't you remember? Miss So-and-So's School in Dallas, in 1928?" Duke ignored her firmly, not because he didn't remember, but because she reminded him of how old he was. The lady finally turned and walked to the back of the club, stood there for a minute fuming, and then took off her expensive Italian shoes and threw them, one at a time, all the way across the room at him.

Duke's music was as much about love and about ladies as it was about black culture. He would play "Satin Doll" and announce that a "Satin Doll" was one "which was just as pretty inside as outside." And "Passion Flower" he defined as "one better enjoyed than discussed." He never made small talk out of a description of "Warm Valley," another of his more romantic numbers, but then he didn't have to. Especially if you listened.

Duke himself was a listener. He claimed to be the best and said that listening was his pleasure. He had to keep that huge payroll of the band going (some got over $600 a week and they were always better paid than their contemporaries) because that was the only way he could hear his music played right after he wrote it.

Ellington was a facile composer who could write swiftly and on demand. He spent huge blocks of time in quiet solitude (huge considering his constant appearances and traveling) either in air-

161

planes or while driving from date to date with his baritone saxophonist Harry Carney. He carefully thought out his compositions. Sometimes, he once told me, the most important things were thought out on the john. Then he wrote. Anything could inspire him. A pretty face, a sound in a city, the view of a mountain.

When he was in a period of productivity, Duke would frequently write all night long in his hotel room after the concert or the nightclub job was over. He trained himself to do this, sleeping during the day. The reason was his need for isolation, for think-time, and those late night and early morning hours were when it was most easily come by.

At times his ability to write in quick bursts of creativity was astonishing. "Black and Tan Fantasy," he once told me, was written in 1927 in New York "in a taxicab. We used to stay in Mexico's juice joint all night long and we'd usually be there until time to go to the recording date which was at nine o'clock in the morning . . . and there I was with a number to write and so I wrote 'Black and Tan Fantasy' in a taxicab on the way to the studio going down Central Park. And 'Mood Indigo.' I wrote it in New York in fifteen minutes while I was waiting for my mother to finish cooking dinner. And 'Solitude' I wrote in twenty minutes in Chicago standing up against a glass office enclosure waiting for another band to finish recording. I wrote the whole thing standing up. 'Sophisticated Lady' is one of the things I struggled with for a month. In 1939 we did thirty-two one-nighters in thirty days and I wrote a lot of things like 'Jack the Bear.'

"I was the yearling," Duke recalled, "and played less than anyone and I had the best job, at Mexico's on Broadway. We had some great sessions. There'd be The Lion [Willie "The Lion" Smith] and James P. [James P. Johnson] to give the keys a dusting and I'd take a shot at it and Fats [Fats Waller] was there. He could play even then. There were some real jam sessions.

"The Lion would put his cigar in his mouth and stomp over to the piano and say 'Get up. I'll show you how it's supposed to be.' And he would.

"If only we had tapes of those nights! And then there was the time Coleman Hawkins and Sidney Bechet tangled at the Candy Club. You should have heard *that!*

"They used to have sessions every Wednesday night at Mexico's. One week they would have the trumpet players, the next week they'd have the tenor players, the next week the trombones. I never will forget the night they had the tubas!

"It was a little joint and you couldn't get them all in it. They were lined up out into the street. There were four tubas on the curb waiting to get in and the tuba players inside were using pots and pans and plungers and anything they could lay their hands on to make that wah-wah effect!"

Ellington chuckled at the memory.

"And it was on the qui vive in those days. No gentlemanly give-and-take. They meant business. We had a small band — six pieces — and we'd run up against some of those big bands and Sonny Greer would walk over to their drummer before the set and look him in the eye and glare and growl out, 'I'm gonna *cut* you!' We scared 'em to death.

"And then there was the night that King Oliver met up with Fletcher Henderson's band. Oh, I wish we had a tape of *that* night.

"I wrote an entire show in one night," Duke told me once. "It was called 'Chocolate Kiddies,' and though it never got to Broadway it ran for two years in Berlin with Josephine Baker and Adelaide Hall. I got an advance of five hundred dollars for it."

Ellington wrote a composition once called "Harlem Air Shaft" (you can hear echoes of it in Paul Simon's "The Boxer") and he described it as straight programmatic music. "So much goes on in a Harlem air shaft. You hear fights, you smell dinner, you hear people making love. You hear intimate gossip floating down. You hear the radio. An air shaft is one great big loudspeaker. You see your neighbor's laundry. You hear the janitor's dogs. The man upstairs' aerial falls down and breaks your window. You smell coffee . . . an air shaft has got every contrast. You hear people praying, fighting, snoring. I tried to put all that in 'Harlem Air Shaft.' "

The previous reference to Paul Simon's "The Boxer" is an illustration of how Ellington's music floats around in the air and crops up in the most unlikely places. Simon, for instance, says he doesn't listen to jazz. The author of "Night Train" certainly did. He's Jimmy Forrest, a tenor saxophone player who once spent a year or so working for Ellington. When he left, he took along a good memory of an Ellington composition called "Happy Go Lucky Local" (part of the Duke's "Deep South Suite," which was never recorded in full). Ellington always claimed to have been flattered by the exact parallel of "Night Train" to the theme of "Happy Go Lucky Local."

There's a bit of Ellington's *Night Creature* (written for Arturo Toscanini and the NBC Symphony) in Leonard Bernstein's *West Side Story*, and the Duke always claimed Count Basie's "One O'Clock Jump" was the child of a phrase he played in an early blues. "Moonglow," the pop song of the 30s which Steve Allen made into a hit in 1955 as "Theme from *Picnic*," is easily recognizable as a reworking of Ellington's "Lazy Rhapsody," first recorded in 1932. And then, of course, contemporary blues fans who dig Junior Parker's version of "Goin' Down Slow" are probably unaware that the instrumental blues figure in the background is an exact reconstruction of Adelaide Hall's wordless vocal on Ellington's "Creole Love Call" (circa 1927).

As far as I know Ellington never sued anyone for any borrowing of Ellington material. He professed to be flattered and in a way he was. There certainly has been no lack of direct Ellington influence, something short of plagiarism, in almost every era jazz has gone through since he first came on the scene.

But in other ways Duke could be very touchy about his prerogatives. He once lectured Dave Brubeck for allowing Dave's sidemen to share his dressing room. "You're a leader, a star," he told Dave, and stars don't share dressing rooms. And once when the Crescendo, a Hollywood nightclub, appeared to be giving top billing to comedian Mort Sahl, Ellington refused to enter the club until the proper order of billing was arranged.

Duke considered himself, at least in his show business personality, an equal with all the stars. And he certainly was. Duke was secure enough in this that he thought it funny when Hubert Humphrey stepped out of an elevator at the George V in Paris, looked at Duke and said "Cab! How good to see you!"

Ellington, as Stanley Dance noted when he delivered the eulogy at Duke's funeral, loved America. He was a patriot in a somewhat different sense from John Wayne. Duke fought racism all his life and he spoke out plainly in his autobiography, saying it was basically an economic disease. "Our major problem," Duke wrote, is "brainwashing of children and adults . . . [it] is the worst in the world. . . ." There are educational institutions in the United States still where he would be barred from teaching because of opinions like that.

Duke's patriotism was not just based on his receipt of presidential honors. He felt this country had been good to him. When Franklin D. Roosevelt died, for instance, Ellington and his orchestra performed a singular service. While the presidential funeral train was traveling from Hot Springs to Hyde Park, the Blue Network (the predecessor to ABC) had Ellington on the air for hours, from the Radio City studios, playing a long program of his own compositions. Ellington was proud of the fact that his was really the only American music heard on the air that dreadful day. He had done the same thing once before under slightly different circumstances. The night in the 30s that the Lindbergh baby was kidnapped, Duke was broadcasting from a Chicago ballroom, and the network kept the band on the air into the early morning hours so that the lines would be open for bulletins about the kidnapping.

Sometimes the black press and his black audience thought he was less than outspoken in his support of the civil rights movement. Yet, as Duke told Nat Hentoff in 1965, "People who think that of me haven't been listening to our music. For the past twenty-five years, social protest and pride in the history of the Negro have been the most significant themes in what we've done . . . we've been talking about what it is to be a Negro in this country for a long time."

All though his career, Duke's compositions reflected this, back to "A Night in Harlem" in 1926 and "Black Beauty" in 1928 (long before black was beautiful) down to his more recent "Togo Brava Suite," "Black Swan" and "Afrique." And back in Harlem in the 20s, Ellington was trying to get other bandleaders like Fletcher Henderson to call their music Negro music, not jazz.

Yet, as I said before, Duke had his earthy side. If you hung out with him for a while, you saw it when he met the night people,

165

the black doormen, the taxicab drivers and the street hustlers, each of whom had a word for him and many of whom he knew for years. They always dug him. He was a soft touch.

Backstage, he could bring off his elegant ambience under the most trying of circumstances. I remember him one night after a concert in a grimy old fraternal hall, standing in an improvised dressing room, just a sheet hung on a clothesline between some posts. Duke was in his shorts, a bandana wrapped around his head, and he sat at a card table greeting one after another of his friends and making the whole shoddy room seem regal. Another time, in a similar dressing room at a nightclub, an old friend apologized for thrusting himself upon the Maestro when he was changing clothes. Duke smiled beatifically and said, "I only take my clothes off with the people I love."

His humor could be sharp. When several of his best men left him in the early 50s, he told me, "I'm just a young bandleader starting out again. I'm not old enough to be historical and I'm too young to be biographical."

Miles Davis has said, "Duke puts everybody on," and there was the usual Milesian truth to the statement. When I made the pilot show for the educational TV series *Jazz Casual*, Ellington was the guest artist. We were all set and waiting for a five o'clock taping. Came 4:45 and no Duke. Came 4:55 and no Duke — and then he walked in. The crew was in a panic. I was sweating like a grand jury witness. I went over to the Maestro and said, "Now Duke, the usual formula is . . ." Duke smiled benignly at me and said, "Anybody can do it with a format, sweetie. The trick is to do it without one. Now I'll sit at the piano and start to play and you walk on and ask me what the tune is and we'll go from there." I said "okay" weakly, did what I was told to do, and we had a half hour of Ellington and Billy Strayhorn piano duets with the Maestro talking up a storm about his music.

Duke could be perverse, too, to put it mildly. When he first appeared at the Monterey Jazz Festival, the same summer he had made a tremendous hit with a long up-tempo number at the Newport Jazz Festival called "Newport Up," Duke asked Jimmy Lyons, the manager of the festival, what he should play. "Anything you want to, Duke," Lyons replied, "except that number about the other festival." So Ellington opened his show with "Newport Up."

A couple of years later, Ellington brought his band to Monterey with two singers, neither of whom Lyons wanted on the show. Instead, he told Duke, he wanted Ellington and the band to accompany blues singer Jimmy Rushing in a special set. "You don't like my singers?" Ellington murmured and then agreed. But what he actually did was something different. When Rushing came on, to great applause from the audience and the band, Ellington went over to the piano and sat there throughout the entire set, conducting from the piano bench. But he never touched the keyboard.

Ellington was a piano player and a great one, but his true instrument was his orchestra. One of his greatest abilities was his gift for creating tension with subtle rather than raucous sounds, as his son Mercer has noted. He wrote, like Bach, for the performer, *his* performers, which is one of the reasons his scores are not published since they changed from player to player. "It's not the notes that are important," Duke said, "it's who they're written for. Before you can play anything or write anything, you must hear it. Some of the prettiest things on paper come off very drab. So you hear, you imagine, you see a note on a piece of paper and you hear it played in the tone personality of a particular musician.

"For instance, here's a guy who uses a mute, and he finds he can get only seven good notes out of it. The problem is to use those seven. Personalized writing is very important. If I didn't know who I was writing for I don't know what I'd do. When we first did 'Black and Tan Fantasy' we found there was a mike tone created by using two horns close to the mike. The problem then, when we did 'Mood Indigo' later, was to use that mike tone!

"I always consider my problems opportunities to do something. Like Jimmy Valentine or Houdini. Necessity, in other words, is the mother! But I couldn't work without a deadline. If I retired to some luxurious home by the sea, you know what I'd write? Nuthin'!"

And so Ellington spent his life on the road with his own self-financed orchestra, writing his music in hotel rooms, taxicabs and airplanes, making the final decisions in the john and hearing it played within hours by the collection of virtuoso musicians he paid so handsomely. Duke thought he was a lucky man to have that pleasure. Money was incidental. "I have to get a bang out of it, not just the money. I'm not worried about writing for posterity. I just want it to sound good right now."

The weekend Duke died, watching the television news shows from the funeral parlor and the church with all those thousands who came from all over to mourn him (singer Alice Babs flew in from Spain), I could not cry for Duke. He was out there living every minute like a teenager right up to the last few months. He had been everywhere, seen everything, knew everybody, and all his adult life he had had the one thing he wanted most, his orchestra ("an expensive toy") to play his music. And what music! As the French poet Blaise Cendrars said, "Such music is not only a new art form, but a new reason for living."

I am honored to have known him. His music gave me countless hours of pleasure throughout my life and I expect it will continue to do so. And it was not just pleasure, it was inspiration. Duke's mystery was inspiring. He made you want to know. As Andre Previn remarked one night after we'd seen Duke's band, "You know, Stan Kenton can stand in front of a thousand fiddles and a thousand brass and make a dramatic gesture and every studio arranger can nod his head and say, 'Oh, yes, that's done like this.' But Duke merely lifts his little finger, three horns make a sound and I don't know what it is!"

Previn's statement, really, says more than a Pulitzer Prize ever could. Duke was a musician's musician and a composer's composer. And one incredible man.

Four kisses. One for each cheek.

1974

# 2.
# A Ducal Calendar
# 1952-1974

What follows is an assemblage, drawn from a variety of sources, of what I saw, heard and experienced of the last twenty-three years of the greatest career in the history of American music. I begin with a piece written in 1966; thereafter the arrangement is chronological, from 1952 to 1974.

## 1966

To LOOK AT Edward Kennedy Ellington and to think about him in terms of his music is to find oneself baffled by the complexity of a personality which can, within seconds, be as youthfully adventurous as in "Stompy Jones" and as explicitly experienced as in the sad, wise line in "Pretty and the Wolf," "Yaaaas, baby, yaaaaaas baby."

The man is the music, the music is the man, and never have the two things been more true than they are for Ellington.

"If society denies someone their reality, then they'll structure their own reality," Nelson Algren once remarked, and I am fond of applying this to Ellington. Denied the reality of his own preeminence as a composer of American music, Ellington immersed himself deeper and deeper into that music until it became him and he it, and the entity, like some swirling, golden globe composed of dozens of flat discs linked together, presented a definite image to any close look from any angle but was, in reality, only a single petal of the rose. The whole being a collection of these facets.

Ellington is a huge compilation of paradoxes and contradictions. "I don't appreciate analysts," he has said. "If you're busy analyzing you can't listen." Yet his music, not only by its very nature but by the mystery with which he deliberately surrounds it, shrieks for analysis. With a tantalizing magician's artfulness, Ellington never lifts the seventh veil. The scores are not published, no one sees them complete; when asked the question direct he answers obliquely. The mystery of how he does it remains a mystery deliberately encouraged and cultivated by the Master.

Or take the question of who writes what, Duke or Billy Strayhorn. At a festival one afternoon a jazz musician, himself a distinguished composer and soloist, expressed his regrets that Ellington had not had the time to work out something really new for the concert and had, instead, thrown together a mishmash. "If only he'd said, 'Strays, we need thirty minutes,' and let Strayhorn do it, at least we'd have had something new." When the comment reached Duke and Strayhorn they doubled up and, like little Audrey, they laughed and laughed because they knew Strays *had* written it.

He did it to me. After one Monterey concert which concluded with "One More Once," that theme of Ellington's late rock 'n' roll and early Twist period, I remarked in print that we must reconsider this number: it was obviously the composer's own choice as among his finest work as he played it at every possible opportunity. I paid for that the following two weeks at the San Francisco nightclub where he then appeared and from which I could not stay away (I am shamelessly addicted to the Ellington music; twice I have made it for almost every hour of a two-week engagement). Nightly, I heard "One More Once" as Duke spotted me in the audience. It was only after hours of scheming that I came up with something to help me escape. Ellington had been retitling it "One More Twist" and I said, one night, that I was disappointed in him. He stopped like a shot, tugged the ends of his tie, raised an eyebrow and asked why. "It's all right for an older man, Duke," I said, "but for someone as young as you, you should be up to date and call it 'One More Bossa Nova!'"

Age interests Ellington and he has said many interesting things about it. Not the least is his standard reply, when someone asks for one of the real old, *old* tunes, that they must mean some other band, perhaps his father's; he himself is much too young to have been playing way back then.

During his recent tour of Japan a reporter asked him why he was the only jazz musician whose name in print is almost always followed or preceded by his age and Ellington replied, "I think it is very gracious of them to give me seniority without my having the chronological majority to be eligible for it."

The outrageous elegance of the language reflects the outrageous elegance of style that he displays in everything. The ice cream, the shirts, the suits, the hats, the manner. Every female of any age whatsoever is greeted by Duke with exactly the same full-blown regal gestures and royal salute and told how her beauty honors and inspires.

And just when I've decided no one in our time has carried elegance to such outrageous proportions, I remember Duke sitting on a whiskey crate at a scratched-up old piano in an upstairs ballroom, the pale blue tie untied and hanging from the super-rolled collar of the ice blue shirt open at the neck, the foot stamping on the creaking bandstand and Duke grunting and groaning to the audience as he played, like some mythological earth god, raunchy as Old King Doojie.

Don't come too close because things are not what they seem. Even when he's angry — and for him to display anger except in private is rare indeed — he is controlled. Duke's polished routine with jazz critics (remember, he hates analyzers, they have no time to listen) is legendary. Yet I once saw him lecture a critic like grandma with a three-year-old who ruined the Irish linen tablecloth. Willie Cook had just left the band in the midst of a performance (another rare moment in Ellingtonia; Duke never fires anyone, they say) and the critic was complaining that the trumpet section, despite the presence of Ray Nance, was weak. Inadvertently (I wouldn't have missed it for the world!) I wandered into the dressing room and found Duke, his finger wagging in front of the critic's nose, eyes blazing, saying, "In fourteen years on this band there has never been one single night in which Ray Nance has not played something beautiful," while Willie Cook, precariously balancing on one leg, the other half-stuck into the trousers of his street suit, called out, "You tell 'em, Duke! You tell him, baby!"

So it is with these records.* Every time you play them you hear more. For me playing them was like a trip back over the years of my own life. Ellington leaning forward from the stage at the Savoy to speak to Jimmy Mundy, who had fought his way through the crowd to request "Birmingham Breakdown." Ellington making the announcements over the radio wire from the Palisades Ballroom in New Jersey on a long-ago weekend, and later that night Rex Stewart riding back to New York on the 125th Street Ferry and a young kid (me) so awed by his presence he was unable to speak. And Ellington at the Apollo and at the Strand with the scrim and that inspired use of the stage lights and Freddy Jenkins joking with Ivie Anderson and Sonny Greer. And that same kid (me!) playing "Reminiscing in Tempo" in the record booth at Bloomingdale's on Lexington and stealing the needles afterwards. And the discovery that the Ellington sidemen took their music along when they went to one of Ernie Anderson's jam sessions at a midtown hotel. And hearing the band on all those late night broadcasts from all those vanished ballrooms and dance halls from the Roton Point Casino to Sweet's. Then the records, "Rose Room" for one, and the first look at the band at the Apollo.

Over the years one of the most exquisite pleasures I have had with the band has been to bring someone to hear it for the first time after years of the records. I did this with Walter Thiers, the jazz critic from Argentina, and with London's Francis Newton, hearing Duke for the first time since before World War II. The effect is shattering. Simply shattering. And wonderful to observe.

The motto of Hans Von Seekt, the chief of the German General Staff after World War I, was, "Be more than you seem." There has been so much more to Ellington than has seemed for so long that it is difficult to believe it isn't obvious. I remember one time when a music paper jazz critic complained about the fact that Ellington never did anything new, he was "unproductive these

* *The Ellington Era*, Volume 2, Columbia.

days." I sat down and made out a list of over twenty titles of numbers I had heard in nightclubs, concerts and dances up and down the Coast that had never been recorded (some of them still haven't). And don't forget that it was, how many years ago? fifteen? that a *down beat* writer called for Duke's retirement and Stan Kenton, returning from Europe, claimed his music meant more there than Duke's.

And yet, as this is being written, Duke is more active than ever. Television programs, Broadway shows, motion picture music, concerts, special commissions (one from Grace Cathedral in San Francisco for religious music — which reminds me of Duke's remark before the California Arts Commission: When someone said jazz came from the brothels of New Orleans, Duke murmured, "They didn't learn it there").

Still Duke never seems hurried or busy. Just as the orchestra seems to function without any discipline (yet its musical discipline is of the strictest), Duke works without seeming to work, swinging from the TV set (he digs the shoot-'em-ups) to the piano during the commercials and, in an aside to Strayhorn, "We must save that." Duke works everywhere all the time.

The show continues. The Master Conjurer says, "Nothing up my sleeve," and never lets you see what he is doing, the hand is quicker than the eye. Yet sometimes we get a glimpse. I would like to think I had one such glimpse the night he played a concert at San Francisco State College's gym. The place was jam-packed and Duke could do no wrong. Everything he played came off perfectly. Even Sam Woodyard's hamming and scene-stealing worked out right. The band was magnificent. The audience went absolutely wild and wouldn't let him leave. It was such a display of outrageous approval that even the Ellington aplomb was shaken for a moment. He forgot his own lines introducing Johnny Hodges' solo on "The Banquet Scene" from *Timon of Athens* and left out most of it. It made no difference, the audience brought them all back for an encore and that time, it struck me, there was no sly cynicism, no subtle put-on when he said, "We want you to know we love you madly." I really believe he meant it, that he did love us all madly. I know we loved him. I expect we always will.

# FEBRUARY 24, 1952

This year Duke Ellington is entering his fourth decade as a name bandleader.

Thirty-odd years is a long time in any business — long enough in most to earn the right to retire. But with Duke it isn't like that. "I'm just starting," he says.

In one sense he really is starting all over again. A year ago some of the most important members of his band left to form their own unit: Johnny Hodges, alto saxophonist; Lawrence Brown, the trombonist; and Sonny Greer, the drummer.

This departure of three key men would have been enough to ruin any band built, as Duke's is, with a careful eye to the abilities and limitations of its individual musicians. Once before, over a period of several years, Duke had lost three men: Rex Stewart and Cootie Williams, the brilliant brass team, and clarinetist Barney Bigard.

But Ellington survived to become even greater, to win the popularity polls three years in a row, to change the sound of his band somewhat and to develop new musical personalities to replace the old.

Last year, however, people thought it would be a different story. Sonny had been with Duke from the start, back before 1920 in Washington, D.C. Hodges had joined in 1928 and Lawrence Brown a few years later. They would be hard, some thought impossible, to replace. And to top it off, vocalist Al Hibbler left.

Once again, however, Duke proved himself more resourceful than the ordinary bandleader (wholesale desertions have broken up dozens of bands through the years). He added Britt Woodman, a young Los Angeles trombonist with a beautiful legitimate tone and flawless execution, to take the place of Lawrence Brown. "You know, that boy just sat down and read the book," Duke says, shaking his head in wonder. Then he brought back Juan Tizol, the Puerto Rican valve trombonist who had been with the band before and whose compositions "Caravan," "Perdido," "Pyramid" and "Azure" are such a part of Ellingtonia.

To replace Johnny Hodges, Duke brought in altoist Willie

Smith, a graduate of the Jimmie Lunceford and Harry James bands and always considered by jazzmen to be one of the few men who could hold his own against Hodges.

For the most important spot, Duke picked a youngster named Louie Bellson, who had drummed for Benny Goodman and Harry James. Considered by drummers as one of the greatest technicians, a student of percussion, Louie is, in addition, an arranger of considerable merit. He is the first Caucasian to play regularly with Ellington and he has brought a new sound and a new life to the band.

These new faces have been with the Duke for less than a year but they have already caused a stir in music circles. "I'm a young bandleader starting out all over again," Duke says wryly.

This time, instead of molding the sound of the musicians to that of the band, Duke has allowed the band to change its group sound. On some numbers, such as their recent "Deep Night," or "Fancy Dan," they are like the old Ellington band, with the liquid flowing swing that has been its trademark. Yet on others, such as the Bellson composition "The Hawk Talks," they sound like the swingingest, shoutingest, stompingest band since the Woody Herman Herd of the mid-40s.

Duke has introduced more new sounds to music than he can remember, from the jungle growls of the early band to the wordless voices used as instruments in recent years. It is a tribute to his extraordinary fertility that after thirty years in the band business he can still produce new and exciting music. Perhaps his best is yet to come.

## NOVEMBER 5, 1952

We were standing in the lobby during the intermission of Duke Ellington's concert at the War Memorial Opera House last February talking to Andre Previn. "Duke Ellington is unquestionably one of the four greatest modern composers," Previn said, and alongside him listed Stravinsky, Prokofiev and one other, I have forgotten whom.

It seems to me that the whole world, not just American jazz musicians, owes a great debt to Ellington for what he has given us these past twenty-five years. Even his early records, for which you almost need an adapter if you want to listen to them now, still have their moments; his great bands of the 30s and 40s were without equal and I think their host of records will give me joy for life. How many times have you listened to the Columbia *Masterpieces* LP? No matter, you'll find something new each time.

As Nat Cole once said, "Duke will always be twenty-five years ahead. He was doing things ten years ago they haven't caught up to today." Amen. Writing about music is at best a frustrating thing, but these stumbling words are especially frustrating because they are only a slight indication of the tremendous respect and admiration I have for the Duke.

# AUGUST 18, 1953

One of the favorite indoor sports of jazz aficionados in recent years has been to complain about the Ellington band. For twenty-five years Duke was unique; his fans broke through the bitter departmental lines in jazz collecting and included lovers of every style associated with the word.

But since the great exodus of stars, which began with Barney Bigard and Cootie Williams and continued through Johnny Hodges and Sonny Greer, his fans have been so busy griping they haven't had time to listen.

And they should have. Ellington's strongest point has always been his living compositions. Standards like "East St. Louis Toodle-oo" and "Mood Indigo" have been written and rewritten constantly to include the talents of new men and to eliminate the spots that called for the peculiar abilities of former sidemen.

Every time a new musician joined the band there was a new sound. But the fundamental, viscous, flowing rhythm and deep, lush tones that characterized Duke in music have remained.

The memories of yesterday are sweeter than the facts of today —

they always have been. But Duke's music is as good right now as it ever has been and it is stupid for his long-time friends and fans not to listen to it.

Would they have him always sound the same, always say the same thing? Do they?

Recently, Duke made two magnificent broadcasts originating in a Chicago nightclub, the Blue Note. There were many new tunes, many revisions of old ones; through it all there was the wonderful Ellington sound and the promise of great things to come.

We may be witnessing the dawn of a new Ellington age that will be even better than the past. Some evidence of this seems to have influenced the country's jazz critics, who have just voted him top band in the *down beat* poll. Further evidence is in a new Capitol LP album, *Premiered by Ellington*. In it, Duke demonstrates again that his is the greatest single talent to be produced in the history of jazz. His music has maintained an astonishing level of excellence over a quarter of a century, and I would like to predict that, a quarter of a century hence, it will be studied in the schools and critics will grant him his true place among the great modern composers.

In the Capitol album, for instance, tunes like "My Old Flame," "Stormy Weather," "Flamingo," and "Cocktails for Two" are played so magnificently that if these were the first versions of the tunes there would be no question of their value.

They sound different from the original recordings, naturally, because Duke and the band have changed since then. But they are proof that the great Ellington talent is essentially unchanged. Today's band may well be, as Duke says it is, the best he has ever had, and young musicians like Clark Terry, Britt Woodman and Jimmy Hamilton have as much to say as their predecessors. Harry Carney continues to make all other baritone saxophone players seem feeble by comparison and Duke, of course, is ageless.

# APRIL 13, 1954

To date, jazz has produced only one man who can stand as a composer among the musicians of the world: Duke Ellington.

Ellington brought dignity to jazz, took its blues and rags and its stomps and melded them into a form of Afro-American music that seems destined to last. One of the most remarkable things about his music is its versatility. He has always had one of the best, if not *the* best, dance orchestras ever since he came to New York from his native Washington, D.C. As a concert artist, he ushered in the concert era of jazz and used the opportunity to present not stage versions of after-hours jam sessions, but legitimate musical works reflecting the moods and thoughts of his people through the medium of some of their most gifted instrumentalists.

As a composer, *Black, Brown and Beige*, "Mood Indigo," "Reminiscing in Tempo" and others of his more serious works qualify him for inclusion in any discussion of American music. His popular songs are among the best in our repertory: "Sophisticated Lady," "Do Nothin' 'Til You Hear from Me," "I Let a Song Go out of My Heart," "Solitude," "I Got It Bad and That Ain't Good."

Jazz is an informal music and it is doubly remarkable that Ellington has managed to retain such informality in his orchestra and in his own personality and yet produce music that, more than any other jazz, seems completely at home in the War Memorial Opera House or in Carnegie Hall.

To laugh, to be joyous, to be sad, and through it all to retain dignity, is a difficult thing. Duke Ellington, it seems to me, has managed to do that better than anyone else in the jazz field. His music is a reflection of his own personality — one of the richest on the music scene.

## MARCH 17, 1957

Ellington has consistently paralleled his career as a dance and jazz bandleader and popular songwriter with a career as a serious composer in the idiom of what he has called Negro music and whose "color, harmony, melody and rhythm" have always been his first interest.

His serious compositions include "Blue Belles of Harlem" (commissioned by Paul Whiteman), "New World A-Coming," *Perfume Suite*, "Reminiscing in Tempo," *Liberian Suite* and others.

Constant Lambert, writing in the mid-30s on contemporary music, noted that Ellington's best works "are written in what may be called 10-inch record form, and he is perhaps the only composer to raise this insignificant disc to the dignity of a definite genre...."

Later of course, Ellington used 12-inch 78-rpm discs for some of his compositions, and now he has the greater scope of the long-playing record. His latest work, *A Drum Is a Woman*, which Columbia's wholly inadequate program notes refer to as "a musical fantasy paralleling the history of the origins of jazz," is on a 12-inch long-playing disc.

In 1941 Duke was asked by Orson Welles to write a musical history of jazz. The project was begun, abandoned and begun again, only to be completed this past year in a three-month rush of work.

It is interesting and attractive, at times deeply moving, and remarkable for the exceptional performance by the Ellington orchestra. Ellington's conception of jazz is in terms of women and drums; this work, then, is the story of both . . . of a drum-woman, Madam Zajj ("jazz" spelled backwards, almost), her unobtainable lover, Carribee Joe, and how she sought him throughout New Orleans, New York and the whole world, only to lose him in the end to the jungle he never really left.

The device Ellington has chosen is a combination of short programmatic pieces, varying in length from two and three minutes (the time segment of the 10-inch record) to ten and twelve min-

179

utes, and the whole tied together with a narration by Duke himself. It is curious to note that this is the first occasion when he has found it necessary to give explanatory narration on record, although he did this for the premiere of *Black, Brown and Beige* at Carnegie Hall. The result is a musical story, perhaps a new convention for the long-playing record.

Duke's voice is the perfect instrument to accompany the band. Its soft timber and the lushness of his enunciation fit the music and the sound of his orchestra perfectly. There are moments, though, when the work seems less neatly put together than one might wish, an occasional blurring of direction that suggests a reading of a musical script, a sort of recorded audition.

But there are also moments of exquisite beauty and humor. In particular there is the wonderful fourth part, "Zajj's Dream," where the chorus recites the names of the Latin musical instruments, "maracas, bongos, claves, timbales," while Duke recites a line that goes straight back to Vachel Lindsay — "She sent Joe a message and the message went ZOOM!" Here, as in other sections, his voice and the meter of the lyrics are perfectly matched to the rhythmic pulse of the band, suggesting the direction a merger of jazz and poetry must take.

"Zajj's Dream" is the most successful portion of the composition, a wild, flamboyant, imaginative series of pictures ranging from the jungle to spaceships and including "Rhumbop," possibly the only individual number capable of standing alone.

Those who look to Duke Ellington only for the brief rhythmic and harmonic excursions of a "Perdido" or "Bakiff" will possibly find this too pretentious. Those who look for a familiar format for serious composition will in all probability dismiss it as slight. But in Duke's own words, "We must try to make our work express the rich background of the Negro." I think that this is in many ways the best of his serious writing and that in it he fully justifies the accolade handed him by Constant Lambert: "A composer of uncommon merit, probably the first composer of real character to come out of America."

## OCTOBER 1, 1957

Earlier this year Ellington presented his new suite, *Such Sweet Thunder* — or almost all of it — at a concert in New York. It was later done in full at the Shakespearean Festival in Stratford, Ontario. Columbia has now released a 12-inch LP containing thirteen short compositions by Duke and Billy Strayhorn — the complete *Such Sweet Thunder* suite. It is played by the Ellington orchestra.

By and large, the repertoire of jazz has been limited in form to either the thirty-two-bar popular song or the twelve-bar blues. Although a great number of classic jazz performances have been produced as mere improvisations on the structure of popular songs, there has always been a movement within jazz to develop original compositions; in no one more than Ellington has this tendency flowered.

Essentially what Duke has done is to write a series of showcases for the different sections of the band and the prize soloists. Everything has the unique Ellington touch which has enabled him many times to take what seems a trivial approach and produce something lasting.

There are fascinating examples of his creative genius in this album and of the solo virtuosity of his musicians. For instance, "Sonnet for Caesar," one of the four musical sonnets Duke has written, features Jimmy Hamilton on clarinet. Hamilton is one of the most consistent clarinet soloists in jazz and one of the few playing today who is always rewarding to hear. On this number he builds a beautiful, almost regal, melodic structure, artfully assisted by the drumming of Sam Woodyard.

Britt Woodman, who possesses possibly a greater command of his instrument than any trombonist in jazz, is featured in "Sonnet to Hank Cinq" (such a beautiful title!). And the other soloists — Russell Procope, Quentin Jackson, Johnny Hodges, Paul Gonsalves, Harry Carney, Ray Nance, Jimmy Woode and Clark Terry — all appear in circumstances designed to give their talents the best possible setting.

*Such Sweet Thunder* runs the Ellington gamut from deep blues to frolicking, humorous dances to languid, romantic alto saxophone solos. Every single moment of it is well done.

## MARCH 9, 1958

When the time comes in future years to write the final assessments of our culture, there is more than a chance Duke Ellington will rank as one of the great American musicians.

Ellington has doggedly pursued his own way in the jazz world. Periodically the younger musicians, infatuated with some momentary wizard, blithely skip Ellington's music. But this lasts only a short time. Very quickly they are jerked back to reality when they find that some flatted fifth, some voicing, some linear writing device which is new to them is old hat to the Duke.

One of the fascinating aspects of the band over the years has been the way in which standard Ellington compositions, such as "Mood Indigo" and "Solitude," have altered, as different versions of the Ellington band have played them, yet have always retained their essential character. In Duke's new Columbia album, *Ellington Indigos* (CL 1085), the two tunes just mentioned, as well as "Prelude to a Kiss," are redone, as well as several other ballads, including "Autumn Leaves," "Tenderly" and "Willow Weep for Me."

The album was recorded under excellent conditions and the performances all have that beautiful warm quality which has always characterized the best Ellington. Harold Baker, usually known for his open horn solos, takes a lovely, graceful, muted solo on "Mood Indigo" and Johnny Hodges is almost frighteningly effective in "Prelude to a Kiss." This LP is a prerequisite for all discussions of Duke these days and, to me, demolishes completely the arguments of those, including André Hodeir, who feel he is no longer creatively important.

## MARCH 13, 1958

It has been Ellington's fate, particularly in recent years, to have been bypassed by public acclaim while younger bandleaders appeared to be doing more exciting things. However much one may enjoy the other good bands of this era, it only takes one evening with Ellington to put things back in perspective. And the perspective reveals over and over that he is beyond comparison.

In his dual function as leader of his orchestra as well as its chief creative talent, he has managed to express his personality more fully than any other composer in jazz. In so doing he has presented the talents of the men who are fortunate to work for him in the best possible light. This is one of the reasons why it is a rare Ellington sideman who maintains his stature upon leaving the Duke, much less increases it.

A recent program consisted of excerpts from *Such Sweet Thunder* and *A Drum Is a Woman*, plus a selection of ballads and blues calculated to display individual soloists. A feature of the second half was a medley of Ellington compositions — a list that now rivals any of our popular composers and offers a variety ranging from "Mood Indigo" to "Diminuendo and Crescendo in Blue."

The continual, flexible use of dynamics and shadings and the unusual voicings of the band gave the performances a richness of texture that only Ellington can supply. Make no mistake: This Ellington is every bit as creative as at any period in his past. It is indicative of his skillful use of his men's talents that two of his newest members, drummer Sam Woodyard and bassist Jimmy Woode, have melded with him into the best rhythm section he has had in years.

# AUGUST 3, 1958

On January 23, 1943, Duke Ellington presented his major composition, *Black, Brown and Beige* in a concert at Carnegie Hall. As the master of ceremonies, he introduced each of the three sections of the composition, explaining that it was "a tone parallel to the history of the American Negro." He had been at work on the composition since the mid-30s and had incorporated into it much of the material he had written originally for an opera.

Regrettably, the full score has seldom been heard since that night. Parts of it were recorded on two RCA Victor 78-rpm discs some years ago and have since become not only collectors' items but legendary examples of the Ellington compositional style.

Early last spring, he once again recorded *Black, Brown and Beige,* this time for Columbia, and again the album contains only excerpts from the full work. However, the moving "Come Sunday" theme (the second part of the opening section, "Black") is sung by the great gospel singer Mahalia Jackson rather than played by the alto saxophone of Johnny Hodges.

The combination of Miss Jackson's voice and the orchestra of Ellington was pure inspiration and has resulted in one of the most magnificent recordings either of them has ever made.

Ellington and Miss Jackson recorded it in Hollywood, and after several abortive attempts to achieve exactly what Ellington wished, he had the lights turned off in the studio and Miss Jackson sang in the dark. (The notes, by Irving Townsend, who deserves great credit for revitalizing Columbia's policy toward Ellington, really should have told more of episodes such as this.) Her voice puts to shame any other which has ever been heard in serious jazz singing.

The Ellington band is more flexible and deeper-toned than the one which originally recorded *Black, Brown and Beige.* And on the second side, accompanying Mahalia Jackson, it rises to heights of emotional intensity even it has scarcely enjoyed before. As her cellolike voice sings the moving message of joy, the band plays a series of deep organ tones behind her that is astonishing. The tonal patterns shift, and when drummer Sam Woodyard touches the cymbal, it has a delicacy and flavor that is exceptionally moving. Ray Nance's gracefully urgent violin obbligato, Harry Carney's stately baritone solo and the brief appearances of Harold Baker, John Sanders, Britt Woodman, Cat Anderson and Quentin Jackson are all renewed indication of the creative reserve of this orchestra.

It is astonishing that after almost thirty-five years as a bandleader, Ellington can still produce performances of such power and startling vitality. Looking back (which Ellington never does) at the body of his work, it is apparent that this man is the full justification for jazz music's existence and that this album is one of his finest hours.

As a finale, Ellington presents Miss Jackson singing "The Twenty-third Psalm." Again, the liquid strength of her voice is matched by the plastic mobility of the orchestra.

After hearing this album, one is reminded of the myopic critical judgment by the Frenchman André Hodeir, who said last year, "Duke is creatively dead," and the petulant echo of this in Nat Hentoff's *Harper's* article last spring. While Hentoff's piece was being written, Duke Ellington was making the music on this album; it is as fine a testimony to his continued creativeness as could have been devised.

## JULY 12, 1959

With the release this month of Otto Preminger's motion picture *Anatomy of a Murder*, jazz fans will have their first opportunity to hear the results of Duke Ellington's first film score.

Ellington, although he has appeared in numerous motion pictures and has composed more extended works than any other jazz musician, had not written a motion picture score until Preminger invited him to do *Anatomy of a Murder*.

"It was a great experience," Duke said. "It's a wonderful education. You know, I learned a lot of things, a lot of things. Music in pictures should say something without being obviously music, you know, and this was all new to me."

Ellington's score, comprising some dozen numbers, four themes all related, has been released on *Music by Duke Ellington: From the Sound Track of "Anatomy of a Murder"* (Columbia CL 1360). Recorded in Hollywood early this summer, the music itself, Duke said, "was written partially in Hollywood and partially in Ishpeming, Michigan, where I went to join the cast of the picture to get the feel of the story.

"Of course *the* tune is 'Flirtibird.' The flirtibird is the girl in the story who's always flirting but nothing ever happens. We've tried to make the tune represent her. It's a flirtibird. The picture people have been very kind; they feel the music is great and they like the songs. Peggy Lee is doing words to 'Flirtibird,' for instance."

The music, as recorded with his full band, comes through as one of the richest and most melodic efforts he has produced in some time. No Ellington album is ever disappointing, but this one in particular is rewarding listening.

Ellington, of course, is modesty itself when it comes to discussing his work. Even though the reports from screenings and from the studio were excellent, Duke kept repeating "the next one will be better. I'll try another one and then I'll show them. I'm young. Give me a chance!"

## JUNE 7, 1960

Duke Ellington's mangnificent musicianship survived a pitifully small crowd, a series of backstage hassles and insufferable programming Sunday night at the Oakland Auditorium Theater to give to those who attended a delightful example of true artistry.

That Ellington is a past master of tonal color, the creating of exquisite tension without sacrificing dynamics, and the utilization of the individual soloist in the settings best suited to his attributes is well established. But Sunday's concert demonstrated once again something we are inclined to overlook. This band has for three decades been so deep in talent it can dispense with the services of three or four outstanding instrumentalists at any one time and, in overall performance, they will not be missed.

The burden of the band's work now rests upon the saxophone section with Johnny Hodges, Harry Carney, Russell Procope, Jimmy Hamilton and Paul Gonsalves. There is such flexibility there, such strength of solo talent, that one does not miss the trumpeters who were formerly starred. The trombone section boasts two versatile men, Britt Woodman and Booty Wood (who plays the plunger mute solos traditional to this band with originality and feeling) and the veteran Lawrence Brown, newly returned and not yet a featured player.

The rhythm section rejoices in the return of Sam Woodyard, by far the most sensitive, swinging and imaginative drummer Ellington has had in years.

The reserves of talent, inspiration and creativity that have made this orchestra and its leader outstanding, produced once again under trying circumstances. The promoters delayed the program thirty minutes; disciplinary action was necessary against a trumpeter who arrived late; for some reason a six-year-old Oriental girl named Jennie Tue did several long numbers midway in the program (thus reemphasizing the need for strict enforcement of child labor laws). Nevertheless the music was grand in scope and elegant in execution as is Ellington's habit.

## JUNE 19, 1960

The remarkably flexible Duke Ellington orchestra and the remarkably flexible Sarah Vaughan voice were both in excellent form Friday night at the Civic Auditorium in a concert that proved once again that even the best of music has a hard time within those walls.

Miss Vaughan came off best, as far as the sound was concerned. The orchestra's setup was such that the drummer played a constant duet with a ghost in the balcony, as the echo of his rim shots and cymbals came tumbling back at him.

Miss Vaughan was in much better voice and in a considerably better frame of mind than when she sang last fall at the Monterey Jazz Festival. Friday night she used her voice, with all its marvelous ability to maneuver the scale and attempt difficult intervals, to scoop and bend notes and indulge in vocal calisthenics, as though she were a jazz soloist in a small combo. On "What Is This Thing Called Love?" she sang the traditional bop interpolation ("Hot House") in scat and ended up in what was apparently a vocal parody of the Dizzy Gillespie trumpet style. When she sang "Misty," she approximated the piano improvisation of its composer Erroll Garner with a series of phrases so far behind the beat one almost lost her. During "Poor Butterfly," to which she sang the verse, Miss Vaughan, never known for lyric retentive powers, came to the line "love in the American way" and, apparently having just read of the Tokyo riots, promptly forgot the rest of the lyric.

Most of her program ranged between such slow, throaty and sometimes ultracute numbers as "Tenderly" and the roaring up-tempo improvisations such as "Cherokee."

Miss Vaughan possesses a truly amazing vocal instrument, one of the best ever applied to jazz, but I never hear her without wishing she could dispense for once with her cuteness and corny milking of lines and just sing. Surely, with a voice like hers, to sing without embellishment should be enough.

## JULY 3, 1960

To have an identifiable, personal sound has been the goal of all jazz musicians since this music started back in the dim regions of the South at the turn of the century.

By and large these have been individual sounds, as jazz itself has been largely an area of individual expression in the form of virtuoso musicians. Even the large bands, back to Fletcher Henderson and McKinney's Cotton Pickers, have had, in the main, only one sound.

Each band has had its sound, but it has been a single thing

hinging on one personality or one manner of collective playing with the same accent. Only the Duke Ellington orchestra has utilized a variety of sounds, a multiplicity of combinations (from trio to full band) in an assortment of interesting and provocative ways.

The band, naturally enough, reflects the complex personality of its leader, just as it is, in reality, his true musical instrument.

Ellington, alone among jazz composers and arrangers, has always written for the specific individual personalities in the band at a given time.

This is why classic numbers such as "The Mooche," "Take the 'A' Train" and "Sophisticated Lady" alter their character as the personalities of different musicians come to bear on the number and the "solo responsibility" shifts from one man to another.

At various times Ellington has remarked that his greatest joy is in the band itself. "Hearing what I've written played by that wonderful orchestra," he said once, is his greatest thrill. Another time he underlined the effect that even slight changes of personnel have in a concept of composing for individual musicians by pointing out that every time there was a change in the band it was a new band. It is.

Bring back Johnny Hodges after an absence of several years and the overall sound of the band remains the same (reflecting as it does Ellington's personality through the continuity of other personnel), but the individual numbers alter in sound and performance as Hodges assumes solo responsibility. Bring back Lawrence Brown after an absence of several years and the brass section takes on a new coloration.

But the individual sound with the most continuity in the Ellington ensemble has been Harry Carney, the baritone saxophone player whose solos and section work have given Ellington's music such solid foundation.

Carney, who is currently celebrating his thirty-fourth year with Ellington, is the one musician whose removal from the ensemble would change that sound drastically.

As he has acquired seniority in the band, Carney's playing has come more and more to mean the "Ellington sound."

Today, he and Johnny Hodges are the living proof that not only is there a future in being a sideman but also that creativity in jazz is not the exclusive property of the very young.

## SEPTEMBER 11, 1960

Even in a world where, as Eric Gill believed, every man is a special kind of artist, Duke Ellington would stand out. In the classic tradition of the original artist, he has not only created his own style, but he has invented the instrument with which to express it.

His orchestra is a collection of artists specially chosen to play Ellingtonia and welded into an instrument for which, one might say, Ellington writes in a very special way.

"Personalized writing is very important to me," Ellington said when I interviewed him early this summer. "If I didn't know who I was writing for, I wonder what I'd write!"

His careers as a dance band leader, a writer of great popular songs, and a composer of longer works have paralleled each other just as the functions of his orchestra exist simultaneously. Everything Duke has done, however, has embodied two things: It swings (as his classic song title declared: "It Don't Mean a Thing, If It Ain't Got That Swing") and it has roots in the blues.

His compositions differ from orthodox works in that, to a greater or lesser degree and varying with the individual composition, the actual score can be either notated or elaborated in performance, though either way it is still codified. There are gaps for individual improvisation, but improvisation in the Ellington sense is not completely ad lib. Varying with the personality of the soloist and his length of service in the band, improvisation can mean the same solo played ninety percent the same way night after night with the other ten percent allowed for interpolation. It can also mean (as with Hodges) solos that are basically the same but which are expandable or contractible at the will of either the soloist or the leader.

After more than thirty years, it is now quite obvious that

Ellington's musicians have always been at their highest peak when with Ellington. On their own they are good men all, but not what they are with the Maestro. It has been his method to let each man sit and grow into the band until the special artist (in Eric Gill's sense) that each is emerges and then can be fully utilized.

Irving Townsend once told of Ellington writing *A Drum Is a Woman* traveling between one-nighters in the back of Harry Carney's auto and stopping the band in the middle of a dance in New Jersey to play excerpts. "I just wanted to hear how it sounded," he told the startled audience.

This illustrates two other extraordinary aspects of Ellington's role as a composer: His work is always done "on the road" and for his entire career as a composer he has been in the unique position of being able to hear today's compositions played back tonight.

Ellington began writing extended works in 1932, with *Creole Rhapsody*. Since 1943 he has produced one each year. It is a high compliment to him (as well as a source of pleasure) that his audiences, bred on dance bands and on the freedom, sometimes extended to license, of the ordinary jazz musicians, have been willing to listen to new, unfamiliar and long works.

For Ellington, this is also a point of encouragement because, as he says, "I never look at the royalty checks. . . . I only go by those who listen. If I go someplace and there are two people who are listening to what I've got to say, this is enough encouragement for me to go on and do what I want to do."

## MARCH 19, 1961

Last summer the Monterey Jazz Festival commissioned Duke Ellington to compose an original work on the theme of John Steinbeck's *Cannery Row* for a premiere performance at the festival.

Ellington's composition, *Suite Thursday*, was recorded by Columbia shortly after its performance at Monterey. It is a major

Ellington work, which is to say it is a major piece of contemporary American music.

*Suite Thursday* shows the fruits of the effort Ellington put into this work. In the past he has been rather famous for last-minute composition. This piece, however, was written while he was on the East Coast, was rehearsed there and in New York, with final touches for the premiere added at Monterey. After the first performance, Ellington played it nightly (sometimes twice) during his two weeks at the Neve in San Francisco. Some parts were altered slightly and the band each night opened the evening playing what Ellington had written during the day so he could hear it.

Saxophonist Johnny Hodges became ill during this period and the notes he was to have played were assigned to Lawrence Brown. (Hodges' place in the section was taken for the recording by Paul Horn.) The piece grew, flourished and matured during those two weeks, and by the time Ellington got around to recording it, it was as ripe as the grapes picked for any Cannery Row winemaker's tour de force.

The suite consists of four parts: "Misfit Blues," a piquant statement of the theme (which recurs throughout and sounds like a musical exposition of the line "Steinbeck is a swinger," which Duke articulated at Monterey) by Lawrence Brown. Ellington has some reflective piano mood setting which leads into a lovely, medium-tempo passage by the reeds and rhythm.

The title indicates, according to Ellington, that the Cannery Row group was a "community of misfits, but they were beautiful people." This movement ends with a bass passage by Aaron Bell and an ensemble chord.

The second movement, "Schwiphti," according to Duke, "is the part that shows the colors. All of Cannery Row had a tempo, colors, moods and variations." It's all in here in ensemble passages with reed section contrasting with brass, interspersed by piano passages by Duke and backed by a strong rhythm pulse from the bass and drums. The trombones shout, the trumpet of Ray Nance hoots and hollers, Paul Gonsalves' tenor coasts along and Andres Meringuito's trumpet wails on high as the music fades to a reed section chorded ending.

192

The third movement begins with a Latin beat, with Duke stating the theme on piano echoed by Jimmy Hamilton's clarinet. This part is called "Zuite Zurzday" ("It has a lilt," Duke says). The reeds follow, still with the Latin beat in the background rather like a Palomino pony (red?) clopping along, and then Lawrence Brown contributes a lyrical trombone statement. Paul Gonsalves ("the fog that clouds" the "beautiful dream" which Hamilton's clarinet represents) appears briefly. There is a low tone like a distant foghorn, more clarinet, more Latin clip-clop rhythm, and then a curious, muted brass ending.

Part four is "Lay-by" ("Doc and Suzy swinging off to La Jolla"). This is a section in faster tempo with reeds and brass now taking over the original theme, fleshing it out and restating it with greater weight. Ray Nance then plays the theme on violin ("this concluding portion of the suite," Duke says, "deals with page 273 of the book") in a bright, witty and swinging solo and with an engaging passage where he plucks the strings (backed by a walking bass figure and the steady drum rhythm). The violin and the band then state and restate the theme, building to a raggy break by Nance, some crashing chords, and a slow, almost sly ending of four two-note phrases by the plucked violin.

Throughout the soloists are consistently good; Sam Woodyard's drumming is admirable and the ensemble work is topnotch. But it is the composition itself, which Billy Strayhorn coauthored with Ellington, that is the important thing.

Not only is it a major Ellington work, but it is quite probably the most important jazz work of the year and an Ellington composition that is destined to take its rightful place alongside his great armada of extended ducal efforts.

# MAY 14, 1961

"You know me, I love problems," says Duke Ellington of his current project: writing the score for the motion picture *Paris Blues*.

Ellington is in Paris and during the rest of this year will probably commute back and forth between the United States and France as he completes his work on the picture.

Working out the score for *Paris Blues* is not, however, according to Ellington, "a unique problem. There's a good deal of onstage music in it," Duke points out, and writing that sort of thing is much easier than doing a music score for straight acting sequences as he did in *Anatomy of a Murder*.

The actual final score to *Paris Blues* has not yet been completed, Ellington says, and this illuminates one of the more interesting customs of motion picture production.

When a score like Ellington's is being prepared and various passages in the film require actors to play music, a version of the music is put on tape first and then the actors are photographed and the music recorded again. Sometimes things alter considerably in this process. Ellington has just completed what is called the "pre-recording." Later this summer the final recording will be done, and Ellington expects there will be numerous changes. "They get ideas for dramatic things after they hear the music the first time, you know," he says.

A number of Ellington's previous compositions are featured in the film, but the Ellington band does not play. Instead, Ellington has directed a group of French studio musicians, for whom he has the highest regard, for the sound track.

Ellington has actually written a good deal of music for *Paris Blues*, whether or not these particular things appear in the final version.

"This is my writing period," Duke says. "I must have written more in the last two years than I've written in my whole life. But it keeps on coming and there's no good in saving it up."

# NOVEMBER 5, 1961

It is a measure of Duke Ellington as a composer and leader that RCA Victor can take twenty-one selections from only a six-year period of his career (1940–1946) and produce a twin-LP package of such beauty as *The Indispensable Duke Ellington* (RCA Victor LPM 6009).

The great music of the 30s and the latter half of the 40s, the magnificent efforts of the 50s and the past year are all bypassed, but it seems to me that one might make a pretty good reputation as a leader and composer on these numbers alone.

The Ellington band of that era — like all his bands except for very short periods of transition — was a uniquely effective mechanism for transmitting the musical ideas of its leader and director while articulating them in the highly individual tongues of the solo members of the orchestra.

Cootie Williams, Rex Stewart, Barney Bigard, Jimmy Blanton, Oscar Pettiford, Al Sears, Ben Webster, Tricky Sam Nanton, Otto Hardwick, Wilbur DeParis, and Sonny Greer are among the men who passed through the band during this period, made their contributions, and thus succeeded in securing for themselves a place in jazz history.

Mercer Ellington, Duke's son, and Billy Strayhorn contributed to the repertoire strongly in those years and are represented here.

But it is not the work of the individuals, great artists though they may be, that marks this collection. Rather, it is the totality of the orchestra and the leader, the sum of the parts, which marks this as one of the most rewarding collections to be issued from the Victor archives.

Included are two of the piano-bass duets which Ellington recorded with Jimmy Blanton, "Mr. J. B. Blues" and "Pitter Panther Patter," the complete *Perfume Suite* and five numbers which have not been issued before: "Blue Cellophane," "Mood Indigo," "Just You, Just Me," "Blue Is the Night" and "Black Beauty."

With the exception of *Perfume Suite*, all of the numbers are confined to the standard time limit of the 30s and 40s, the three-minute single disc. *Perfume Suite* is a four-part suite made up of four elements of that same standard size, and here one can see the classic miniature Ellington composition at its best.

The richness of his recorded output during these years makes any selection arbitrary and it is certain that even in as extensive a compilation as this, there will be gaps that some would have liked filled. However, on its merits alone it is, in the best sense of the word, "indispensable," not only to Ellington fans but also to anyone genuinely interested in American music and jazz.

## APRIL 29, 1962

Broadway musicals have certainly produced some of the best songs in our history, but I confess that with rare exception, original cast recordings bore me even more than the original productions.

There have been few collections to reduce me to the sudden numbness achieved after five minutes of *Oklahoma* and/or *The King and I.* It is, I have decided after long analysis, the fact that the American musical is firmly based in a nonswinging idiom that does it. The only original cast album I have ever wanted is the one that does not exist: Duke Ellington's great revue, *Jump for Joy* (and why doesn't Columbia redo it?).

This brings me to the subject: Ellington has issued an album of the score of a musical, *All American* (Columbia CL-1790), that is a masterpiece of a particular genre.

*All American* is the current Ray Bolger musical. There are numerous albums in release devoted to the Lee Adams–Charlie Strouse score, including an original cast LP. To play them all several times, as I did, and then to play Ellington's album is most illuminating. That Ellington has had a multilevel career, one portion of which has been devoted to the interpretation of other people's music, is no news. But I have never had such a dramatic illustration of exactly how good he is at this task as here.

Ellington took the cream of the *All American* score (the authors wrote *Bye Bye, Birdie,* by the way) and has obviously devoted great thought and concentration to its performance. Each of the numbers is done in terms of one of the soloists of the orchestra and each of the soloists "sings" the number as if he and he alone were in the composer's mind when it was written. Duke's achievement is to extract every possible ounce of lyricism and beauty from the score and to enhance it all by his arrangements and by the stark emotional fiber of the soloists.

On the other hand, melodies which in Ellington's hand become simply lovely and which stick in your mind after hearing him play them are muddied up, distorted and out of focus in the hands of others. Even the original cast LP, which one might assume would have authenticity going for it, does not come within a country mile of Ellington's beautiful performances.

It must be a great thrill to a composer to hear his music played by Ellington: It all comes alive with none of the studied, unmusical pretense of the original cast type of performance. I am well aware that *Oklahoma* is one of the best-selling LPs of all time in the original cast version. You take it; I'll be content with *All American* as Duke Ellington recorded it — a classic example of the way in which the best of jazz can enhance anybody's music.

# JUNE 19, 1962

In the past week I have had the opportunity to make an interesting experiment. Every night I listened to a two-hour concert of recordings by Duke Ellington, going back to the first days of the band, thirty-five years ago. They were played for me after dinner and interspersed between symphonies, concertos and string quartet recordings by the greatest classical artists and composers.

It is not necessary to equate Ellington with Bach to observe that one can listen to both almost indefinitely. I was aware of some of Duke's staying power, but to listen to this much music by one band, and mainly by one man, was a revelation.

In the course of this excursion into Ellingtonia I heard many, many recordings that I have never heard before. They, like the ones with which I was already familiar, emphasized Ellington's consistency. From the beginning down to today, all his music has had form as well as inspiration. And over the years, it has gained — not lost — in depth, in texture, in interest. Duke Ellington today is a greater composer than he has ever been and his music is richer. In only one respect has this band lost with the years: There never was, nor will there ever be again, a vocalist of the caliber of Ivie

Anderson. She was unique and irreplaceable. There have been other good singers with the band, but only Ivie sounded as if she was born to sing to this music.

## OCTOBER 15, 1962

In some societies great artists are considered a national asset, nurtured, encouraged and supported by the state. We are a long way from that in the U.S. of A., but listening to Duke Ellington's orchestra play at Friday night's opening at New Fack's, I couldn't help but think how good an idea this is.

It would not be out of line to declare, by a special Act of Congress if need be, the Ellington musical workshop a national property. Federalize it or whatever you wish, but set it up so it can function without economic worry and perform at the maximum level for the benefit, not only of the composer-conductor and the individual members, but of all the citizens of this land and the world.

Very frankly, I think that the cultural contribution of an Ellington cannot be assessed in terms of money. The amount necessary to arrange it so that this orchestra and its leader would be permanently supported by the government is small in relation to other sums we throw around.

I would like to see Ellington resident one semester at one university, next semester at another, and then for periods of weeks giving concerts in major cities with periodic tours to the rest of the country. And all the while the composer given the facilities and encouragement (relief from economic problems) to compose.

If the government won't do it, I suggest it as a project for one of the foundations, more worthy than many they undertake.

That so much is accomplished now under the strain of hurtling across the country from one-night stand to one-night stand, riding in buses and playing everywhere from concert halls to Elks Clubs' dining rooms, is a tribute to the talent, tenacity and dedication of the musicians and their leader.

Friday evening's first two sets were among the most memorable orchestra performances I have ever heard. Ellington has never sounded better to me. The orchestra as a whole, the individual men, their solos — all seemed inspired and part of a great pulsating unity.

As some indication of the resources of this band, it should be noted that in two full (and long) sets Friday night, they actually didn't get all the way down the batting order.

Johnny Hodges crept in only at the tail end of the second set with his exciting performance on "Passion Flower" and "Things Ain't What They Used to Be." Cootie Williams was featured all too briefly in two selections (in which he was highly impressive) and Harry Carney really had no solo spot at all.

I have the greatest respect for the creative jazz musician of any style (especially since, under our system, he is creating art in a supermarket), but my admiration for the Ellington organization knows no bounds.

Theirs is real American music, not just nightclub entertainment. It should be treated as a national treasure. When that sad day comes when it exists no longer, this country and the world will be immeasurably poorer.


# FEBRUARY 3, 1963

It took almost twenty years for Duke Ellington and Coleman Hawkins to record together, with special music by Ellington for the very special saxophone playing of Hawkins.

The result is now available on a new Impulse album, *Duke Ellington Meets Coleman Hawkins* (Impulse A-26), and it was worth waiting for, a classic example of the melding of two extraordinary musical personalities. Each seems to complement the other, and Hawk sounds as though he has been playing with Ellington for years.

The feeling of the accompaniment — Ray Nance, trumpet and violin; Lawrence Brown, trombone; Johnny Hodges, alto; Harry

Carney, baritone; Aaron Bell, bass; Sam Woodyard, drums; and Ellington himself — is one of continuing excitement. The eight numbers were played as for the ages.

One of the nicest things about the LP is the spirit demonstrated by the participants. There's an informal version of "Limbo Jazz," a Latin rhythm number, which was recorded without the musicians knowing it. Sam Woodyard hums and sings a refrain all through it.

Lawrence Brown, usually such a sober, undemonstrative man, gets a feeling of positive exuberance in his solos, and Duke himself gets into the same sort of groove.

"Jeep Is Jumpin'" is one of the most exciting mainstream-style jazz tunes of recent recording history, a wildly swinging, stomping excursion. "Mood Indigo" is an absolute masterpiece. Hawkins comes in for his chorus as though he had been waiting twenty years to speak his mind. "You Dirty Dog," a blues, has solo after solo of such classic dignity that you realize this particular jazz genre is sufficient unto itself musically.

Hawkins' big tone and sturdy sound, along with his remarkably full conception of playing, has always made him an outstanding tenor soloist. For many, he is the man who invented the saxophone in jazz. And it is quite obvious from this LP that he is not about to turn over his rights in it to any successor. This is by far the best album that Coleman Hawkins has made in years, perhaps has ever made.

## APRIL 1963

To criticize any art form effectively postulates love. If you do not love this art form with which you are occupying your days and nights there are only two other possible attitudes: neutrality or distaste. Either of these makes you a hatchet man or a ghoul. At the very best you can be an educated, intelligent cannibal living off the artistic carcass. We have plenty of examples of this in literature and the other arts. Sadly enough, we also have plenty of examples in jazz of educated and articulate cannibals whose main purpose, regardless of their posture, is to chop down and devour great artists like Erroll Garner and Duke Ellington.

It has recently been my pleasure to listen to eight full evenings of the Duke Ellington orchestra in nightclub and concert performances. It has been a musical experience of a richness, variety and depth unrivaled in my jazz listening. At no point was I bored. At no point did my mind stray from the music to the irritations of clumping chairs or chattering couples at the bar.

It was precisely the same order of experience as I have had with a serious novel, a play or listening to Brahms or Mozart.

At least once every night, Ellington played a medley of "The Mooche," "Creole Love Call" and "Mood Indigo." On some evenings I heard this medley three times. Over the years I have heard it countless times. It has no more palled than have the Bach Partitas, and for the same reasons as well as some additional ones.

Ellington's music bears repeated hearing. If it is listened to with concentration, something new will be heard each time. The operational phrase is "listened to with concentration." Most jazz critics are victims of the economy of abundance. They haven't got time to listen to Duke on record except for the first time 'round. They never have a chance to go back. This is understandable if not excusable, but where they are in clear violation of the moral responsibility of the critic to the artist is in their failure to make any attempt to hear this orchestra at length and under a variety of circumstances over the years. You cannot listen to Duke, any more than you can to Bach, merely in a saloon, at a cocktail party or while yapping during a concert. You are required to work at listening in order to hear.

True, Ellington plays many of the same things again and again; so, I might point out, do symphony orchestras. That Duke has been playing "Mood Indigo" for over twenty years is not an indication of laziness or sterility at all. It is a testament to his remarkable musical imagination which has created an infinite variety within the melodic structure of this composition. That variety is present night after night, though it may be cloaked in a subtlety not obvious to the critic.

Ellington, for thirty years or more, has been engaged in supporting a continuous musical workshop in which his ideas can be revised, altered and reconsidered. What he writes in the morning can be played at night. That our society has refused to accept him as a serious composer and has insisted upon the entertainer image and the jazz and dance band image produces a situation which forces this workshop to support itself by almost constant travel. But the product that has reached phonograph records is of remarkable consistency: there is no Duke Ellington album not worth owning. The sad part is that there is so much of his music that has not been preserved for the world.

## SEPTEMBER 22, 1963

Columbia has just released a three-LP package of Ellington recordings dating from 1927 to 1940, a highly creative period in the band's history and including some of the greatest jazz recordings ever made. It is called *The Ellington Era* (C3L27).

Ellington's work is fascinating to listen to in a decade's chronology. In the beginning there was much more evidence of direct relationship to the rest of jazz music, to the trumpet playing of Louis Armstrong, to the soprano saxophone of Sidney Bechet, to the big bands of Fletcher Henderson and King Oliver, for instance, than there is later on when the full flower of Ellington originality came into being.

As these recordings — which come from what might be called the Ellington preclassic and classic periods and do not give more than a hint of the great scope of the Ellington modern period — clearly show, Ellington has conducted a large-scale research project in the blues. His music has been written to explore all the possibilities inherent in the blues form and the blues gestalt. And just as the sonnet has not been exhausted by one poet, the blues have not yet been exhausted by even so prolific a composer as Duke Ellington.

Jazz musicians, especially those young enough to have missed the Ellington band during this period, might consider these recordings an invaluable casebook of jazz exercises, ranging through the gamut of jazz expression, all the scope of the jazz orchestra. For the music lover it is a treasure trove.

The list of instrumentalists includes Rex Stewart, Cootie Williams, Ben Webster, Arthur Whetsol, Bubber Miley, Jabbo Smith (in a rare and rewarding "East St. Louis"), Otto Hardwick, Jimmy Blanton, Joe Nanton, Johnny Hodges, Harry Carney, Lawrence Brown, Juan Tizol and Barney Bigard.

Playing through the forty-eight tracks, one is struck by the fact that there is a changing pattern of soloists but the band retains its individual character always. Barney Bigard in the context of the Ellington band was magnificent. So were Stewart and Williams.

One is also struck by the unique quality of Ivie Anderson as a jazz vocalist and by the consistently deep and diverse nature of the Ellington compositional talent.

There is a fascinating booklet with essays by Irving Mills, Stanley Dance (the best of the Ellington historians) and Leonard Feather, plus some wonderful photographs.

Feather ends his essay thusly: "As you reach the final sides, you may be reminded . . . of the oft-repeated and crushingly apt summation by Andre Previn: 'Another band leader can stand in front of a thousand fiddles and a thousand brass, give the down beat and every studio arranger can nod his head and say "Oh yes, that's done like this." But Duke merely lifts his finger, three horns make a sound, and nobody knows what it is.'"

Let's be reminded of that quote by all means, but also let us quote it right. What Previn said was, "Stan Kenton can stand in front of a thousand fiddles and a thousand brass." And Previn didn't say, "Nobody knows what it is"; he said, "I don't know what it is," meaning Previn.

Previn said it in 1952 at the Opera House in the intermission of an Ellington concert. He said it to me and it was first published in *down beat* later that year. It has been frequently quoted since, and not always accurately.

# DECEMBER 15, 1963

Quite possibly no musician in history, certainly in jazz history, has engaged in such a deliberate camouflage over an extended period of time as has Duke Ellington. It is possible to attribute his behavior to various things, such as the refusal of his audience ever to accept him for the serious musician that he really is. But no matter what one credits as the cause, it is a fact central to Ellington's personality, character and music that he will never be direct or orthodox. One cannot expect him to react in any predictable fashion. His truth is in his music.

Part of the image Ellington has perversely presented to the public through the years is that he is only the "piano player" in the band.

Actually, he is a psychologist, choreographer, thinker, counter-thinker, plotter, enticer and master musician. As well as several other things.

And, in order to make it harder for the public and the critics to discover that he is also not just the piano player but a damn fine piano player, Ellington has always concealed his real ability on that instrument.

What I mean is this: As if to prove that critics don't hear and audiences won't listen, Duke has always made it seem as if his piano playing were not to be taken seriously. He has always implied this in what he said and occasionally he has said it half seriously, or at the least with his tongue in his cheek. And, seated at the piano, he has made a ritual out of pretending not to play. His hands fly, his arms wave and if you *want* to think he isn't much of a piano player, he'll be delighted to show you visually that you are right.

But when the hands touch the keyboard, Duke is true to his art. Then he is the pianist supreme. But by that time he has flashed the symbols and distracted, like a musical magician, not the eye but the ear. Duke plays the piano seriously. But he is not heard. He has carried this into his recording, eschewing solos and making only two solo LPs in all of the dozens of albums he has cut in the past decade.

"I am a listener," Duke has said. And like all musicians he digs listeners. He is not only the boss, but the boss musician.

# JUNE 7, 1964

In the summer of 1927 a Boston saxophone player named Harry Howell Carney was working with a band in a Chinese restaurant in New York. One afternoon in June he met a piano player named Duke Ellington on the street, was asked if he could fill in for a while in Ellington's saxophone section, took the job and has been there ever since.

To this day, Harry Carney insists, Ellington has never told him the job was permanent. When the band opens tonight at Tin Pan Alley in Redwood City, the temporary saxophonist will be sitting there behind the baritone sax as always.

Harry Carney has, in the thirty-seven years he's been with Ellington, gradually become such an integral part of the band's sound that it would be inconceivable without him. He is also one of the master soloists in jazz.

Carney didn't really start playing baritone until he joined Ellington in 1927. "At that time the baritone was not very popular. Most players doubled and the instrument was only used to play parts, although a few people like Joe Garland and Foots Thomas played solos. My favorite was Adrian Rollini, who played bass sax. I used to listen to him on records whenever I could.

"Rollini was playing melodies with such a beautiful tone so I tried to imitate it. In fact I was trying to make the baritone sound like a bass. And also Coleman Hawkins was an influence and I used to try to make it sound like a tenor as well!"

A couple of years ago, Harry Carney jotted down some notes for me on the years he'd spent with the Ellington band.

"Some of the thrilling points of my career came when I was still cutting my wisdom teeth," Carney wrote. "One was our engagement with the Broadway musical show *Show Girl*, starring Ruby Keeler and Jimmy Durante . . . our first movie, *The Black and Tan Fantasy*, which at that time gave me kid ideas about becoming a movie star . . . our first Carnegie Hall concert with Benny Goodman . . . our first trip on the road, coast to coast, when I had trouble believing I was really in all the places I had so recently studied about in school . . . how I knocked myself out visiting points of interest everywhere we went and taking pictures . . . the excitement of touring Europe for the first time at the tender age of twenty-three, still knocking myself out sightseeing. . . ."

There have been a lot of laughs in the years with Duke, such as guys stuffing horns full of paper or towels so when Harry would step forward to solo there would be no sound. Back at the Cotton Club, Carney recalls, "new band members would be initiated into our group by two obviously incompatible musicians who would set a scene by constantly bickering with one another; then, when the new man was undressed in the crowded dressing room, go for each other with a toy gun and knife and send the newcomer racing out into the club!"

When the Ellington band made its debut at The Palace in New York, a very important date, all rehearsals were complete and everybody apprehensive, and then Duke "decided at the last hour to add an introduction to the opening number which was hurriedly put on manuscript strips at each musician's chair. The curtain opened and the stage lights went out!"

All over the world, Carney says, people ask the same questions. His standard answer to one standard question, How do you get a job in a big band? is: "Join a small group playing in a Chinese restaurant where people like Duke Ellington come to eat on their nights off!"

Do it and who knows but you'll have a temporary job that lasts thirty-seven years, like Harry Carney!

# JUNE 10, 1964

When Duke Ellington introduced a new composition called "Skilipoop" Sunday night at Tin Pan Alley in Redwood City, he defined it as "the art of making what you're doing look better than what you're supposed to be doing."

Sunday night's opening performance was really a combination of several concert programs and consisted of two very long sets. It was all something of a definition of antiskilipooping, or making what you do look less serious than it actually is.

Duke's charm and outrageous elegance were a complicated cop-out on one of the most glorious evenings of music I have ever heard. This band and this man (despite the fact that I have been listening to them as attentively as I know how for most of my adult life) are a continuing source of surprise and delight.

The orchestra, and the Maestro, were in rare form Sunday night; even the presence of a group of idiotic loudmouths ("Duke, play 'Never on Sunday'") couldn't stop him.

He came to Redwood City with a program that offered an entirely new face to most of his standard music (it is the first time we have heard the band in over fifteen years without either a vocalist or Ray Nance's trumpet and violin) and with a portfolio of new things that were exquisite.

The audience kept insisting on standards and finally Ellington said, "We must be playing all the wrong numbers," and then did a medley of half the standards in the ASCAP catalogue, or so it seemed. Actually, it was just a part of his own compositional output.

The variety of the band's repertoire, from the solo numbers to the great shouting and swinging ensembles on "Rockin' in Rhythm," "C-Jam" (with a fine Buster Cooper trombone solo) and "Skilipoop," is almost infinite.

An exposure to Ellington is essential to any involvement with American music — a moral duty, in fact, for critic and musician and fan. And in addition it's a helluva lot of fun.

## OCTOBER 9, 1964

In the past week, Ellington has presented his current basic concert program at San Mateo College, at Foothill College, at the Richmond Auditorium and at the San Francisco College State gym.

After hearing all but one of these, it strikes me that the Ellington orchestra is in magnificent form, playing more interesting new music and doing so with a consistent grandeur that is remarkable.

The "new" Ellington, for me, dates back a few years and covers such works as the *Timon of Athens* score from which Johnny Hodges' featured number, "The Banquet Theme," is currently being played. A lush, creamy, deeply rich impression of a royal feast and festive evening, it combines the Ellington master touch in background and shifting coloration with the warm and full-throated Hodges alto saxophone in a sensual, exultant cry of joy.

On the surface, at any rate, early Ellington compositions depended greatly on the individual voices which were featured. They still do but, I believe, to a lesser degree. Today more emphasis seems to be placed on the total orchestral effects, where the Ellington gift for texture and tension has been brought to higher peaks of perfection.

At the same time, the casualness which has been an Ellington trademark for years continues. Yet in pieces such as "Mynah" (featuring clarinetist Jimmy Hamilton) from the *Far East Suite*, the seemingly casual approach is highly deceptive. And even in the accompaniments to the solos in the current selection of standard ballads, there is a great deal more than meets the ear at first hearing.

Still the classic delights remain. The "Mood Indigo" trio of Russell Procope, clarinet, Lawrence Brown, muted trombone, and Harry Carney, bass clarinet, produces one of the most sublime sounds in American music. Brown and Cootie Williams in "The Mooche" evoke memories that go back beyond the life span of the youngest members of the band.

The pianist is also the band's vocalist these days. His introductions to the numbers are essays in semantic virtuosity, and he has even resurrected, as a regular part of the program, "Monologue" (or "Pretty and the Wolf"), which is not only a sharp-edged sociological comment, but also one of the most delightfully witty and intriguing numbers Ellington has ever created. It is interesting to note that this composition, which dates back to 1951, has been discovered by the hip youth to be very much right now.

## AUGUST 20, 1965

It was a glorious opening night, Duke and the orchestra were in rare form, and the audience was delighted.

The music was superb. There were two performances of "Rockin' in Rhythm," for instance, both of which contained moments of sheer exuberance that seemed to lift the whole mob, audience and band alike, right off the floor of Basin Street West.

There were the usual outrageously elegant Ellington gestures and words: "Eveeeeeeeerybody look handsome!" as he waved the band to rise; "A request from a 'Satin Doll' for a 'Sophisticated Lady' "; and, in response to an intriguing "Ad Lib on Nippon," "All the kids in Japan want you to know that they, too, love you madly."

But, of course, the richest, the most elegant and eloquent moments were in the music. In "Satin Doll," for instance, bassist John Lamb, a remarkable soloist, has created a whole new bass sound in this number combining bowing and slurring and picking in a manner which seems to have distilled the influences of half a dozen masters of the bass. In "Fade Up" (a new "Tutti for Cootie") trumpeter Cootie Williams growls and sings out majestically on his trumpet for a rousing finish.

During "Ad Lib on Nippon," a composition resulting from the Ellington tour of Japan, drummer Louie Bellson provided a surprise in the opening portion. He produced a group of temple bells strung on a stick like shish kebab which, when shaken, emit a mysterious metallic, ringing tone. It delighted Bellson, pleased

Ellington and gave an added touch of the mysterious to this most exotic number.

Throughout the night, as evidence of his musical inspiration, Ellington himself played introductions on the piano which were of a marvelously varied and intricate nature, and periodically, on some well-known composition such as "Newport Up," whole new — or apparently new — backgrounds for solos would appear.

As always when the house is full of celebrities from show business, Ellington was effusive. His monologue "Pretty and the Wolf," which relates the story of a country girl who comes to the big city, was masterful. I firmly believe it should be preserved on film for university speech departments as an essay in communication far past the literal word.

The entire Woody Herman band, en route to Los Angeles, was in the audience. None of them played. Judy Garland, who was also in the audience, sang "Mood Indigo" as the last event of the evening. It was an interesting experience in listening.


## AUGUST 23, 1965

Never once in the years I have been writing of performances at concerts and nightclubs by the Duke Ellington orchestra have I said all I wanted to say. Always there are dozens of things which have had to be left out because of space.

Or perhaps space is the wrong word. They are left out because there is too much, because the Ellington music and the performances work on such a multiplicity of levels that you really do not get it all at once. Some things take a while to sift through.

At the moment there is no vocalist with the band. That is, there is no one whose sole role is to appear out front and sing lyrics. The vocalist at the moment is the piano player, who does quite well, come to think of it.

Take the little matter of the sign-off music. He didn't use it the other night and he may not be using it on this tour, but it makes no difference, it should be mentioned anyway. Ellington goes through an elaborate ritual to discuss finger-popping and earlobe tilting in time to music (all his philosophy is publicly clothed in elaborate garments) as he admonishes the audience not to pop the fingers on one and three (tilt the left earlobe on *those* beats) because, he says, "it is considered aggressive." One who has listened to upper-middle-class WASP audiences try in vain to clap on anything *but* one and three can read a great deal into that comment. And consider the final touch, with the left earlobe dipping on one and three and the fingers popping on two and four, The Maestro remarks that "one can be as cool as one wishes to be." I like that.

Then there are the elaborate, almost Oriental, applications of hyperbole to introductions to tunes, to announcements to the audience, in elliptically worded announcements of simple things like the end of the set.

And while this is going on, before it and after it, the Ellington music is there.

Take the playing of Paul Gonsalves. It was a long time before I really heard him. There was too much else going on and his style, which is entirely his own with its runs and weavings, was too subtle for me at first. Then one day I suddenly actually *heard* something he played on a ballad. I might have known that any musician who stayed with Ellington as long as Gonsalves has and for whom Ellington had written compositions was unique. He certainly is.

Since then some of the most moving things I have heard by the band have featured Gonsalves, whose style of playing soft, lyrical ballads is agonizingly beautiful in a bittersweet fashion. I am often just bowled over by a little phrase he has blown behind someone else. Or the way he works his way in and around the ballad themes.

Then there are Harry Carney and Johnny Hodges. These are, of course, two of the original sounds of the Ellington ensemble and as such have a number of standard costumes in which to appear.

But even in "Things Ain't What They Used to Be," or one of the other standards in which Hodges is featured, the performance is never quite the same. There are subtle shifts in emphasis; the same is true of Carney, especially on "Sophisticated Lady." And just when I am hung up listening to something going on in the saxophone section, I hear all this activity in the trumpets and Cat Anderson or Cootie Williams will be adding some little touch.

This activity from the individuals goes on into the arrangements which constantly shift around and, although remaining superficially the same, they have, over the years, acquired innumerable little subtle differences.

"He not busy bein' born is busy dying," Bob Dylan has sung, and it certainly applies to Duke Ellington and to the Ellington orchestra. It is in a continual state of resurgence. You never know what will happen next.

## SEPTEMBER 5, 1965

Downstairs on the site of the old Neve and Fack's No. 2 and, much earlier, the Balalaika, there's the topless club The Cellar. Upstairs, Coast Recorders has a studio designed by Bill Putnam, where Duke Ellington recorded Monday afternoon.

Ellington sessions have been legendary in their impromptu aura, but this one went down as if it were following a script.

At 4:30 the musicians began arriving — Paul Gonsalves arrived in a taxi, others came in cars or on foot — carrying their instruments. The studio was already set up with the saxophones bunched around one microphone, the trombones around another, the trumpets stage left on risers, the piano across the room from them and the drums and bass on the stage behind.

The old theater-restaurant had been adapted to a sound studio but signs of its former role were still visible, not only the stage and the curtains, but an old chandelier. Baffle boards ringed the room to control the sound and huge tricolored panels with a similar purpose were mounted on the walls. In one corner, the control booth was set up with a row of seats for visitors.

By the time Ellington arrived, resplendent in a blue polka-dot shirt and clutching a case of music, the other music stands had been set up and the charts laid out by "Brother" Hodges, Johnny Hodges' son and summertime band boy.

Nat Adderley, in a cap and sunglasses and holding his trumpet under his arm, climbed on the trumpet stand. Joe Zawinul, the pianist in the Adderley band, squatted in a corner obviously in rapture. Allen Smith walked calmly in. Smith and Adderley were to be in the trumpet section in place of Herbie Jones and Mercer Ellington for the recording.

Other musicians clustered around the room. Grover Mitchell, home on vacation from the Count Basie band, talked trombone talk with Lawrence Brown and Buster Cooper. The saxophones ran down their parts.

Duke looked around and said, "Isn't this upstairs from the Neve?" John Lamb bowed his bass in the box he was placed in on stage, smiling out over the rim like an observer. Mercer Ellington walked around the room passing out music.

Duke looked up at the control room. "Alllll right! The solo is always here," he said, pointing to the solo mike in the center of the room, "and the band plays pretty loud. Johnny Hodges! Just when he's feeling his worst he can blow the blues!"

Lawrence Brown got up and walked over to the pile of instrument cases. "Bring back the soprano trombone, Lawrence," Chuck Connors called after him.

The engineer, Don Geis, spoke over the intercom. "You play alone, Duke?" Ellington spread his arms wide and hollered back from the piano bench, "I don't *ever* play alone." The band ran down the chart for "Feelin' Kinda Blue."

In the control room we could hear Nat Adderley's aside, "That's the one you should have." Grover Mitchell was leaning on the lip of the stage with a broad smile on his face. Duke said, "I think that should be ten bars of the piano," and turned to the control booth, "Roll it!" and they started to play the tune again, Hodges holding up his hand with two fingers showing as a signal to the band.

During the playback after take 1, Duke leaned on the piano music stand, his head down in his arms, occasionally raising it to peer under the slightly raised lid on the grand piano. Almost to a man when the take was finished, the saxophone section rose, took out cameras, and began to snap photos of everybody in the room.

And so it went for four tunes. "I like first takes," Duke said later when he decided that, in fact, the first takes were best. The band had left then and Ellington was winding up his own listening to the recordings.

During the session the band was a study in casualness. They moved slowly and deliberately whenever they walked, and Hodges, who played so beautifully, seemed to be determined to demonstrate that it's easy when you know how. Cat Anderson, who took several magnificent solos and who wrote two of the tunes, ran the trumpet section through their parts and listened to everything with a quick ear for comment.

Mercer Ellington was in action all through the session, making notes, arranging the music, giving cues to the engineer and making suggestions. Duke sat at the piano, stood in the midst of the band and conducted dramatically in a highly unorthodox manner, supervised the sound setup and handled runthroughs from the sound booth — "Let's have that again without the solo" — and in general was a volcano of activity.

Two of the musicians from the band at the Cellar stood in the corner agape with awe at the Ellington sound. Singers Bill Hawkins and Jon Hendricks sat in the booth, rocking in silent admiration. Later, Ellington, just before he went home, asked Hawkins to sing and, in the empty studio, played the piano for him on "Body and Soul" while the sounds of "Hello, Dolly," played by the group at the Cellar, came up through the open door of the exit.

A few minutes earlier, half the band stood around while Joe Zawinul played "Come Sunday" with Ellington leaning over him at the piano. When it was over, Duke shook his hand and Joe removed his Alpine hat and bowed. "That's how I got these bags under my eyes," Duke said. "Leaning over pianos like that listening to Tatum and Fats Waller and James P. Johnson."

"Thank you, Maestro," Louie Bellson said as he left, and added a moment later in an aside, "It was a ball." The engineer smiled his delight as he wrapped the tapes for Ellington. Duke had sat in the control booth and played back every one of the takes on the four tunes to choose the ones he liked best.

It was dark when we got outside but everybody felt good. "It isn't always as easy as this one, but it all went good today," someone remarked.

And that was the truth.

## OCTOBER 2, 1965
*"With trumpets and sound of cornet make a joyful noise before the lord the king." Psalm 98:6.*

When William "Cat" Anderson, the high note specialist of the Duke Ellington orchestra, lifted his horn towards the five-story-high ceiling of San Francisco's Grace Cathedral and produced his soaring tones, the biblical admonition seemed to have been brought thoroughly into the twentieth century.

Ellington's appearance belonged to the cathedral's Festival of Grace, celebrating its consecration. Previous events in the year-long festival included a presentation of Benjamin Britten's "War Requiem," a communion service by jazz pianist Vince Guaraldi, and talks by Paul Tillich, Martin Luther King, and Archbishop Joost de Blank, late of South Africa.

Ellington's Sacred Concert was the idea of Canon John Yaryan, a former vice-president of Libby-Owens-Ford Glass Company turned cleric and a lifelong admirer of the Ellington music. "I have every one of his records back to 1927," Canon Yaryan says.

Ellington had been working on the concert program for two years. He brought his fifteen-piece orchestra, with baritone saxophonist Harry Carney, alto saxophonist Johnny Hodges, and trombonist Lawrence Brown to the cathedral, wrote a new composition, "In the beginning God," and combined the new music with excerpts from his older compositions.

Over two thousand people packed the gothic cathedral on top of Nob Hill; hundreds were turned away. Added to the orchestra for the occasion were Esther Marrow, a young gospel singer from Detroit; jazz tap dancer Bunny Briggs; a fifteen-voice choir from San Diego; the cathedral choir; jazz singers Jon Hendricks and Jimmy McPhail; and West Indian singer Tony Watkins.

215

Miss Marrow's voice rang out in clear and vibrant tones on Ellington's "Come Sunday" theme from *Black, Brown and Beige* and in two gospel songs. The two choirs added their voices on old spirituals, and the orchestra, obviously inspired by the surroundings, played magnificently. Briggs, in a number titled "David Danced Before the Lord with All His Might" (II Samuel 6:14), performed a blazing exhibition of virtuoso dancing behind the solid redwood table that serves as the cathedral altar.

The ecclesiastical and musical hierarchy, including Bishop James Pike, Benny Carter, and Rex Stewart, packed the first rows and the interior of the cathedral echoed to the sweet thunder of Louie Bellson's drums and Harry Carney's saxophone. But the front rows could hardly hear, and in the center the rows of bowed heads represented not religious contemplation but an effort to listen to the music from the small sound boxes located under the pews.

However, in the low-priced seats for the general public the sound was excellent. The irony of this caused one observer to remark that not only had the church failed to enter the twentieth century electronically but, since the first could not hear and the last could, the biblical parable had been extended.

Ellington's own composition "In the beginning God" was, in his words, "the most important thing I have ever done . . . the whole story of everything." Jon Hendricks, the son of a Baptist preacher, recited a lyric commentary on society that included lines such as "In the beginning, no symphony," "no jive, no Gemini Five," "no birds, no bees, no Beatles." In spite of the acoustical disaster, the audience was obviously entranced by the program, which was recorded and filmed for educational television.


## NOVEMBER 3, 1965

Sunday's concert by Duke Ellington and Ella Fitzgerald at Frost Amphitheater at Stanford was one of the most glorious afternoons of music I have ever experienced. Both were in superb form, each inspired by the presence of the other; the amphitheater was packed to overflowing, the weather was lovely (though a mite chilly at the last moments) and the sound (by Swanson) really first rate.

Ella Fitzgerald, of course, is one of the great voices in the history of jazz. I have never heard her sing as well as she did Sunday afternoon, both in her own portion of the program (backed by pianist Lou Levy, bassist Joe Comfort, drummer Gus Johnson and guitarist Herb Ellis) and in the marvelous postscript of four numbers at the end of the concert with the Ellington band.

"Don't go!" she cried out to a couple who had to leave during her solo set. "I'm gonna sing with Duke! You'll miss it!" She was right. It was worth waiting for, as her voice blended with the band, rang out like a horn on the scat portions of "Cottontail," and brought out the deep luster of "Azure" and "What Am I Here For?"

Ellington's men, who had been playing with great spirit and sensitivity all afternoon, were obviously delighted at the opportunity to play behind her. Before the concert Ella Fitzgerald herself referred to appearing that afternoon with Ellington as "an honor."

It was certainly a privilege to be present. Major artists do not always meld together perfectly in any of the performing arts, but this particular union enhanced both parties for the benefit of all.

Ellington, resplendent in a dark jacket, four-inch cuffs and blue suede slippers, opened the program with "Ad Lib on Nippon," as yet unreleased on disc, which presents Jimmy Hamilton in some exquisitely moving clarinet solo work on the theme. Tenor saxophonist Paul Gonsalves was next on "Chelsea Bridge." While he was weaving his way rhapsodically through the lacy melody, the musicians who were later to accompany Ella Fitzgerald stood over to one side of the stage raptly listening. His stomping tenor style was featured next in "Newport Up" and then Cat Anderson did "El Viti."

Gonsalves returned for "The Opener" and then Johnny Hodges played a magnificent solo on "Passion Flower" followed by his guaranteed "breakup" number, "Things Ain't What They Used to Be." It did indeed break it up and he got an ovation.

Louie Bellson's percussive showcase "Skin Deep" and an Ellington medley closed the first half.

217

The second half included a fine "I Can't Get Started" and a wildly swinging "Them There Eyes" by Ella Fitzgerald, plus the best blues I have ever heard her sing, a long version of "St. Louis Blues" with Cat Anderson softly playing an obbligato to her voice. She moved the audience to rapturous applause singing "Lover Man" and then Ellington came on, took over the piano, and his orchestra and Ella Fitzgerald really tore it up.

Even though it was coming on chilly, no one wanted to go home. The afternoon had been too good to admit it was over.


## NOVEMBER 7, 1965

"I've never heard anything like this," the jazz fan from London said with a dazed expression as we wandered into the home economics buldings of the Sonoma County Fairgrounds near Petaluma and found the Duke Ellington orchestra playing for a dance.

What he had forgotten — or perhaps never knew — is that jazz was dance music long before it entered the hallowed halls of the concert houses, and the few remaining big bands, such as Ellington's, Count Basie's, Woody Herman's and the Harry James unit, must function as dance bands even today in order to keep working year round.

Something new he learned that night was that the great jazz bands are also great dance bands and that the program they play for dancing is varied, fascinating and a great deal different than the one they use at concerts.

Ellington's dance fans, at least in Petaluma, are not specialists in the Hully Gully, the Twist or the Locomotion. They are dancers from the 30s, now middle-aged, who move around the floor in the staid motions of the fox-trot although, to judge from the expressions on their faces, in seventh heaven.

Dances start slowly. The band plays quietly and the tempos are slow to medium. Sometimes to end a set or almost always to end the evening the band will play a flag-waver. Louie Bellson's "Skin Deep," the long drum solo, ended the midnight set and a vigorous

version of Billy Strayhorn's " 'A' Train" was the closing number
for the night.

All big bands I have ever heard love to play dances as a contrast
to the concert and nightclub circuit, especially when the dance is
a successful and well-attended one such as the Ellington appearance in Petaluma.

"You get a good feeling," tenor saxophonist Paul Gonsalves
says. "The band gets feeling like the audience when they're having
a good time." Johnny Hodges, who maintains a resolute attitude
of stubborn severity alternating with detached boredom (possibly
as compensation for the terrifically effective lyric and blues messages he gets into his solos), shook his head and admitted, "This
was a pretty good one."

It certainly was, and the audience — including those who drove
from as far as seventy-five miles away to hear it — were not dis
appointed. "You seldom have a chance to hear a band like Ellington play a dance," said Nico Bunick, the jazz pianist, "and it's a
wonderful experience." The jazz world will be the loser when this
dying phenomenon exists no more.


## JANUARY 23, 1966

The phone rang the other evening and a pleasant voice inquired:
"Would you like to hear the theme of the new Sinatra movie,
played on the electric piano by the composer?"

"Yes," I gulped, and then over the long distance wires came the
lovely sound of Duke Ellington playing some extraordinarily
romantic and melodic music from the score of *Assault on a
Queen*. When it ended he came on the phone again. "That was
the theme for the girl," the Duke said. "She walks well. That's the
description in the script. I'm sitting down here on the Paramount
lot in an office. I have four instruments in it. A desk. A piano. A
telephone. And a davenport.

"I'm sitting here looking like a composer. I know all the positions, what angle to tilt the cigarette holder, when to lie down,
when to lean back. Would you like to hear the *Queen Mary*

music? The *Queen Mary* is in the Bahamas and they decide to stick it up."

Ellington then played some more melodic and fascinating music. I said as much. "Oh," he replied, "I didn't do that very well. I always was a lousy demonstrator. That's the reason I never could get the publishers to take my songs!"

I expressed my regret at not having a closed circuit TV setup so I could enjoy watching the composer at work. "Would you like me to come up and play it in your parlor?" he asked. "I always was a parlor piano player. I won't open up the left hand on you," he said. "But I did it to Willie 'The Lion' Smith in Pittsburgh last summer." And then Duke played something echoing all the parlor piano playing that made jazz history. "I did a new version of 'Portrait of the Lion' in Pittsburgh. It was a reflection of him," Duke said.

Ellington is busy these days (and nights) wrapping up the score for the movie. He then takes off this month for an extended tour of Europe with Ella Fitzgerald and later goes to Japan once more. Meanwhile, his musical *Pousse Café* opens in Toronto tomorrow night and tonight he is on the Ed Sullivan show.

"Why aren't I in San Francisco?" he asked. And I apologized for the city shirking its artistic duty. "But I'll be there May eighth," he added. "In a concert. See you then."

He will, God willing.

## JUNE 30, 1966

"I have to get a bang out of it, it can't be just for the money," says Duke, who opens tonight at Basin Street West with his orchestra.

Ellington, who recently was given an honorary degree of Doctor of the Arts by the California College of Arts and Crafts, was speaking of the various suggestions for concerts and performances that come to him.

This summer, for instance, he'll fly to Antibes, play concerts there, return to the United States for dates in the East, fly out to

California for dates in Los Angeles (a Hollywood Bowl date with the symphony and an appearance here at the Mt. Tamalpais outdoor amphitheater in late August) and then fly back to New York only to return in a few weeks for the Monterey Jazz Festival.

Some years ago a friend of mine asked Billy Strayhorn how everyone stood all this traveling and last-minute arrangements and general panic. "If you don't learn how to relax on this band, you'll never make it," Strayhorn replied.

Ellington writes for the men in his band. "And every time you get a new cat, you get a new problem," Dr. Ellington says. "You say, well how do I do *this*, because this guy isn't as effective on the top notes of his horn; you can hear the struggle he's having and it's a little wavy. Or something like the bottom note. He doesn't hit them with a *whoom!* you know, with the guts it should have. You know some people are better in the middle, some people are better on the bottom and some of 'em are better on the top. You know, and you figure these things out and it's very interesting to do.

"Our personalized arranging is a matter of arranging with all of the better characteristics of the performer in mind and with deep consideration for the limitations of each one. As you know, there's no musician in any kind of music who doesn't have some limitations. He may be the world's greatest concert trumpeter, I mean actually play *anything* technically, but there are certain things in, say for instance, our field, where he wouldn't handle it so well because he probably wouldn't feel an accent on a certain beat, or something like that.

"I've gotten a tremendous bang out of working that way. I started working with cats who had limitations.

"This is the thing I've always done, all down the line. I've always had some little limitation to deal with, and of course it enhances the joy of doing it, more so than a guy who has the good fortune of having a big fat symphony all the time and he can do anything he wants to."

Ellington's ability to rise to the occasion is legendary. At Fack's eating a bowl of ice cream he told me how he once wrote an entire show in one night, when he was working at the Cotton Club. He grinned and remarked, "Necessity, after all, is the mother!"

# SEPTEMBER 4, 1966

When Ellington presented his Sacred Concert at Grace Cathedral a year ago, he did not think that he was beginning a series. He thought only in terms of that one concert.

The concert was a huge success and since that time Ellington has repeated it with different casts in Coventry, England; New York; and other cities; and will present it Friday night at Oakland Auditorium.

In November, the National Educational Television network will release a one-hour version of the Grace Cathedral Sacred Concert filmed there last year as part of a two-hour profile of Ellington done here by the KQED Film Unit.*

CBS-TV broadcast an hour-long version of the New York Sacred Concert last December performed at the Fifth Avenue Presbyterian Church and RCA Victor has now released an album extracted from that concert, *Duke Ellington's Concert of Sacred Music* (RCA Victor LSP 3582).

As Ellington announced when he held his press conference at Grace Cathedral last summer, the Sacred Concert consists of new music, excerpts from older Ellington compositions, adaptations and pieces which he wrote for other productions.

There are eight tracks on the LP. The first is devoted to the new music, "In the beginning God," which Ellington took as the theme of the concert, using the cadence of the syllables as a foundation for the composition. "We say it many times in . . . many ways."

"In the beginning God" runs for fifteen minutes and twenty seconds and is divided into four parts. The first is a long statement of the theme led off by baritone saxophonist Harry Carney. Clarinetist Jimmy Hamilton weaves the theme into the higher registers, Brock Peters does the solo vocal part rather stiffly and formally, and then Louie Bellson's drums introduce the up-tempo

* Produced by R.J.G.; each hour show was nominated for an Emmy.

portion with Peters chanting the humorous lines about "no bottom, no topless," "no birds, no bees, no Beatles," "no jive, no Gemini Five" and ending with "No heaven, no earth, no nuthin'!"

Then follows the medium-tempo Paul Gonsalves tenor solo with the Herman McCoy Choir chanting the name of the books of the Bible as riffs in the background. There is a kind of coda, with Cat Anderson's trumpet high above the band playing the theme. "That's as high as we go," Ellington remarks before the applause. The final section is a recitation of the New Testament books by the McCoy Choir with Ellington accompanying, a Bellson drum solo, and the choir singing the theme. Cat Anderson's trumpet on top again ends the number. Highly effective, beautifully recorded, it is a fine piece of Ellingtonia.

"Tell Me It's the Truth" is a gospel number with tambourines, hand clapping and a moving exchange of statements between saxophonist Johnny Hodges and trombonist Lawrence Brown before Esther Marrow sings the vocal. And there's an exquisitely beautiful clarinet obbligato by Jimmy Hamilton.

"Come Sunday," one of the themes from *Black, Brown and Beige*, is used three times in the concert. Here it is sung by Esther Marrow, whose warm, emotionally exciting voice gets great dignity and feeling into the lyric. The band plays behind her in an intriguing manner, almost seeming to moan.

Next is a swinging version of "The Lord's Prayer" in which Ellington and the orchestra combine with Esther Marrow to produce a different and tasteful rendition of the prayer as a sort of gospel song. Cootie Williams' growl trumpet appears throughout.

The second side opens with "Come Sunday" again, now as an instrumental selection by the orchestra, a sweet-sounding arrangement with solos by Jimmy Hamilton, Cootie Williams, and Johnny Hodges, who literally makes the alto saxophone sing the melody.

Next are two songs by Jimmy McPhail, who sang them in the production they were originally written for, *My People*. The first, "Will You Be There?" is really a sermon on the subject "Will you be there, will your name be called?" The McCoy Choir and the orchestra accompany him on part of this number and on all of "Ain't But the One," a strong statement of the doctrine of one God.

"New World A-Comin'," written in 1943 and performed then in Carnegie Hall as an orchestra and piano concerto, has been redone as a piano solo and it is beautifully played here. The finale is "Come Sunday" once more, only now played up-tempo with a baritone saxophone lead as a basis for Bunny Briggs' tap dance, "David Danced Before the Lord with All His Might." The choir recites the lyrics and Briggs taps delightfully, though this number is really more visual than aural.

The album is a thrilling performance. It is cleaner than the Grace Cathedral performance, which Ellington at the time wryly called a rehearsal. Still, it lacks the special flavor and some of the deep intensity of the premiere. This is particularly true in the vocal portions. Nevertheless, that it will rank as one of Ellington's finest works, I am sure.


## SEPTEMBER 17, 1966

Duke Ellington's concert Thursday night at the Palace of the Legion of Honor gave the Patrons of Arts and Music a generous sampling of the multi-faceted Ellington talent.

There were his hit songs and standard compositions strung into several medleys; there were Swing Era big band numbers that those in the audience who were dancers then remembered with glee, and there were excerpts from Ellington's *Shakespearean Suite* and a relatively new composition, "La Plus Belle Africaine," to illustrate his deeper compositional talents.

Not that even the most trivial of Ellington's work is without deeper significance. Thursday night his opening numbers, "Black and Tan Fantasy," "Creole Love Call" and "The Mooche," written more than thirty years ago and long before the band had established itself as a concert attraction, were deeply moving, the shifting colorations evoked from the reed section blending with the growling trumpets as soloist after soloist stepped forward.

This is the thing about Ellington. He has evolved the most efficient orchestral machinery in music. It functions in a variety of ways. As an orchestra it can pit section against section, the reeds rhythmically blowing a countermelody to the trumpets or the trombones. It can, like a pocket kaleidoscope, quickly shift into a chamber group as three clarinets, or a trumpet, trombone, and clarinet trio, step forward and with only the rhythm section backing them produce chamber music sounds.

Ellington's use of unexpected voicings, the delicate shading obtained from the different clarinet sounds of Jimmy Hamilton, Russell Procope and Harry Carney, the use of the muted trumpets for the growling effects and the mutes in the trombones — all provide a diverse palette.

Having a roster of soloists that includes at least half a dozen unique in jazz, including baritonist Harry Carney, alto saxophonist Johnny Hodges, trumpeter Charles "Cootie" Williams, trombonist Lawrence Brown and his own individualistic piano, Ellington is able to present a series of miniature concertos in which the soloists perform and then step back to add their sound to that of the full orchestra.

The Shakespearean excerpts are seldom heard these days and their inclusion made the Patrons of Art and Music concert a memorable experience. Ellington has a particular affinity for the Shakespearean plays and gets something of their quality into his music. *Such Sweet Thunder* with the Cootie Williams solo, "The Star-Crossed Lovers" with Hodges and Paul Gonsalves on tenor, and "Madness in Great Ones" with its wild dissonances and counterrhythms were extraordinary.

## JUNE 2, 1967
*How "Strays" looked at life: Billy Strayhorn*

Billy Strayhorn was a sweet and gentle man and he died Wednesday after almost two years of an agonizing and dramatic struggle with cancer.

They called him "Swee'pea" and "Strays" and everyone who ever knew him loved him. All his life he lent grace and style to everything he did. He could even order a drink — some kind of gin — at Tin Pan Alley down the Peninsula and explain how to make it and sip it and discuss its virtues and compare it to a whole lifetime of gin drinks and do it all with the most elegant style and make of it a moment of delight.

It would be presumptuous of anyone but Duke Ellington, for whom Strayhorn was the perfect alter ego, to assess his musical contribution. All that the rest of us know is what Strayhorn and Duke have allowed us to know — that he wrote "Take the 'A' Train" and "Lush Life" and "Chelsea Bridge" and "Raincheck" and other beautiful and swinging things the Ellington band did. And that he worked so closely with Duke on all kinds of longer compositions — *Drum Is a Woman, Suite Thursday, Such Sweet Thunder, Perfume Suite* — that where the Master's hand stopped and Strayhorn's began only he and Duke knew.

In his twenty-eight years with Ellington, Strayhorn came to the point where he could provide what was needed in the Ellington style at any time so well that many famous musicians have themselves been fooled into thinking Duke wrote something Strayhorn wrote or vice versa.

Last year, after he had had his first desperate operation, Strayhorn came to San Francisco when Duke was playing at Basin Street West. He looked thin and wraithlike, but that beautiful smile was still there and that glow in his eyes.

Everybody was worried about him, but he had been up for three days, ever since an all-night party in New York with his friends in a theatrical club, and life was beautiful.

I think that may be the clue. Life *was* beautiful for Billy Strayhorn and he put that beauty into his music and into his lyrics. And when the band swung "Take the 'A' Train" it was Strayhorn's statement of what a ball it all can be, and when they played "Daydream" or "Passion Flower" it was his picture of a world that was packed with beauty and bursting with emotion and from which the only sane thing a person of sensitivity could do was to extract the utmost. And I am certain Strays did that.

## JUNE 18, 1967

For the past couple of years, audiences at Duke Ellington concerts and nightclub appearances have had the pleasure of listening to excerpts from *Far East Suite,* a nine-section work inspired by his tours of Japan and other Far Eastern countries.

RCA Victor has finally recorded *Far East Suite* (RCA Victor LPS 3782). It runs to forty-three minutes and fifty-one seconds in this version, and I doubt if it is complete. I suspect there are other pieces which have not been included.

The compositional credits indicate that Ellington and the late Billy Strayhorn wrote it together, with the exception of "Ad Lib on Nippon," which Ellington is credited with writing alone.

"Tourist Point of View" opens the suite and is a vehicle for tenor saxophonist Paul Gonsalves. "Bluebird of Delhi," known previously as "Mynah," is the second number and it is a showcase for Jimmy Hamilton's beautiful clarinet sounds which state the theme and alternate with long soaring brass, resolving down to the clarinet phrase again and again and going out with a lovely bass slur. The number was written, Ellington indicates in the notes, for a bird which appeared in Hamilton's hotel room.

"Isfahan," titled after a Persian city in which the band played on the tour, features Johnny Hodges in a creamy, melodic solo. It dissolves into a languid brass section after which Hodges returns and ends his solo with a repeated note. Audiences before whom this has been performed will remember the stage business with Ellington and Hodges at this point, when Ellington held up the music for Hodges to read.

"Depk" was inspired, Ellington says, by a dance performed by six boys and six girls. It has a lovely introduction by Ellington and a bright mood generated by an artful contrast of the reeds and brasses. This is a wildly swinging number played with abandon.

In "Mount Harissa," named for the mountain outside Beirut which is crowned by the statue of Our Lady of Lebanon, Ellington's own piano playing dominates the first part of the seven-and-a-half-minute number, then retires behind Paul Gonsalves' tenor solo. The tension mounts and is dissolved in an ensemble passage followed by more piano solo and ending on a slurred bass note.

"Blue Pepper," also known as "Far East of the Blues," is a bluesy number featuring the brass and Ellington's piano and an insistent drum rhythm. Johnny Hodges solos (with low, moody Ellington chords behind him), and shouting trumpets end the number.

"Agra," which Ellington says is a portrait of the Taj Mahal, is a vehicle for the baritone saxophone of Harry Carney. He begins with a low rumble, plays a beautiful lyric line with muted trumpets in the background, and ends with a baritone coda and a drum roll.

"Amad" Ellington wrote two months after the trip and implies it represents the general coloration of the journey. There are wild brass passages; Ellington's piano in a four-note repetition sets the theme. It is a hard-driving number in which the trombone section sets the framework for Lawrence Brown to end with a long "call to prayer" which sings out of an exotic figure played on the cymbals by drumsticks.

"Ad Lib on Nippon," which completes the suite, is the longest of all the compositions (over eleven minutes). It begins as a duet between the piano and bass with sticks-on-cymbals in the background. The tempo increases until it becomes almost a stomp, still the piano and bass, and Ellington plays a modernized stride piano. Then the brasses and reeds enter, echoing the theme set by the piano. A soft reed passage ensues and the piano and rhythm take up the theme again, alternating between the orchestra and the piano and bass.

A piano interlude follows and then a bowed bass statement, then the piano again introduces the clarinet, which is heard alone for a moment before the whole orchestra comes in, furiously wailing, with the clarinet taking breaks and alternating with the bass and drums. Then the entire orchestra comes in wailing a second time.

Clarinet breaks reintroduce ensemble passages alternating with mounting brass chords to a final clarinet interlude and the end, a low rumbling chord.

The suite is an impressive work. It contains all of the Ellington elements and has a unifying thread of the East about it, a kind of strangeness in sound and color that makes it very attractive. The band has been working at this a long time and has really gotten it down. Ellington himself emerges more obviously than usual as the control factor in the music; you can hear his piano directing the band throughout, shading the solos, filling in bits of color, and in general acting both as the conductor and as the choreographer.

*Far East Suite* certainly ranks among the most impressive of Ellington's long works. That is saying a great deal.

# NOVEMBER 13, 1967

An orchestra is a living, breathing, human thing, and despite the static nature of written music, what you hear with a group as individual as the Duke Ellington assembly, which is currently at Basin Street West, changes from night to night and from set to set.

No matter how many times you have heard a particular number, it is different by a shade of emphasis, a slight alteration of tone, or phrasing, even of lines, every time it is played.

Listening to the Ellington band the other night I was struck by this. I heard Sam Woodyard, Ellington's imaginative and sympathetic drummer, make accents during "Caravan" I had never heard before, and this shift in emphasis opened up new meanings of the composition for me.

At another point in the evening, Ellington played the medley of "Black and Tan Fantasy," "Creole Love Call" and "The Mooche" which provides the orchestra the occasion for a thrilling blend of instrumental sounds. I don't know how many times I have heard this medley. It has grown, now, to become a kind of concerto for orchestra, each number melding into the next, with the growl sounds and the supremely rich and lasting music of the reeds. When Lawrence Brown and Cootie Williams played their two-part section, the house hushed down to almost a religious quiet.

This is real music, make no mistake about that. When you have produced something that can last, as this music has, and which continues to give the listener something new each time he hears it, you have dipped into the magic that is art.

Ellington's art is the product of an extraordinarily complex and fertile mind. To dismiss it because the compositions have been heard before or because they bear a relation to one another is to dismiss one mountain because you have seen others. It is also, of course, to miss the whole point. The Ellington music, over the years and right up to the present, is the product, basically, of the genius of the composer and the work is of a whole. There is, really, no Ellington composition, however casually done for whatever immediate purpose, that is not related to the whole body of his work. The Ellington point of view, one might call it. The result has been to create a musical universe with its own traditions, its own conventions, its own sounds and its own leading voices. It is complete in itself and it bears infinite study just as — again a tribute to its depth and its complexity — it bears infinite hearing.

In "The Twitch," a relatively new number, the other evening Ellington urged that brilliant trombone soloist Buster Cooper, whose sharp, biting edge is so exciting, to "tell your story." Ellington's music, in whole or in part, never fails to tell a story, and in that story there is room for an infinite variety of changes.


## APRIL 28, 1968

Periodically the argument is made that jazz is unsuitable to be played in church.

Aside from quoting the Hundred and Fiftieth Psalm, "Praise him with sound of trumpet . . . praise him with high sounding cymbals," the argument becomes moot when the music of Duke Ellington is concerned. Empirically it is obvious that his music is suitable to be played anywhere, just as is the music of Bach and Beethoven. His Second Sacred Concert this month at Grace Cathedral seems to me to prove that beyond question.

Ellington began his series of sacred concerts at Grace Cathedral two years ago. His concert this month was entirely new music, composed for this tour and heard previously only at the Cathedral of St. John the Divine and at the other churches in which it has been presented this year. It was, in its performance here, a most rewarding musical experience.

Ellington will celebrate his sixty-ninth birthday tomorrow. No longer does he try to appear nonserious when he is serious, except when he cannot avoid the temptation. In the first place, he can't afford the time, and in the second, there isn't the need to present his music, even when he is having fun and making jokes, as if he did not consider it every bit as serious as Stravinsky considered *his* music.

Ellington uses in his Sacred Concert the orchestra ensemble, individual instrumental voices, words which he and occasionally another reader speak, the vocal ensemble or chorus, individual human voices and, in the finale, dancers.

The band was set up on a platform with a ledge in front of it for the chorus. In front of the chorus was a piano, and Ellington worked either on the main stage with the band (for his speaking role or for the electric piano) or down in front when he played with and accompanied the individual singers and the chorus.

He combined all of these elements into another expression of the themes which have been implicit in his work over the years. I am not sure that any of Ellington's music can be taken any less lightly than this concert program. I suspect that any of it is suitable, within the proper context, for inclusion in such a program. The failure to understand his deep seriousness characterized the critical reaction to his early work, and the obtuseness of this is graphically demonstrated by the continuity of work which is evident now.

Ellington's ability to combine lyricism, vocal and instrumental, into a deep, emotionally stimulating mood and to space it all out with vocal utterances which give a perception, and, sometimes, a lightness, is quite astonishing. He preaches sermons even though, as he said in the documentary film *Love You Madly*, he is not a preacher.

At one point in his use of the individual soloists, Ellington presented Cootie Williams playing "The Shepherd Who Watches over the Night Flock," a tribute to the pastor John Gensel of New York. This must be the umpteenth piece Ellington has written over the years for Williams to play on trumpet and yet it had a freshness about it that was stimulating. And it still combines all the old sounds.

"It's Freedom," one of the featured numbers, presented the three voices (Peggy Flake, Tony Watkins and Trish Turner) sequentially with the orchestra and a series of instrumentalists accompanying them. Changing tempos, swinging movement and the blending of the voices made it as entrancing as anything Ellington has ever done.

The qualities of pageantry which Ellington has always displayed came into their own at the end of the concert when the Xoregos Dance Company spun up the aisles to form a whirling line of flashing colors in front of the altar. Tony Watkins, possessor of one of the most beautiful male voices Ellington has ever used with his orchestra, moved down into the audience to sing the finale, "Praise God and Dance."

"I am only a messenger," Ellington said of his role in the sacred concerts. He is most certainly an eloquent messenger. As a postscript to the Grace Cathedral concert, I heard Ellington last Sunday night in a concert at the Oakland Coliseum with Tony Bennett and a comedian, Jack E. Leonard. He played his current standard concert program and reprise of Ellington classics. It seemed basically religious to me. I doubt that I shall ever hear Ellington play again, in any context, without thinking of it as religious music.

Jazz did, of course, come from the church in the beginning and Duke Ellington has put it firmly back there now.


## JANUARY 13, 1969

The Duke brought his portable music workshop to Bimbo's Thursday night and he concludes his winter seminar with the last show Wednesday night. Thus you have three full evenings in which to alleviate your personal cultural impoverishment.

Ellington's library is so extensive that he can program several

232

concerts a night for more than these three nights (or three weeks, for that matter) without repeating, and the trick is that, in the nightclubs which have become his concert halls, he casts his performance in the image of entertainment. On one level it is entertainment, but Ellington, like all major artists, refuses to work on but one level at a time. It is always fascinating to listen, when the band is at its most entertaining with Trish Turner and Tony Watkins dancing and singing out front, to all that is going on under the sugar coating.

Ellington is deceptive. A great deal is said these days about "new forms." Listening to Ellington opening night I was struck by the real key: He began by playing Billy Strayhorn's classic "Take the 'A' Train." I have heard Ellington play that number countless times — at least several hundred — thus it must be true that he has played it thousands of times. Would you expect it to dry up? Would you expect him to become bored? Remember that at least two trumpet players were driven to alcoholism in the Tommy Dorsey orchestra by playing the same solo on "Marie" five shows a night. Would you expect the band to be tired?

And that is the remarkable thing. Ellington superficially retains the form, but inside it changes around so much that it might as well be a new composition. On " 'A' Train" he began with a piano introduction (and continued playing on through the ensemble of the band) that was absolutely exhilarating to hear.

You can't do this kind of thing unless you possess the caliber of artistic gifts of an Artur Rubinstein, or the Boston Symphony. Does that sound fulsome to you? I submit the comparison is apt. No pianist ever retained his magic capability to give new life to familiar music year after year any more fully than Ellington has as a soloist. As a composer, his task has been unique. To his songs, his progammatic pieces, his excursions into longer themes and the rest, he has applied a mind that continually reinjects the music with new ideas so that it always keeps, despite the degree of organization, the spontaneity of improvisation.

It is a display of musicianship that is blinding in its virtuosity. How sad it is that generations of American college students have been denied the opportunity to enhance their appreciation of good music by the absence of the Ellington ensemble from the regular college and university cultural programs, which are clogged with German tenors, string quartets and classical pianists ad nauseam.

## MAY 7, 1969

"Hayakawa Smells — He's the Racist, Not Duke." The sign was hung around the neck of a black student who slowly paraded around the audience at the Duke Ellington concert Monday in the S.F. State Gym.

As he walked alongside the students squatting on the gym floor, he was applauded and cheered. Earlier Dr. S. I. Hayakawa had walked up the aisle to squat among the students in the front row to a mixture of hisses and boos and an occasional "Hiya Haya!"

Duke's concert was a free admission affair and the students jammed the gym, even overflowing onto the stage itself, carefully let in one at a time by business-suited, crew-cut men stationed at the stage area. Ellington, whose $3,000 fee was paid out of Hayakawa's contingency fund (the initial $50,000 of which Chicago millionaire W. Clement Stone contributed), came onstage his usual dapper and ebullient self and played several numbers before making his dedication.

There had been a lot of behind-the-scenes activity concerning Duke's appearance. The Black Students' Union, the AFT chapter and other groups were deeply concerned that Ellington "did not know where Hayakawa was at."

In the *Daily Gator*, the Black Students' Union had announced that there would be a surprise at the concert, that Duke would endorse the BSU. That wasn't precisely what happened, but Ellington, instead of introducing Hayakawa as he had done at Bimbo's earlier this year, did make an announcement. "This concert is totally dedicated," he said, "to those of us who are determinedly dedicated to developing the Black Studies program." He was cheered.

Later the band ended the concert with a highly rhythmic number; Hayakawa danced, as the pictures have shown, but when Duke mentioned him as "our choreographer" he was strongly booed. And still later at the reception planned for Duke, a BSU member, smarting from Ellington's even mentioning Hayakawa, put the Duke down in plain terms.

But all in all it was an honorable day and a victory for the students, though not a total one.

## OCTOBER 3, 1969

Duke Ellington "is certainly the greatest American composer," the president of the New England Conservatory, Gunther Schuller, said last weekend at the Ellington Symposium at U.C. Berkeley.

Later on the same program, John Lewis of the Modern Jazz Quartet, who is a trustee of Manhattan School of Music, said much the same thing and wondered why this glorious music and the methods, standards and devices of its creator and his gifted ensemble were not taught in the nation's educational system.

It is a question worth thinking about. Note that the Ellington symposium was not given as part of the regular University of California curriculum, nor as part of the cultural concert events, nor as part of the music department, but as an event in the Extension Division's Lifetime Learning Series for adults on weekends and at night.

Thus it was necessary to charge a special fee for the symposium and to set tickets for the magnificent concert which ended the symposium at unusually high prices.

Earlier in the program, sociologist Ortiz Walton had noted that Ellington had never had his own TV show nor had any of the foundations, which have been so generous in support of symphonies and the rest of America's exponents of the European tradition of music, underwritten Ellington's activities. Instead, Ellington has had to subsidize his own composer's workshop by touring the country constantly, working in nightclubs (Las Vegas at this point; Bimbo's in December) and giving concerts.

One wonders just exactly what is meant by "culture" on the level of those whose grants and gifts are aimed so exclusively at a musical culture which, no matter how worthy it may be, is never-theless something other than that which is truly of this nation.

I submit that if culture meant American culture, Ellington's music would be supported in precisely the way the symphonies and operas are supported and that he would be in residence a month at a time in all our major cities in the best hall available. In addition, his music would be as much a part of the standard educational system as the symphony is, as a regular part of each year's curriculum.

Ellington's production has been enormous despite his having to be self-supporting. He has written thousands of compositions which grow in importance over the years. Young people are less acquainted with him than with classical composers because he is offered to them only on a TV show or in a nightclub, never as part of our heritage and of the same importance as something called classical music.

The Extension Division and Dr. Marvin Chachere are to be congratulated for leaping in where stiffer academicians have faltered. It was a grand program, a historic event.

One of the foundations could do a lot worse with its money than to underwrite a twenty-six-week series by Ellington on National Educational TV. He already has more than enough original works of importance to do it. An accompanying project could be a lecture series on TV by Gunther Schuller, whose examination of the Ellington music was brilliantly done. I am quite serious about this dual project. It really does seem to me to be of considerably more cultural and historical importance than what most foundation cultural expenditures achieve.

## OCTOBER 12, 1969

Last week, commenting on the University of California's recent Duke Ellington Symposium, I quoted pianist and composer John Lewis, who asked at the symposium why the music of this great man was not taught in our educational system.

A step in that direction is being taken this week by the Berkeley Unified School District, where Duke Ellington and his orchestra will appear in a special concert at the Berkeley Community Theater Thursday evening.

The Ellington appearance is a project of Dr. Herb Wong, the modest principal of Berkeley's Washington Elementary School and a disc jockey on KJAZ.

Ellington has agreed to fly in from Las Vegas on the band's day off, bringing along the entire orchestra which played such a memorable concert last week at the university. Several students from the Community High School project, a special school-within-a-school at Berkeley High, are making filmed impressions of various Ellington recordings this month which will be shown for Ellington's comment Thursday.

Ellington will also spend some time with the students themselves late Thursday afternoon and the concert is scheduled for an early, 7:30 P.M. start in order that schoolchildren will be able to attend.

Along with the introduction of Ellington's music into the Berkeley school system, this concert and Ellington's appearance will celebrate the second year of integration in the Berkeley school system.

Berkeley students through the sixth grade will be admitted for $1 each. Older students will have tickets available to them at $2 each.

Ellington's recent concert at U.C. was one of the most interesting he has done in this area. His own performance in several solo piano compositions was outstanding. Some of the band members who have been with him twenty years or more said later that week that they had not heard Duke play so well in years.

Dr. Wong's idea for the presentation of Ellington in this manner is an excellent one and should, really, be brought a step further along next time. Ellington, as well as other great jazz musicians, should be brought to the schools exactly as the symphony is, as part of the regular daytime curriculum. It would be a tragedy indeed if the full realization of the greatness of his music came to our educators only when he was no longer with us to perform it in person.

237

# DECEMBER 15, 1969

It was such a pleasure to hear Ellington's music last week at Bimbo's. It was so serene, so creative, so alive and so right.

Duke is almost seventy-two, and he is the youngest man in the band. The reason he is so much on top of everything, so utterly relaxed in the midst of the hurricane, is an interesting study in psychology.

Duke picks the moments he will deal directly with whatever is coming at him. He chooses the terrain. You can't engage him in the direct entanglement that tears us all apart in daily life because he won't entangle.

Thus Duke is able to relax in his dressing room in between sets, conduct two interviews simultaneously (one on the phone), play host to a long line of beautiful females of all ages (some of the matrons trouping up the stairs to that dressing room looked like Ponce de Leon on his search for the fountain of youth).

His mind must work on several tracks simultaneously. He reminisces, tells stories, attends to current business, gives his visitors individually four kisses ("one for each cheek") and philosophizes.

"Some of the best ideas come when you're in the john," he said the other night. "I just found a bag of papers, little scraps, maybe only a single word on a piece of paper, but I'd been looking for that one word for months. I knew there was a reason I'd left that bag to be saved. There are some gems there."

The phone rang and he picked it up. "Oh, I'm not a teacher, I'm a learner," he told a reporter. "I watch children and dogs — and you learn. Especially if you try to teach them something."

Duke turned to the room. "What do people do who rest?" he asked. A photographer took a picture of Duke and Johnny Hodges posing with a young saxophonist. Duke began to change his clothes. "Don't take this picture with my pants down," he said.

Duke's mind turned to his recent Sacred Concert in Barcelona. "That Spanish choir sang the words in English but with a Spanish accent." Duke then did a perfect imitation. "I got so carried away after they sang and Alice Babs got nineteen encores I forgot to ask for a copy of the audio tape. You get so involved in the music." He paused and then added casually, "That's why I can never discuss finances."

I asked him, "Was it in stereo?" Duke looked at me for a minute and said, "Whatever happened to binaural? Remember binaural? That was the best, really, you only have two ears."

What's it like to work in a band like that? What do the musicians think of Duke, people ask? Well, Russell Procope, the saxophonist who has been with him over twenty years, told the NET filmmakers in *Love You Madly* that it was the best years of his life and it was worth it.

And the other night Willie Cook, who has played trumpet in Duke's band on and off for fifteen years, spoke about how he felt playing the muted trumpet solo on "Black Beauty" at the U.C. Berkeley concert in October. "You know, I was honored. Honored. Duke never let anybody play that solo since Arthur Whetsol died in 1940. Ask him to let me play it again."

And then Duke followed the band out on stage, bowed, and fielded a request from Tom Fleming of the *Sun Reporter* for "Stompy Jones," an old Ellington swinger, played it and the set was on. Art in a nightclub. Culture with the waiters walking back and forth. Statues to whom in the opera house?

## FEBRUARY 22, 1970

Duke Ellington is heading towards his seventy-second birthday on April 29, an age when most people think about slowing down a little. Duke, on the other hand, seems to have his own artistic version of the expanding universe. He's busier now than he has ever been in his life.

Only a few years ago, Ellington insisted on traveling in autos, buses and steamships. He would not fly. Last week he arrived at the Los Angeles airport from Australia and immediately took a plane to Buffalo, New York, where he conducted the Buffalo Philharmonic Friday night. Saturday he flew to Toronto for a similar appearance with the Toronto Symphony and Sunday night he conducted the Ottawa Symphony

Tomorrow night Ellington appears at Madison Square Garden in New York to receive a tribute from dozens of artists covering the whole spectrum of black music. The evening is entitled *Sold on Soul* (a perfect Ellingtonian phrase) and the participants include Sammy Davis, Jr., Stevie Wonder, Leslie Uggams, Tony Bennett, Ray Charles, Ossie Davis, Dave Brubeck, the Modern Jazz Quartet, Lena Horne and folk singer Richie Havens.

Ellington will be honored for his achievements in music which have made him the official goodwill ambassador of the United States. On his recent tour, he carried letters from President Nixon authorizing him to fill that role and asking him to report on his tour when he returned. Ellington performed the same function last fall on a five-week tour of Europe in which he played thirty-five concerts in thirty-two days and then returned to the United States and, instead of taking a vacation, immediately went to a Las Vegas nightclub engagement prior to leaving for Japan.

His recent tour took him to several cities in Japan where he has appeared before, but it also took him for the first time to Thailand, Okinawa, Singapore, Hong Kong, Taipei, Australia, New Zealand and the Philippines. In Australia, Ellington did concerts in Perth, Sydney, Adelaide and Melbourne, and in New Zealand he played in Wellington and Auckland.

Ellington works constantly. He is currently, in addition to his regular concert schedule, working on plans for an opera (in which the San Francisco Opera has expressed interest), two musicals and a play.

How does he find time? Ellington works when least seeming to. He composes late at night, after he has ended his public appearance at a concert or a nightclub, taking advantage of "those last hours and that last cigarette" to think out some new musical idea. He composes driving from concert to concert in Harry Carney's car or while ostensibly sleeping during a long plane ride. Some of his most famous compositions have been worked out while riding in a taxi, or leaning against a wall in a studio waiting for someone else to finish work.

The Ellington method is to waste nothing, neither time nor ideas. He records endlessly, keeping even scraps of things he may improvise on the piano and saving them for future use. And all the while he appears to be unconcerned, unworried and in no hurry at all.

He deserves his tribute at Madison Square Garden. Ellington has packed more creativity into his lifetime than one would expect from a dozen men and he is still going strong. He is simply remarkable.

## JUNE 11, 1970
### *The sunlight and beauty of Johnny Hodges*

When the ambulance arrived at Harlem Hospital the evening of May 11, Johnny Hodges was dead. He'd been stricken in the dentist's office and like the tough independent man he was he hadn't said a thing, but had gone out to the head. That's where they found him.

His full name was John Cornelius Hodges and the musicians and his old friends called him "Rabbit." He played the alto saxophone for Duke Ellington's orchestra and most of the time since 1928, when he joined Duke, he sat there in the reed section.

He played with love and with beauty and if ever a man made an instrument sing and talk, Johnny Hodges did. He played so well and with such an individual sound and concept that, for the purposes of jazz, he really invented the alto. He really did. Even after you pass the horn through Charlie Parker and then Phil Woods to come out with the Fred Lipsius solo on the Blood, Sweat & Tears album, there is still in it some of the sunlight and beauty of Johnny Hodges.

He was a master musician — one of the most incredibly prolific improvisers that has ever existed — and his strong and personal style on the alto influenced generations of musicians and set the stage for others to develop on their own.

He believed in music — as many of his generation did — not only as a way of life but as a mystic force for good. He played for people and he would help people, and the last time I saw him he was posing with some twelve- or fourteen-year-old youngster who had taken up the alto and Hodges was giving him pointers on its use.

Duke Ellington wrote for Johnny Hodges to play. So did Billy Strayhorn, and the magnificent, warm, flowing tones of Hodges' solos were an outstanding characteristic of the Ellington orchestra.

Hodges began as a drummer. Sidney Bechet, the master of the soprano saxophone, had him briefly on that instrument but there was really no room while Bechet was there (no one did anything with the soprano until forty years later when John Coltrane took it up) and Hodges switched to alto.

In 1951, after twenty-two years with Ellington, Hodges split and formed his own small group which he led for four years and with which he recorded his instrumental R&B hit "Castle Rock." Then he went back to the Duke and had been there, looking like the chieftain of some ancient tribe, ever since.

Hodges recorded innumerable times with Ellington, for his own groups and with other people. He never played a wrong note. Extravagant as that might seem, I mean it and it's true. Hodges could improvise endlessly and perfectly. He had a unique and mysterious ability to conceive of phrases to play which not only fitted together into perfectly constructed architectural lines but which, when you heard them, seemed so logical they were inevitable. He played the blues like he had invented it. Like B. B. King plays it. As though it was a personal possession.

He could swing a room full of lead balloons, he was so powerful. Chorus after chorus on the blues would flow out and fill whatever hall he was in, each phrase adding to the next to make a longer, perfect structure and each structure building on the others to create waves and waves of emotion that flowed with the pulse of life itself.

Musicians always listened when Hodges played. Even the musicians in the band who had heard him for forty years. He never played a wrong note and he never had a bad idea. Ellington featured Hodges a great deal, it was like having a Heifetz in the string section, and one of the numbers he played a lot was "Things Ain't What They Used to Be." Years ago some salty-minded musician had said the line that fitted the opening phrases of that number and from then on it was always in my head, incongruity of context notwithstanding. "All the boys in the band eat pussy," the words would come as the music sounded out and Hodges played. And no matter how many times he played it, he made it new and fresh each time. That is magic. Truly.

When Hodges played the soft, dreamy songs with what Ellington called his "slurpy" tone, it was disgraceful what it could do to you. His specialty was songs like "Warm Valley" and "Passion Flower" and you didn't have to have too vivid an imagination. All you had to do was remember that the Ellington music is basically about women.

Back in the 30s, Hodges did a little swinging blues instrumental which he titled "Jeep Is Jumpin'," and from that song they named the Jeep. No kidding.

Hodges on stage was beautiful. Not only did he look like a prince, but he had the most incredibly bored facial expressions. He could look out under his eyebrows with the pain of infinite patience at some nut in the hall. When he got up to play, it was an exercise in time: Hodges never rushed. He was as deliberate as an ocean swell. He would get up, walk out from his chair, and get to the microphone in time to adjust it and start to play. Not an extra second. But my God how he could play! Rocking those blues out line by line with the horn singing to you and the ends of the phrases giving him time to take it out of his mouth and run his tongue across his lips, put it back, and sing out another line.

"All the boys in the band eat puss-eeeeeeeeeeey!"

All my life, since I discovered the Ellington band on the radio from Chicago, I have had the sound of Johnny Hodges in my ears. I got goose pimples when I first saw him with the Ellington band. I will never forget it. There they actually were! They were really and truly alive and I was going to hear them do this wonderful thing right there in front of me!

One night I heard the band when Wellman Braud, who hadn't

played with them for fifteen years, came in with Barbara Dane and sat in. Braud was the original bassist with Ellington and he took them back to tunes Duke had forgotten. But not Hodges. Braud would play a bit of the bass and then Hodges would stick the alto in his mouth and play the line for Duke and they'd be off. He could smile when he played. I saw him do it one night at Monterey when Jimmy Rushing (the blues singer who did that line "Don't the moon look lonesome shinin' through the trees" forty years ago) came on stage. Hodges turned to him, still blowing, and smiled.

In the intermissions he used to walk around, stocky, rolling, like a banker. Dignified and almost somber. Beautiful deadpan sense of humor.

In the TV film of Ellington's Sacred Concert, there is a short bit when Hodges steps out to take his solo in the beautiful "Come Sunday" portion. He stands there in the area in front of the altar of Grace Cathedral and lets his eyes roll up . . . up . . . to the top of the cathedral while he plays. Wow!

Like I said, I have had the sound of Johnny Hodges in my ears all my life. And I can tell you that things ain't what they used to be now that he's gone and they never will be again.

Johnny Hodges was a real musician and a real man. I was always proud when he recognized my face.

## FEBRUARY 20, 1972

The visits of America's most important composer to the West Coast are governed by economic laws, and the ones which dictate to seventeen-piece orchestras involve the availability of halls and the logistics of travel. So it is that Ellington manages to get here every year but some years he manages to be here for more appearances and for a greater length of time.

This year, he will ameliorate the cultural poverty of northern California with a series of appearances beginning Wednesday at

San Jose State, Modesto Thursday, then U.C. Berkeley's Zellerbach Hall on Friday, followed by a Saturday date at U.C. Santa Barbara, one at the University of the Pacific in Stockton next Sunday and, after a sojourn in Los Angeles, returning for a March 5 date at the Marin County Center Theater, a March 6 date at Sierra College in Auburn and one on March 7 at Chico State.

Ellington has been on an almost continuous world tour for the past two years. He made a triumphant series of appearances in Russia last year and then right after New Year's went on to the Pacific for a series of appearances in Japan.

Each of Ellington's overseas tours has in recent years resulted in a special composition or series of compositions. When he premiered his "Afro-Eurasian Eclipse" at the Monterey Jazz Festival, for instance, he said, "It was inspired by a statement made by Marshall McLuhan of the University of Toronto. He says the whole world is going Oriental, and that nobody will be able to retain his or her identity, not even the Orientals. Now we travel around the world quite a bit and during the last few years we have noticed this coming about. So we wrote this suite, adjusting our perspective to that of the kangaroo and the didgeridoo, which automatically puts us Down Under or Out Back. From this viewpoint, it is most improbable that anyone can tell who is enjoying the shadow of whom. So now we give the responsibility to Harold Ashby, who will scrape off a little of his chinoiserie almost immediately after the piano player completes his riki-tiki."

That flowery introduction by Ellington struck me at the time as indicating his oblique acknowledgment of the international influences which have entered his music in recent years. His tours of Latin America, his visits to the Caribbean countries, his State Department–sponsored concerts in such exotic places as Asia Minor — all have entered into his music.

Ellington, unlike many composers, seems to have the ability to absorb the sounds of a country and a culture rather than to hear them just as a continuing chatter of airport, concert hall and motel noises. He can get the flavor of a new place into his music with a faithfulness that is quite effective.

245

It has never been part of the Ellington style to be flat-out open about what he is doing. "Duke puts everybody on," as Miles Davis once remarked. And the put-on is really only a kind of magician's sleight of hand to enable Ellington to perform as a serious composer while masquerading as an entertainer and as a nightclub attraction. The Ellington music has always been serious, even if it is serious music with a sense of humor. And his music is deeply emotional even if he, in his sleight-of-hand style, remarks from time to time that he approaches all of his composing as exercises in ingenuity, seeing each piece as a challenge to his creativity. Ellington is not involved in games when he is dealing with music, but in almost pure emotion, both in the organization of his material and in the choice of colors, patterns and individuals with which to express whatever it may be that he wishes to express.

American society has confined Ellington by limiting him to functioning for many years solely within the entertainment world. Despite that, Ellington has managed to create music that has stood the toughest of all tests, that of time. All one has to do to demonstrate this is to go back over the wealth of material he has been recording over the years and play the albums. They sound — with rare exception — as if they had been written last night. They have fire and energy and the thrill of discovery over and over again for the listener.

One of the results of this tremendous outpouring of music is that it is impossible for Ellington to present concerts consisting exclusively of new material. His audiences will not stand for it. They demand some of the older numbers every time they hear him, either from fondness or for a sense of familiarity. They greet each new departure with a delayed reaction and then, after a time, accept the new work as another of the Ellington standards which must be referred to again and again.

For years I have thought it would be economically feasible and artistically thrilling to have the Ellington orchestra in residence in San Francisco for a month, giving a whole series of concerts of his music from the shorter pieces of the early era on through the longer and more ambitious compositions of the past twenty years.

There is another thing. As the vicissitudes of the world of travel and of life itself have caused gradual changes in the personnel of the Ellington orchestra, some familiar faces are no longer present. They cannot be replaced, but the genius of Ellington is expressed nowhere more directly than in his utilization of new members of his ensemble. Each change means a change in the composition itself.

The result, once one is able to achieve a little objectivity, is really to renew the composition in terms of the expressiveness of the new voice. Ellington is past master at that, as anyone who has listened to the various medleys of Ellington standards over the years has found out.

If Marshall McLuhan's prediction of the end of identity ever comes about, it will be in a world that is without the kind of genius Ellington personifies. And that will be a sad world, indeed.

## JUNE 3, 1973
### A moment of magic: Elmer Snowden

One of the biggest disappointments of my life was the fact that we had no camera available when Elmer Snowden came to Duke Ellington's dressing room downstairs at Basin Street West one night. It would have been a great filmic moment and it certainly would have had historic significance, for Elmer Snowden was Ellington's first employer (Duke played piano in Snowden's band in Washington, D.C.) and old Elmer passed away recently.

We had been making a film documentary of Ellington for National Educational Television and had followed him around San Francisco and Monterey as he recorded in a studio, as he rehearsed for his Grace Cathedral Sacred Concert, as he capped the Monterey Jazz Festival with his performance and as he played at Basin Street West.

Ellington, by the time we were through, wanted to keep us around indefinitely. He liked the presence of the cameras, having gotten over his initial suspicion of them. But the trouble was, we had run out of money and couldn't film at all anymore. And so, while we were sitting around in Duke's dressing room one night during an intermission, the door opened and in came Elmer Snowden.

Duke is tall, heavy, chesty, majestic. Snowden was short and very black and shiny and it was hard to think of him as bossing Ellington around. They hadn't seen each other in years. Duke was constantly on the road and Snowden was hidden away in Philadelphia most of the time, barely working at all and only now and then appearing in public. The problem was that in the 30s, Snowden, who had led a band all through the 20s and most of the 30s, got into a jam with the musicians' union and, for a time, was outlawed by them. Things such as this were hard to get around traditionally in the music business, and even though Elmer got straight with the union eventually, he never really was able to recoup his position.

But the two of them, Duke, the piano player who went on to the heights of show business success, and Snowden, the man who gave him his first job and had gone down steadily ever since, just radiated love and delight at seeing each other. For an hour they sat there, Duke on the cot and Snowden on the chair, and reminisced. "Remember the night . . . ?" "How did such and such go?" "What ever happened to . . . ?" It was a magic moment and I felt privileged to be present as they played the game of Remember When, each one trying to catch the other out by bringing up an old nickname or the title of a song neither one of them had played for forty years.

Bitter and broke, Snowden had given up on the East and, lured by the aura of North Beach and the San Francisco folk music scene, had come here to try again. He didn't think it was too late. He put guitar strings on his banjo and he rehearsed a trio, using the veteran New Orleans bassist Pops Foster.

They had several pretty good jobs. They were at the Coffee Gallery and later at the Cabale in Berkeley with Hugh Romney on a show that, had all gone well, should have been San Francisco's first glimpse of Tiny Tim, years before he ever made records or got on TV. It was Hugh's idea, and it almost worked except that

Tiny Tim's mother wouldn't let him go that far away from home then and he canceled out.

Anyway, Elmer played around here a little bit and for a while toyed with the idea of opening a local club. He had a backer or almost had a backer and he thought he would make it. I tried to do a television show with him for NET because he was, far and away, the most interesting banjo player I had ever heard, but even though he thought he had a chance to get a career going again, Snowden couldn't bring himself to say his trio was good enough for the standard he wanted to maintain on TV. So we never did it.

What did happen, though, was a gig at the Monterey Jazz Festival (the same one Duke appeared at, although on a different day). Elmer was in his late sixties at the time and Pops Foster had just turned seventy-one. They needed a drummer for the afternoon at Monterey and did not have one. It was a big problem until someone, I think it was Jimmy Lyons, came up with the suggestion of Tony Williams. Tony was just making his reputation then as the percussionist with Miles Davis. He was seventeen and he had never heard of either Elmer Snowden or Pops Foster, but he played with them that afternoon and, since Tony is now — and was even when he was seventeen — a musical genius, the result was spectacular. It was one of the finest moments of that whole Monterey festival.

I'm glad I saw it, just as I'm glad I saw Elmer and Pops Foster at the Coffee Gallery and the Cabale, because those real old-timers are getting fewer and fewer; and even after they are in their seventies and can no longer be as dexterous as when they were sharp young kids coming up, they can still do it. If you ever get the power, it never leaves you altogether. Bunk Johnson and Louis were proof of that.

The impact of that afternoon at Monterey was intense on many people. Jon Hendricks, for instance, was so struck by the coincidence of Tony being seventeen and Pops Foster being seventy-one and he, Jon, being the seventh son of a seventh son that he skipped and danced all along the side of the festival arena testifying to its magic.

I hope somewhere in Philadelphia — because Elmer went back there the winter after Monterey and never left — some dedicated jazz or folk fan has recorded Elmer's reminiscences. They should have been priceless. They must have been. After all, he and Duke were almost the same age and their careers were intermingled. Elmer went to New York first with a band that had Sonny Greer and Otto Hardwick (two musicians later associated with Ellington for many years). Fats Waller was supposed to join them and when he didn't, Duke came up from Washington to be the pianist and the group was called The Washingtonians.

Right there the history gets muddy. One version is that Duke took over the band, and without Elmer's permission. Another is that it just happened. In any case, Snowden was replaced as leader by Ellington, and in all the recordings Ellington made in those early years before establishing himself as a leader, the guitarist or banjo player was always Freddy Guy, not Elmer. It left a bitter taste, and the files will never be complete because who knows if Arthur Whetsol and Sonny Greer and Otto Hardwick would have ended up with Ellington making such historic music had they not been with Elmer Snowden first.

## NOVEMBER 8, 1973
### Ben Webster — Another giant gone

When, a couple of years ago, I did the notes on the back of Miles Davis' album *Bitches Brew*, I said that there would always be time to listen to Ben play "Funny Valentine."

Ever since, people have been asking me — not jazz fans, because they know, but people from the rock audience — just who was Ben?

Well, Ben died recently of a heart attack. He was a tenor saxophone player and he had lived in Europe for most of the past ten years. His name was Benjamin Francis Webster and if you want comparisons, he was to the tenor saxophone, perhaps, what Szigeti has been to the violin. What I mean is that Ben did not invent concepts and styles of improvisational playing on the tenor, but he developed a highly personal sound and the ability to phrase and to invent astonishing solos, all of them delivered with a special sort of high-voltage emotional content.

The analogy doesn't quite work, of course, because classical violinists are not composers; they are interpreters, and Ben was both. Not that he wrote that many original compositions (though every one of his improvisations was in itself an original composition even if based on or inspired by someone else's work). Ben was a superb interpreter and a magnificent jazz instrumentalist, some of whose solos on Ellington records, for instance, have become in themselves traditional ways to play those compositions. Sometimes — once at the Monterey Jazz Festival — instrumental arrangers have scored a Ben Webster solo for an entire saxophone section, it had such originality and form.

The essence of jazz artistry is the ability, developed over years and years of assiduous practice, listening, and absorption of music, to step to the front of the stage and, right off the top of the head, improvise enchanting melodies and moving variations on themes. Ben knew no superior at this kind of thing and the fact that he was able over a long, long career to do it every time in that astonishing combination of hard tenor tone and breathy sensual sound established him early on as one of the true kings of that instrument.

They called Ben "Brute" because he was built like a wrestler with a severe face and a scowl when he played. He looked like a black version of the guy who turns you down for credit at the used car lot. Yet he was gentle and romantic and sweet and it all came out in his playing.

He could be, in person, far from gentle and romantic and sweet, as anybody who knew him was well aware. A few days after he died, Dizzy Gillespie and John Levy, who used to play bass in jazz groups before he became one of the top managers in the world of entertainment, were talking about Ben. John told us that day about a night, years and years ago, when he was playing in a Harlem club. The club had a long bar and Ben came in "carrying that long, gold-topped cane he used to have, and he just swept it along the bar knocking off all the glasses to the floor," John said. "And then I got down from the bandstand and took him by the arm and walked him out around the corner to another bar and sat there and told him how he didn't have to act like that, how everybody really loved him. And it ended up with Ben sitting there crying."

"You always were the peacemaker," Dizzy said.

Ben was a man who needed a peacemaker because he was, for all his talent and his incredible musical gifts, a troubled soul. And when his trouble was deepest, he tended to let it erupt in such capers. But, as John Levy noted, Ben always knew who not to fight!

The reason Ben was a troubled soul was that he knew his art and he knew how little it was appreciated. In our world the innovator generally gets the attention and the interpreter may completely miss it. Many of us, myself included, tended to overlook Ben in our search for innovators and I know that hurt. But there was more to it than that; Ben was a black artist in a white society and it drove him to despair and eventually into exile. The first deep, poignant hint of that I had was when a British jazz critic who met with Ben in New York told me of the experience. He and Ben talked very frankly for an hour or more and then an American jazz critic, white, came into the room, and right in mid-sentence, Ben began to change what he was talking about. That episode tells a lot of how it seems to a black artist here in the land of the free and so on.

Ben's life (he was sixty-four when he died) paralleled much of the history of jazz and the list of people he played with reads like the roster of the great. Ben started out as a violinist and switched to piano (self-taught) and then took up tenor when he went to work in a band led by Lester Young's father. He followed Coleman Hawkins in the Fletcher Henderson band and was a star of the big black bands in the 30s, but he came to his full fame with Duke Ellington in the 40s and rued the day he ever left. In fact, I think if Ben had not wanted so badly to be back with "the Governor" he might have accomplished his dream. But the Duke digs cool and Ben was a flat-out unashamed admirer of everything Ellington did and knew where his true home was. After all, they never had a tenor in Duke's band until Ben joined them in Boston, and when, a decade later, Paul Gonsalves took over that chair, what Duke dug the most was Paul's ability to play Ben's solos.

Ben made jazz history at the Monterey Jazz Festival more than once. He "wrote his name" there with a blues solo following Jimmy Witherspoon's ode to balling in the rain and he wrote it on the stages of many clubs and concert halls as well.

But he couldn't make a living at it in his native land. And his spirit, that glorious, loving spirit which imbued his playing with that incredible human quality, could not be nurtured in this society.

So he left.

Ben playing "Funny Valentine"? God yes. He played all of it every time he blew and he opened his heart to us and we let him down and so he went away. He's going to be hard to forget, though, as long as those albums last.

# 1974

Duke Ellington has always been in a most peculiar position. His biggest rival is himself. People are always coming up to him and asking him to play some masterpiece he wrote ages ago, whereas the Maestro himself wants to play the music he was working on last night.

But from any objective standpoint, Ellington's problem is one which can happen only to a genius and thus is, in one sense, no problem at all, but a continual series of tributes to his remarkable creativity.

Ellington, like all complete artists, has created his own world, at times entering the one inhabited by the rest of us, but returning again as soon as he can to the beautiful world of sound which he has invented. There are many ways to view the world any such artist has created. But that world is really the artist's vision, the way he sees the world he finds himself in and the way he projects the possible world, the world he wants, through the medium of his art.

Ellington's world has great, singing beauty, it has snorting, chuckling humor and it has amazing subtlety. Above all, its beauty is consistent because Ellington believes it is a simple choice: It is better to surround oneself by beauty than not. And he has done it.

The music in a recent set, *The Golden Duke,* dates back to the late 40s. Ellington was surrounded then by the greatest array of virtuoso solo players ever assembled in one band. It was a sticky time; World War II had just ended and the economic adjustments that followed resulted in, among other things, a strike against recording companies by the American Federation of Musicians. The record business itself had gone through a stringent shortage of shellac during World War II and was just getting back on its feet. The monopoly of the old record companies was breaking down and Duke signed with a new, upstart company named Musicraft which had ambitious plans and an impressive series of artists but was, really, before its time and did not last.

However it lasted long enough to give us some beautiful examples of the Ellington of that time. They are all the more fascinating because, for instance, "Happy Go Lucky Local" is the only section of a lost work of Ellington's, *Deep South Suite,* which was never recorded except for transcriptions for the Armed Forces Radio. Thus the work is lost to history since the Duke never looks backwards, but always dead ahead.

In the 40s, Ellington made a yearly journey to Carnegie Hall and was in the habit of writing new compositions to present at that concert. A good deal of the program of these two orchestral sides was originally put together for a Carnegie Hall concert in December 1946, at which Duke presented the great French guitarist Django Reinhardt. W. C. Handy was in the audience that night, too, and it must have been a unique occasion.

This was all before the era of tape recorders, so there was no chance, actually, to record the entire concert. But the band went into the studio during that same period and did record the music we have here.

The Ellington organization had a very special asset for many years and that was Billy Strayhorn. It is a plain statement of fact that Ellington could ask Strayhorn for eight bars of something to finish a composition and Strayhorn could produce it so perfectly in the Ellington style that no one could tell the difference.

254

In addition, Strayhorn was a prolific and remarkable composer in his own right, as generations of Ellington fans have discovered, through the longevity of his magnum opus, "Take the 'A' Train," which Ellington has used for a theme for many years.

Over the years Ellington and Strayhorn frequently played the delightful musical game of letting people be confused over who wrote what and never telling them. That would have been very uncool.

Mary Lou Williams, the greatest woman musician in the history of jazz, arranged "Blue Skies" for Ellington using the title "Trumpet No End" to pay tribute to the succession of trumpet players who solo on the number. It was such an excellent arrangement that it has remained in the Ellington book ever since and is still played upon occasion.

"Happy Go Lucky Local" (like "Overture to a Jam Session," this Ellington work was too long for a three-minute shellac 78-rpm disc and was originally recorded in two parts but has been edited together here into one) is now an Ellington standard. It is also, oddly enough, a standard in another milieu. A tenor saxophonist who worked for Ellington briefly in the 40s recorded the opening theme of the song under the name of "Night Train" and it has been a hit several times in that version. Ellington never got around to suing, so a generation of strippers who disrobed to it and a generation of rockers who rocked to it may never have known its genesis.

"Golden Feather," incidentally, is named for Jane Feather, wife of Leonard Feather, the British jazz critic who was Ellington's publicist in the 40s; and "Jam-a-Ditty" was originally called "Concerto for Jam Band." Three Ellington singers appear in this set, too. Kay Davis, one of the most beautiful women ever to grace the stage with an orchestra, is heard on "Minnehaha"; Al Hibbler, the blind singer from the Southwest who later was to make such pop hits as "Unchained Melody," sings "It Shouldn't Happen to a Dream"; and Ray Nance sings the lighthearted "Tulip or Turnip."

A word about Ray Nance: At the end of the 30s, Ray came into the Ellington band, replacing Cootie Williams who had been there for a decade. Ray doubled on trumpet and violin, which was one of the reasons Ellington hired him away from Earl Hines. It gave the band another sound. It also gave the band one of its great comics as well as a soloist on two instruments who was consistently artistic and entertaining all the long years he was with the band.

Whenever you hear the sound of a violin with Ellington it is Ray Nance. I remember one night listening to Duke in San Francisco with Mary Travers when she said, "I didn't know a violin could play jazz." It was difficult to explain in one brief conversation the misconception that statement implied.

Ellington used to refer to Ray as the violin section. Duke would start the band with a downbeat, slip onto the piano bench, and start tapping out an A for Nance to tune by. Nance, who extended the art of procrastination to ultimate limits, would slowly get up from his chair, take the violin in his hand, and tune it while walking around the side of the band, arriving at the microphone at the exact, precise moment his solo was to begin. I watched him do this for years. He would hold back to the last microsecond, pretend to trip, talk to other band members along the way, do anything he could think of to prolong the moment and yet never miss. And he plays the violin sublimely for its role in the Ellington constellation.

As to his trumpet playing, I once heard Duke explain to a critic that in fourteen years in Ellington's band, there had never been one single night during which Ray Nance had not played something of extraordinary beauty. Ray Nance is no longer with the Ellington orchestra. I am truly sad about that and so is everyone else I know of. He was so versatile a performer that Duke once toured Europe with just a rhythm section and Ray. But that's another story.

One more bit before we go on to the duets in *The Golden Duke*. This Ellington band had the rhythm section of Freddy Guy, the Ellington guitarist for many years, Oscar Pettiford, one of the greatest bassists ever to play jazz, and Sonny Greer, the drummer who was with Ellington in the very beginning and who gave such a tasty quality of humor to the band. In addition, it had the all-time reed section of Harry Carney, Johnny Hodges, Jimmy Hamilton and Russell Procope with the tenor soloist Al Sears (who replaced Ben Webster). The trumpets and the trombones were equally versatile with Cootie Williams, Shelton Hemphill, Taft Jordan, Harold Baker and Ray Nance, trumpets (Cat Anderson is heard on "Blue Skies" and "Happy Go Lucky Local"), and Wilbur De Paris, Claude Jones and the incomparable Lawrence Brown, trombones.

Ellington could stand in front of that assembly, point his finger at any one chair, and the musician was capable of standing up immediately and taking a solo. There have been very, very few bands like that.

Ellington recorded the rest of the material in this package for his son's label, Mercer Records, in 1950. The duets are utterly fascinating examples of the empathy which existed between Ellington and Strayhorn. They have been unavailable for many years now except for a brief 1964 reissue release on Riverside.

Some few years after these records were made, I did a television program which was to serve as a pilot for a proposed series of jazz programs on National Educational Television. Ellington and Strayhorn played a long duet on that pilot program, the only time they ever did it on TV as far as I know. The program was completely successful as a pilot and a series of twenty-six programs resulted, but the musicians' union insisted that the tape be erased since it had been approved only for local TV and not for the network. I have always wondered just what that union thinks music is.

Sadly, both Billy Strayhorn and Oscar Pettiford (a most forceful man, part Indian and, like Lester Young and Wes Montgomery, a member of a large musical family) are dead now. The final track on the collection is a composition by Duke and his son Mercer, in memory of Jimmy Blanton, who had died a few years before it was made. Blanton was, like Charlie Christian, a man who brought a stringed instrument out into the solo field in jazz. Blanton was an incredible bassist and after his breakthrough the instrument was never again just a part of the rhythm section.

The thing about the music in this double-LP package is that it is perfect Ellington: By that I mean that the music works on many levels simultaneously. The more you listen to it, the more you hear. Late at night, when your mind is clear and uncluttered, you can hear the Duke turning things around, making string sections out

257

of saxophones, making vocalists out of violins and adding his own, personal instrumental sound at the appropriate moments.

I bought these records when they were first released. They thrilled me then and they thrill me now, all these years later. Why not? If it's good it's always good, and this music is very good indeed.


## MAY 19, 1974
*On the road with The Duke: Paul Gonsalves*

It's sad to see the way the creative forces in jazz are dying off or have been turned off by the relentless pressures of the world we live in. Of course, the generation of musicians who took the musical idea that Buddy Bolden and those other anonymous New Orleans musicians made into· jazz and forged it into a world-renowned art form are old men now. In their seventies and eighties, those who are left, and even the younger men who came along in the early 20s and who picked up their style and their approach from the giants like Armstrong and Hawkins, are themselves well into middle age and dropping like flies.

Paul Gonsalves died the other day, in London, from a heart attack. He was in Europe for some concerts because the Duke Ellington orchestra, in which Paul had been for twenty-four years one of the most original and lyric voices, was not working. The Ellington band is not working because Ellington himself, just turned seventy-five, is seriously ill in New York, has been, in fact, since the beginning of the year. Harry Carney, who joined Duke in 1927 as a temporary member of the band and has been there ever since, just had a heart attack and has been told he can't travel anymore. Tyree Glenn, that remarkable trombonist who also played vibraphone, died just last week, and within the past couple of years Ellington has lost a number of veterans including Ben Webster and Johnny Hodges, in addition to Paul Gonsalves.

It is sad. Of course it's sad, but it is also inevitable, and when these men die, I can't help but think how little the world knows about them, about their art and why it was that during their lives, even though they had and have this mysterious power to create music and affect the lives of their listeners, so little of the perquisites of such artistic achievement came their way.

Paul Gonsalves, like so many other great musicians, spent his life on the road, with those rare interruptions when the Ellington band bedded down for a month at some hotel or other. He traveled with Duke all over the world and he played his music in all the centers of civilization except for Siberia and mainland China.

And everywhere he went he made friends. No other musician I have ever known was his equal at spreading a kind of universal love as he went. Everybody liked him because — and this is not to say he was a simple man — he truly liked everybody. I cannot even imagine him having an enemy. And in the absence of any, he took on the role himself and did his best to beat his body into submission with everything he could lay his hands on.

But no matter how knocked out he was, how sick he was, he played like a saint. His solos were marvels of harmonic and lyric invention and sometimes it even seemed, as he would struggle to his feet and squeeze his eyes shut and begin to blow, that his very life was coming through that tenor saxophone, carried on his breath.

He played for laughs, too, and Duke played it with him. Visually they made a great contrast in their high jinks on stage to the sober, almost somber faces of Harry Carney and Johnny Hodges and Russell Procope. Paul looked a little like a dark-skinned Stan Laurel and his mugging accentuated it. But he never failed to bring his solos off successfully and his humor added to them.

He went through his life determined to be sweet to anyone, especially if that anyone was involved in helping him down the path of dissipation. Sometimes he would slouch there in the saxophone section, apparently unconscious, but when the musical cue came he would somehow find the strength to stand up, move to the microphone, and play.

Back when George Andros operated a club on Bay Street called Fack's II (it was once Turk Murphy's Easy Street), the Ellington band played there for two weeks — twelve nights, since they had one night a week off. Upstairs in the tiny balcony you could sit, almost in darkness, and look down on the band. It was like a private concert because you never saw the audience, just the band playing its hour or hour-and-twenty-minute sets and then the Vernon Alley Trio came on and sometimes some of Duke's men, especially Cat Anderson, but now and then Paul Gonsalves, too, would play with Vernon's trio all during the intermission.

I must have been there ten of those twelve nights. It was an ecstatic experience, the band played so beautifully, and I remember Paul night after night blowing solos that could really take your mind, tow it by the ears, right on up into the clouds with him.

He had a highly individual sound, a very individual touch on his instrument. The musical son of Coleman Hawkins and Ben Webster (he idolized Ben, knew his solos by heart but never imitated Ben's sound), Paul gave a quality to the Ellington band that was deeply personal. If that band ever plays again, that personal sound will be deeply missed. The last time I saw Duke, a couple of years ago when the band came back from some overseas tour, Paul was ill and out of the band. It was not the same. Just simply not the same.

Artists like Paul Gonsalves have had a bitter battle in our society. Even when they made money and gained fame, they have never been — and still are not — treated with the kind of attention they have deserved. They are still classified as "entertainment" and the music they create as something less valuable than that other music we seem to place such value on.

When will it ever end, I wonder? When will we really acknowledge that the music of, say, the Duke Ellington orchestra and its members is music of very real and special value to us in this society, of greater and more special value than most that goes on in conservatories and the opera houses all over the land? That's not hyperbole. It's really true and one day, pray, we will all know it.

But it will have been too late then for Hawk and Pres and Ben and Hodges and Paul and all the rest.

What a shame.

## MAY 27, 1974

Three days before he died last week, Duke Ellington's Christmas card arrived. The Duke was always late — he got his first job at the Cotton Club in Harlem because the man who did the hiring was also late and so never heard Duke's competition. But his Christmas card this year was even later than the usual February and it seemed significant.

Duke had been ill almost all the time since he came back from a long tour last December — more gravely ill than he knew — and when I heard he had pneumonia, I thought it might be the end.

It was a full life, God knows. For better than fifty years he led his own orchestra, writing his own music for it and surrounding himself with the sound he loved. Ellington lived for music, and he made that music into a voice of his time in a very special and unique way.

For at least the first half of his career, his managers and others did their best to keep that music and to keep Duke firmly in the category of entertainment. But Ellington knew from the beginning that he was more than a bandleader and more, even, than the composer of popular songs. His mother told him he was "blessed" and he believed her and proved throughout his life that the blessing of creativity was not wasted upon him. There are more than a thousand compositions, from "Soda Fountain Rag" right up to whatever he was working on at the end, to testify to that.

Duke Ellington was an amazing man in a whole variety of ways. He loved challenge. He luxuriated in the capability of composing late at night (he regularly worked until six or seven A.M.) and then hearing his orchestra play the new music that evening. He delighted in improvising, but he was absolutely serious behind that suave, often ironically jovial exterior about his music.

Ellington matched the elegance of his music with a personal style that included his lush and sometimes purple prose. But at the least he proved that elegance has more dimensions than a velvet suit. Style meant a lot to him and so did psychology. He analyzed

261

his musicians and his friends and he loved to stage their actions as well as their playing. He wrote in such a way that when the time came for his soloists to improvise, he knew them so well that he could almost predict what they would play.

It wasn't until long after we had completed the documentary *Love You Madly* that I realized Ellington had really directed the whole thing. Once he made up his mind to be filmed, he carefully led us along the precise path he wanted us to follow.

He was so alive, so creative, that he was the youngest man I ever met. It is true, really, to say he dwarfed all his contemporaries and it is also true that he was the greatest composer this nation has produced. His music is everywhere. In rock 'n' roll, in jazz, in pop songs, in symphonies.

"Kisses, kisses, kisses" he is supposed to have said before he died. I believe that. Duke was dedicated to one other thing as much as to music and that was love. He loved people and they loved him. Russell Procope said the best years of his life were spent playing in that band and he loved every minute of it.

The best years of all our lives were spent listening to Ellington's music, and we all loved it and him madly. Friday morning's news bulletin that he was dead ended an era. There will never be another like Edward "Duke" Ellington. He was truly an original.

# 3.
# Coda:
# The Piano Player

WHEN DUKE ELLINGTON came onstage to open the show at a nightclub, he would walk out just as the band was finishing the theme
"Take the 'A' Train," welcome the audience, thank them, tell
them the boys in the band all loved them madly, and then say,
"And now we'd like you to meet our piano player."

Duke loved the effect he would get occasionally from some member of the audience uneducated in Ellingtonia. As Duke finished
saying "meet our piano player" he would put out his arm towards
the piano, turn his hand palm up, and look expectantly towards
the empty piano bench. For a split second he was the master of
illusion. There was more than one nightclub patron over the years
who *saw* a pianist on that bench when Duke made that gesture.

Then, of course, as the appreciative applause arose, Duke would
smile his elegant smile and stride over to the piano. It always
amazed me how quickly he could move when he wanted to. He
could sure move faster than I could.

263

Once across the stage and on the bench, Duke would stretch out his arms again to remove any tension from a tight sleeve, sometimes touch his hands together and look down at the keys. Then he would play.

Make no mistake about it: In addition to all the other things Duke Ellington was, and was superbly, he was also one hell of a piano player. Anytime.

Duke dominated the keyboard. He played *all* of it, sometimes his long arms extending from the bottom of the bass to the top of the treble. He not only had the scope to play the entire instrument, but he understood, as very few pianists understand, the use of the pedals for special effects. Duke was a master at this.

He played the piano in a constantly shifting way. I don't mean he had different styles. He did not. He had his own, personal, unique style, and what is even more important, he had a personal *sound* on the piano. Let Duke strike a chord or a note and you knew it was Duke and no one else.

But what I mean is that sometimes he played the piano as if he were playing an orchestra or as if the sounds he made were parts of an orchestral sound. And sometimes he played it like a rent party bluesman at nine in the morning after a long night. And sometimes he played it like a lover with his guitar serenading under a lady's window. And sometimes he played it like a man possessed, as if there would not be time even to get out all he wanted.

Duke came up on piano in a tough school. When he was first in New York the city was full of hard-playing keyboard men and they played against each other — like Minnesota Fats and Willie Hoppe. Competition was not only the spice of life, it was the act of survival, in a sense, as the musical underground grapevine established a pianist's reputation by the contests at Mexico's or other after-hours clubs, and that reputation was what got the jobs.

Throughout his long career after his orchestra became established, and after Duke himself became established as a composer, his gifts as a pianist were generally treated casually when they were not ignored. To a degree, Duke's other talents obscured his piano playing and his role as pianist in the orchestra was not obvious at all much of the time.

However, there was a clue for all who wanted to see it. The Ellington orchestra in stage shows and in nightclubs always began to play before the Maestro appeared. Duke would enter from the dressing room and walk up to the stand as the band was playing. You could always tell the moment he came into sight. The musicians sounded different instantly. It was like a change in the electric current. And the moment he sat at the piano and struck the first note, the whole thing tightened up into a cohesive unit.

Then, throughout the performance, Duke would subtly feed chords, drop in rhythmic figures, add a special sound to underline the soloists or the ensemble passages, and literally drive the band.

He rarely recorded as a soloist, but when he did he showed that he could extend to an entire number the brilliance he exhibited in the short solos he took in the orchestra's arrangements.

Ellington's roots as a pianist went back to the era of ragtime and stride piano, to a time when both hands and all ten fingers were needed because the pianist played alone, hour after hour, without the aid of other instruments. And thus he had to supply it all — melody, harmony, and rhythm — himself. Duke did not, as some of the modern jazz pianists did, play the piano like a horn. He could play hornlike figures and he did, but Duke heard the instrument on a larger scale than that, and thus made it *sound* larger.

No one in my memory has ever had the ability to make the piano growl and rumble the way Duke could, with those low clusters of notes and that heavy rhythm. He could stomp, in the old-fashioned sense, and he could rock like the all-time swinging pianist. And, of course, he could be melodic and rhapsodic, sometimes playing melodic lines that truly seemed to sing almost as if they had words.

Many times Duke worked out ideas for compositions at the piano after the concert when the stage and the hall were empty. Many times he sat at the piano during intermissions in clubs, if the circumstances were right, and worked on some idea, letting the audience assume he was aimlessly doodling. But that was pure deception. Duke Ellington did nothing aimlessly. Ever.

The most amazing thing about his piano playing, to me at any rate, was the way in which he could switch moods. On one number he would be the suave, international boulevardier, and in the next tune he would be as down-home funky as the raunchiest back-room, after-hours piano player. He could become positively earthy in an instant.

Sam Woodyard, who played with the Ellington band on and off for a decade, used to call Duke "Piano Red." That was a tribute to his basic funkiness because Duke Ellington's drummers, who had to work with him night after night knitting together the rhythmic basis for the band, really knew as no one else could know just how good he was.

# Selected List of Available Records

I have attempted in this list of long-playing albums to provide references for listening to go along with the various subjects in the book. Although I have been assured that all of these LPs are currently available, I am enough of a cynic to take that with a grain of salt. Albums tend to become unavailable quickly but also, like living things, they change their skins and reemerge in different covers, with new titles and new numbers! This is beyond my control, but if you persist, you should be able to find any of these albums you are interested in, remembering only that it may be necessary to insist that your neighborhood record store special-order for you.

In several instances I have referred to albums which were not available when this list was being compiled but which are planned for release before this book will be published, hence I have listed them and noted this fact.

In general, any major artist is worth hearing on any LP on which he appears. You could do a lot worse, in the process of examining the sounds of jazz, than just taking that approach. You will never go wrong with any album by the Duke or the other heroes. Anything they have recorded is worth your listening time.

The quality, incidentally, of almost any LP manufactured today is quite good and one should not worry about buying an LP on an unfamiliar label. Naturally, recordings made years ago, before high fidelity, will not sound as clear and live as recent ones. But the music is still there and it repays listening. You'll quickly adjust, believe me, and when you do, you'll find that Louis Armstrong circa 1923 is just as interesting a player as he was by the time they got around to inventing tape recorders.

Following is a list of recordings arranged to correspond with the sequence of articles.

### BESSIE SMITH

*Nobody's Blues but Mine* (with Louis Armstrong), Columbia G-31993 (2 records)
*Any Woman's Blues*, Columbia G-30126 (2 records)
*Empty Bed Blues*, Columbia G-30450 (2 records)
*World's Greatest Blues Singer*, Columbia GP-33 (2 records)

### LOUIS ARMSTRONG

*Early recordings:*
*Louis Armstrong/King Oliver*, Milestone M-47017 (2 records)
*West End Blues*, King Oliver with Louis Armstrong, Columbia J-21
*Young Louis, The Sideman*, Louis Armstrong, Decca 79233
*The Louis Armstrong Story*, Vols. 1–4, with Johnny Dodds, Earl Hines, et al., Columbia CL-851/854 (4 records)

*Later recording:*
*Rare Batch of Satch*, Louis Armstrong, RCA LPM-2322

### JIMMIE LUNCEFORD

*Lunceford Special*, Jimmie Lunceford, Columbia CS-9515E
*Rhythm Is Our Business*, Jimmie Lunceford, Decca 79237E, Vol. 1
*Harlem Shout*, Jimmie Lunceford, Decca 79238E, Vol. 2
*For Dancers Only*, Jimmie Lunceford, Decca 79239E, Vol. 3
*Blues in the Night*, Jimmie Lunceford, Decca 79240E, Vol. 4
This comprises the bulk of Lunceford's best recordings.

## SELECTED LIST OF AVAILABLE RECORDS

BILLIE "LADY DAY" HOLIDAY

*Lady Day*, Billie Holiday, Columbia CL-637
*The Billie Holiday Story*, Columbia KG-32121, Vol. 1 (2 records)
*The Billie Holiday Story*, Columbia KG-32124, Vol. 2 (2 records)
*The Billie Holiday Story*, Columbia KG-32127, Vol. 3 (2 records)
*Lady in Satin*, Billie Holiday, Columbia CS-8048
*Strange Fruit*, Billie Holiday, Atlantic 1614
The last LP above is a reissue of Lady Day's classic discs for Commodore
Records made in the late 30s and early 40s. It has been dropped recently
from the Atlantic catalogue though some stores may still have it.

LESTER "PRES" YOUNG

*Super Chief*, Count Basie, Columbia G-31224 (2 records)
*Best of Basie*, Count Basie, Decca DXS-7170 (2 records)
*Young Lester*, Lester Young, Columbia J-24
In addition, Lester Young may be heard on many of the Columbia Billie
Holiday LPs listed under her name.

CHARLIE "BIRD" PARKER

*Greatest Jazz Concert Ever*, Parker, Gillespie, et al., Prestige 24024 (2 records)
*April in Paris*, Charlie Parker with Strings, Verve 68004
*Echoes of an Era*, Parker, Gillespie, et al., Roulette RE-105 (2 records)
*Bird and Diz*, Parker, Gillespie, et al., Verve 68006
*Swedish Schnapps*, Charlie Parker, Miles Davis, et al., Verve 68010
*Now's the Time*, Charlie Parker, Verve 68005
*In the Beginning*, Dizzy Gillespie with Charlie Parker, Prestige 24030 (2
records)

JOHN BIRKS "DIZZY" GILLESPIE

*In the Beginning*, Dizzy Gillespie with Charlie Parker, Prestige 24030 (2
records)
*Dizzy Gillespie*, RCA LPV-530
*Greatest Jazz Concert Ever*, Parker, Gillespie, et al., Prestige 24024 (2 records)
*Echoes of an Era*, Charlie Parker with Dizzy Gillespie, Roulette RE-105 (2
records)
*Bird and Diz*, Charlie Parker with Dizzy Gillespie, Verve 68006

THE MODERN JAZZ QUARTET

*The First Recordings*, Modern Jazz Quartet, Prestige 24005 (2 records)
*European Concert*, Modern Jazz Quartet, Atlantic 2-603 (2 records)
*One Never Knows/No Sun in Venice*, Modern Jazz Quartet, Atlantic 1284
*At Music Inn*, Modern Jazz Quartet with Sonny Rollins, Atlantic S-1299
*The Art of the Modern Jazz Quartet*, Atlantic 2-301 (2 records)
*Fontessa*, Modern Jazz Quartet, Atlantic S-1231
*Pyramid*, Modern Jazz Quartet, Atlantic S-1325

*Space*, Modern Jazz Quartet, Apple STAO-3360
*Under the Jasmine Tree*, Modern Jazz Quartet, Apple ST-3353

CARMEN MC RAE

*Woman Talk — Live at the Village Gate*, Mainstream S-6065
*Live & Wailing*, Mainstream S-6110
*In Person — San Francisco*, Mainstream MS-6091
*In Person*, Carmen McRae, Atlantic 2-904 (2 records)
Atlantic has scheduled for release late in 1975 *The Art of Carmen McRae*,
a 2-record set selected from her recordings for that company.

JOHN COLTRANE

*Olé Coltrane*, John Coltrane, Atlantic S-1373
*My Favorite Things*, John Coltrane, Atlantic 1361
*John Coltrane*, Prestige P-24003 (2 records)
*More Lasting than Bronze*, John Coltrane, Prestige P-24014 (2 records)
*Giant Steps*, John Coltrane, Atlantic 1311
*Blue Train*, John Coltrane, Blue Note 81577
*A Love Supreme*, John Coltrane, Impulse 77
See also: *Miles Davis, Kind of Blue*, Columbia CS-8163; *Miles Ahead*,
Columbia CS-8633; *Milestones*, Columbia CS-9428; *'Round about Midnight*,
Columbia CS-8649; *Miles Davis*, Prestige P-24001 (2 records); *Workin' and
Steamin'*, Prestige P-24034 (2 records); *Miles Davis*, Prestige 24001 (2
records).

MILES DAVIS

*Complete Birth of the Cool*, Miles Davis with Gil Evans, Capitol M-11026
*Miles Davis*, Prestige 24001 (2 records)
*Workin' and Steamin'*, Miles Davis, Prestige P-24034 (2 records)
*'Round about Midnight*, Miles Davis, Columbia CS-8649
*Milestones*, Miles Davis, Columbia CS-9428
*Kind of Blue*, Miles Davis, Columbia CS-8163
*Sketches of Spain*, Miles Davis, Columbia CS-8271
*Miles Ahead*, Miles Davis, Columbia CS-8633
*Something Else*, Cannonball Adderly with Miles Davis, Blue Note LA-169-F
*In Person at the Blackhawk*, Miles Davis, Columbia C2S-820 (2 records)
*In a Silent Way*, Miles Davis, Columbia CS-9875
*Bitches Brew*, Miles Davis, Columbia GP-26 (2 records)
*Live-Evil*, Miles Davis, Columbia G-30954 (2 records)
*Get Up with It*, Miles Davis, Columbia KG-33236 (2 records)

ALBERT AYLER

*Spiritual Unity*, Albert Ayler, ESP-1002
*Bells*, Albert Ayler, ESP-1010

SELECTED LIST OF AVAILABLE RECORDS

EDWARD KENNEDY "DUKE" ELLINGTON

Any of the Duke Ellington albums is worth owning without exception and there are dozens of them. However, for a skeletal listing covering his career, this list should suffice:

*Early years:*
*Complete Duke Ellington*, Vol. 1, Columbia J-29 (2 records)
*Flaming Youth*, Duke Ellington, RCA LPV-568
*In the Beginning*, Vol 1, Duke Ellington, Decca 7922E
*Hot in Harlem*, Vol. 2, Duke Ellington, Decca 79241E
*Rockin' in Rhythm*, Vol. 3, Duke Ellington, Decca 79247E

*Middle period:*
*Ellington Era*, Vol. 1, Duke Ellington, Columbia C3L-27 (3 records)
*Daybreak Express*, Duke Ellington, RCA LPV-506
*At His Very Best*, Duke Ellington, RCA LPM-1715
*This Is Duke Ellington*, RCA VPM-6042 (2 records)
*Jumpin' Pumpkins*, Duke Ellington, RCA LPV-517
*Golden Duke*, Duke Ellington, Prestige 24029 (2 records)
*World of Duke Ellington*, Columbia G-32564E (2 records)
*Monologue*, Duke Ellington, Columbia J-20
*Liberian Suite/A Tone Parallel to Harlem*, Duke Ellington, Columbia J-6
*Masterpieces*, Duke Ellington, Columbia CSP-JCL-825
*A Drum Is a Woman*, Duke Ellington, Columbia CSP-JCL-951
*Such Sweet Thunder*, Duke Ellington, Columbia CSP-JCL-1033
*Black, Brown and Beige*, Duke Ellington with Mahalia Jackson, Columbia CSP-JCL-8015

*Later period:*
*Duke Ellington Meets Coleman Hawkins*, Impulse A-26
*Afro-Bossa*, Duke Ellington, Reprise 6069
*Great Paris Concert*, Duke Ellington, Atlantic 2-304 (2 records)
*Second Sacred Concert*, Duke Ellington, Prestige P-2405 (2 records)
*Latin American Suite*, Duke Ellington, Fantasy 9433
*Yale Concert*, Duke Ellington, Fantasy 9433
*New Orleans Suite*, Duke Ellington, Atlantic 1580
*Toga Brava Suite*, Duke Ellington, United Artists UXS-92 (2 records)
*The Pianist*, Duke Ellington, Fantasy 9462
A number of albums are scheduled for release in 1975 and 1976 of later-period Ellington recordings. Watch for them.

271

# Index

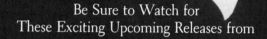